MW00528010

ALSO BY DAVID BROCK

*The Fox Effect*
*Free Ride*
*The Republican Noise Machine*
*Blinded by the Right*

# STENCH

# STENCH

## THE MAKING OF THE THOMAS COURT AND THE UNMAKING OF AMERICA

## DAVID BROCK

ALFRED A. KNOPF · NEW YORK · 2024

THIS IS A BORZOI BOOK
PUBLISHED BY ALFRED A. KNOPF

Copyright © 2024 by David Brock

All rights reserved. Published in the United States by Alfred A. Knopf,
a division of Penguin Random House LLC, New York, and distributed
in Canada by Penguin Random House Canada Limited, Toronto.

www.aaknopf.com

Knopf, Borzoi Books, and the colophon are registered trademarks
of Penguin Random House LLC.

Library of Congress Cataloging-in-Publication Data
Names: Brock, David, author.
Title: Stench : the making of the Thomas Court and the unmaking
of America / David Brock.
Description: New York : Alfred A. Knopf, 2024. | Includes index.
Identifiers: LCCN 2024009528 | ISBN 9780593802144 (hardcover) |
ISBN 9780593802151 (ebook)
Subjects: LCSH: United States. Supreme Court. | Political questions and judicial
power—United States. | Political corruption—United States. | Thomas, Clarence, 1948- |
Judges—Selection and appointment—United States. | Republican Party (U.S. : 1854- ) |
Conservatives--United States. | Opus Dei (Society) | Secret societies—
Religious aspects—Catholic Church.
Classification: LCC KF8742 .B735 2024 | DDC 347.73/26—dc23/eng/20240310
LC record available at https://lccn.loc.gov/2024009528

Jacket photograph by Olivier Douliery/AFP/Getty Images
Jacket design by Tyler Comrie

Manufactured in the United States of America
First Edition

# CONTENTS

# PROLOGUE: APRIL 1993

# THE CLARENCE THOMAS INNER CIRCLE AND ME

I n 1993, you could argue, I was one of Clarence Thomas's best friends. He and I never met, but we didn't have to. His inner circle embraced me in my days as an attack journalist for a then-influential magazine called *The American Spectator.* They were there for me when I was researching and writing my book-length assault on Thomas accuser Anita Hill, published two years after her explosive 1991 testimony before the Senate Judiciary Committee accusing Thomas of sexual harassment. Hill's televised appearance upended the confirmation hearings and very nearly derailed Thomas's nomination to the Supreme Court. When my book *The Real Anita Hill: The Untold Story* was published and caused a media sensation, the Thomas inner circle—including his wife, Ginni—was there with me to celebrate our mutual triumph in undermining Hill and Thomas's other accusers, and also, it's fair to say, to gloat.

In retrospect, it seems to me more than passing strange that a book with so partisan an underlying purpose, no matter how adroitly argued, could have received such a warm reception in so many ostensibly critically minded quarters. Christopher Lehmann-Haupt, a respected daily reviewer in *The New York Times*, gushed about my "impressive investigative study," and concluded that it was "extremely damaging to Anita Hill's case." A reviewer in the Sunday *Times* echoed that conclusion, and the *Washington Post* reviewer sanctioned the book as a "serious work of investigative journalism." These credible voices were perhaps influenced following a careful rollout—first, excerpts on the *Wall Street Journal* editorial page, to confer the imprimatur of the conservative establishment to my arguments, then a George Will column in *Newsweek* in which the bow-tied pundit cheered as loudly for my book as he famously did for baseball, praising its "avalanche of evidence that Hill lied" and adding that it would surely be "persuasive to minds not sealed by the caulking of ideology." Best of all, as I saw it at the time, Rush Limbaugh himself, then at or near the peak of his fame and influence, gave over the better part of three of his shows to read from my book out loud, word by word, to his massive radio audience. I had clearly triumphed in my mission to prop up Thomas's reputation, at whatever cost, and halt a slide in the polls that showed public opinion moving from support of Thomas to siding with Hill. (According to Gallup, by the end of his confirmation hearings, fully 54 percent of Americans said they believed Thomas, versus 27 percent who said they believed Anita Hill; those numbers, by October 1992, showed 43 percent believed Hill, and only 39 percent believed Thomas.)

Then came a bombshell report in *The New Yorker* by two highly respected reporters, Jane Mayer and Jill Abramson, an "investigative review" that went to great lengths to discredit my book—and me. I flipped through the pages of their review in a kind of nervous fever. The truth hurts, and this was the truth, ladled out for me. "He is not an unbiased journalist, as he represents himself; he is a polemicist who writes," the two said of me, accurately enough, I can say now.

I could have seized that moment to snap out of the mindset into which I had sunk in those years, an us-against-them tribalism in which pro-Thomas voices were ipso facto credible and worthy and anyone presenting the other side of the story so suspect as to not even warrant a hearing. Instead, as a natural fighter, a scrapper and a battler, I doubled down. Rather than accepting the truth of what Abramson and Mayer had reported, I would lie in the weeds and wait for my time to counterattack with all I had. What's remarkable to me, looking back, was that obsessed as I was with fighting for my own reputation, stung by having been dubbed "sleaze" by one *New York Times* columnist, Anthony Lewis following the *New Yorker* broadside, I waited so long to ask myself hard questions about what the progression of events said about Clarence Thomas himself and his closest circle.

Looking back now, as demonstrated in the chapters that follow, I can state very clearly and forcefully that, based on information I was given once the hearings concluded and Thomas was confirmed to the Supreme Court, as well as subsequent revelations, I'm absolutely sure that Anita Hill told the truth and Thomas perjured himself to win Senate confirmation, which I would call the original sin of the far right's court-packing scheme. Hill explained under oath in October 1991 to the Senate Judiciary Committee—and a live audience of tens of millions tuned into TV coverage—that Thomas harassed her many times during her two years of employment in Ronald Reagan's Department of Education and then at the federal Equal Employment Opportunity Commission (EEOC). "He spoke about . . . such matters as women having sex with animals and films showing group sex or rape scenes," she testified. Thomas often graphically described "his own sexual prowess" and the details of his anatomy. One of the films Thomas talked about, Hill said, was titled *Long Dong*

*Silver.* Hill also recounted a bizarre instance in which Thomas asked, "Who put pubic hair on my Coke?"

Snap polls showed a country divided on the question of Hill's veracity; I was one who initially believed her. Sitting in front of a TV screen at my office at *The Washington Times,* Rev. Sun Myung Moon's right-wing answer to *The Washington Post,* I couldn't imagine why this thirty-five-year-old law professor from Oklahoma would volunteer for the scrutiny of the klieg lights and make up such a vividly detailed account of sexual harassment. "Houston, we have a problem," I thought.

I later learned that Thomas's closest friends, who helped source *The Real Anita Hill* and assured me then of his complete innocence, didn't believe him either. Mark Paoletta, a deputy counsel in the White House counsel's office under President George H. W. Bush, where he worked on Thomas's nomination, later told me he knew that Thomas had a penchant for the kind of raunchy pornography Hill was describing, a key proof point in her testimony. Though he denies it, the admission was shocking as it was the opposite of what Mark had said previously. Ricky Silberman, Thomas's vice chair at the Equal Employment Opportunity Commission, which ironically enforced sexual harassment laws, later told me she had heard stories of Thomas hitting on female subordinates at the office.

"He did it, didn't he?" she blurted out to me at one point after Mayer and Abramson weighed in.

In fact, I had heard that the Silbermans—Ricky and her husband, Laurence, who sat on the D.C. Circuit Court with Thomas—had such grave doubts about Thomas's plan to flatly deny Hill's allegations that they had quietly pulled Thomas aside and counseled him to withdraw his nomination. They didn't think he could lie his way through this one and survive. Thomas apparently never forgave them for their blunt honesty. And yet, the conservative power couple had insisted to me that Thomas was completely innocent.

One of the most insidious realities of what transpired next was not only that Thomas lied, but that he caused so many others to lie for him. The Thomas circle launched an unprecedented and truly evil smear campaign against the victim of Thomas's predations. Hill was portrayed not only as a bald-faced liar with a left-wing political agenda but also as mentally ill and even a sex pervert herself. In his testimony, Thomas inverted the story, portraying himself as victim, claiming he was being subjected to a "high-tech lynching for uppity blacks" by white liberals who were trying to block a Black conservative from taking a seat on the nation's highest court.

Orrin Hatch, the Utah Republican who was the lead defender of Thomas on the Senate Judiciary Committee, suggested preposterously that Hill had lifted the anecdote about pubic hair on a Coke from the horror movie *The Exorcist*, which had contained a reference to "an alien pubic hair floating around in my gin." Alan Simpson, the GOP senator from Wyoming, was next up to bat. "And now, I really am getting stuff in over the transom about Professor Hill," Simpson said, menacingly. "I have got letters hanging out of my pockets. I have got faxes. I have got statements from her former law professors, statements from people who know her, statements from Tulsa, saying 'Watch out for this woman!' But nobody has the guts to say that because it gets all tangled up in this sexual harassment crap."

Sexual harassment crap? These were my allies.

The Thomas-Hill case is often cast as a "he-said, she-said," but it's not. Three female witnesses waited in the wings to support Hill's story and her credibility, including Angela Wright, who had worked with Thomas at the EEOC and had corroborative testimony. They were not called, due to what the *Los Angeles Times* described as a private compromise deal between Republicans and the Judiciary Committee chairman, Joe Biden. Wright was interviewed by committee lawyers for the record, but she was not permitted to tell her story to the public; she was kept off national television. Biden apparently saw himself not as a partisan Democrat prosecuting a case but as a neutral arbiter of fact; as head of the committee, his role was to conduct a fair hearing—even though Republicans like Hatch and Simpson adopted their usual approach of all-out combat and scorched-earth tactics.

On the morning of October 10, 1991, with the Thomas hearings scheduled to open the next day, Senate staff members from both parties interviewed Wright by telephone. She described several instances in which Thomas had made sexual remarks to her and said that he had once stopped by her apartment uninvited and stayed until past midnight. She claimed that he pressured her to go out with him and once asked her breast size. "You look good and you're going to be dating me," she said Thomas told her in 1984, soon after he had hired her as director of media relations at the EEOC. Wright came across as articulate and credible and was firm in relaying her certainty that Hill was telling the truth, based on her own experiences with Thomas. The committee released the Wright statement late the night before the Thomas vote so that it would attract little attention. After extensive debate, the Senate confirmed Thomas by a vote of 52–48, the narrowest margin since the nineteenth century.

In the wake of the hearings, Thomas was deeply wounded and his reputation sullied; his supporters were angry and out for blood. Thomas could be on the court for decades, they knew, and there was his legacy to think about. Hill's testimony had created a political backlash that threatened to elect a wave of Democratic women and derail the Bush presidency. That was when a right-wing tobacco heiress from North Carolina made a telephone call to an editor at *The American Spectator,* a small right-wing magazine publishing some of my freelance writing at the time. Elizabeth Brady Lurie wanted to donate money for an investigation of Anita Hill. I got the assignment. My article, "The Real Anita Hill," the one in which I called Hill "a bit nutty and a bit slutty," caused a sensation in right-wing circles. Soon I had a contract for a full-length exposé of Hill to be published by a conservative imprint, the Free Press, part of an established and respected mainstream publishing house, Simon & Schuster.

I convinced myself I was telling the true story, but I relied solely on the Thomas camp for my research and interviews. I wholly adopted their point of view. The Republicans pulled out all the stops to help me, providing me with an "erotomania" diagnosis for Hill that some random psychologist had sent in to the committee; an affidavit filed by former law students of Hill's who attested—unbelievably—to Hill having inserted pubic hairs into their exam papers; and even the FBI background report on Angela Wright, the leaking of which was a federal crime. There wasn't anything in the Wright file that at all impeached her credibility, though there was a stray account of a neighbor who had allegedly seen Wright vacuuming her house in the nude. What? It meant nothing, but I tossed it in for effect. That's the kind of book it was.

That was tame compared with what came next. The success of *The Real Anita Hill* cast me into the role of foremost defender of the biggest hero on the American right. I embraced it. Two years later, in January 1994, when Mayer and Abramson published their own book, *Strange Justice: The Selling of Clarence Thomas,* which provided fresh reporting showing that Thomas had certainly lied under oath, I was ready. I had not forgotten the two journalists' epic takedown of my book *The Real Anita Hill,* showing all its many flaws in high relief, and I wanted revenge.

The duo had produced a new witness, Kaye Savage, a onetime friend of Thomas's who said that when she visited Thomas's apartment, she had been taken aback by graphic porn pinups he had plastered all over his walls. To undermine Savage, I called Mark Paoletta, by now a close friend of both mine and Thomas's.

"Savage is a problem," I told Mark.

He called Thomas about the "problem," and Thomas passed on to me negative personal information about Savage that he said had come up in her divorce proceedings. I should have been appalled. I should have recoiled. I should have instantly extricated myself from playing any role in such garbage tactics. Instead, in menacing tones, I confronted Savage with the information. I hinted darkly that I would publish it if she didn't recant her story. In effect, I was now engaged in blackmailing sources and terrorizing innocent women in the cause of defending Clarence Thomas against testimony that I knew was likely true. When I published my review of *Strange Justice* in *The American Spectator,* I smeared Savage, Mayer, and Abramson and called them liars. But I knew better. This time I was the liar.

I spent years after that working on a brutally honest and self-critical book, *Blinded by the Right: The Conscience of an Ex-Conservative,* in which I came clean and repudiated my years as a tool of radical-right-wing interests. I hated writing that book. That old line about writing being easy, you just open a vein, never hit home harder. The book was "the result of harrowing experience," as former *New Republic* editor Hendrik Hertzberg put it in a long, favorable review in *The New Yorker*. "What drove Brock was the wrongness of what he did, not of what he thought," Hertzberg wrote. "As a frontline machine gunner in the Washington scandal wars of the nineteen-nineties, Brock inflicted heavy political casualties. But his own wounds came mostly from friendly fire, and many of these, he eventually realized, were self-inflicted. *Blinded by the Right* . . . is the story of a change of heart, not of mind."

When that painfully honest book hit the *New York Times* bestseller list in 2002, it energized me on a crusade to help the Democratic cause. Working with Bill and Hillary Clinton, I founded the watchdog Media Matters for America, widely hailed in Democratic Party circles as a game-changer, which put in place the first system to monitor, analyze, and expose right-wing disinformation in the media. Also revolutionary, in tame Democratic Party circles, we used the word "lie" to describe what the other side routinely did. I knew it because I had lived it. Later I also founded the oppo-research powerhouse American Bridge, responsible for upending countless campaigns with our exposés on GOP candidates. I morphed into an effective operator supporting Democratic Party causes and candidates in the country, working to counter the influence of the organized right in our politics and culture.

Nothing can expunge my regrettable early years in GOP politics. Full stop. Nothing. I live with that reality. At the same time, my own lived experience from that period of my life gives me the tools to make something good of a bad situation. I understand the machine I served better than any outsider can, and that places on me the responsibility to do everything I can to speak out and articulate what I see as a genuine menace to the American way of life, so that these forces can be opposed and, ultimately, defeated.

Having spent years in close proximity to the Thomas inner circle, I watch current events with a knowing eye. As news organizations raced each other in 2022 and 2023 to publish more sordid revelations about Clarence Thomas's serial corruption and abuse of power as a Supreme Court justice, it felt like déjà vu all over again watching the Thomas network mobilize. When Thomas had a "problem" years earlier with a witness whose real-life recollections could upend the lies Thomas and his supporters had told, our approach was always to smear and attack, never to acknowledge the truth. There was no thought given to the reality behind her words. The actions taken were purely tactical. They were reactive and self-justifying, putting Thomas in the role of wronged party even if facts did not sustain that picture. Thomas's friends had confided in me that they knew the allegations of sexual harassment that nearly denied him a place on the Supreme Court had ample basis in fact; still the pivot was made to pretend it was all a monstrous outrage. From there, once the fabric of reality had been severed, it was easy enough to adopt a mindset that any flak directed at Thomas was offensive and illegitimate, whatever reality in the fact-based world might be, and to dig ever deeper to launch a Forever War on Thomas's behalf with steadily multiplying assets behind it.

Mark Paoletta, the Thomas apologist I'd called a close friend, often came across as shrill and witless in his strident, knee-jerk defenses of Thomas over the years, but at the same time he demonstrated a spectacular resourcefulness in seeking to create an entire industry of hagiography to bolster the cause. *ProPublica* revealed in 2023 that Thomas had failed to report $150,000 that conservative billionaire Harlan Crow—a backer of groups and causes with ideological interests before the court—paid in tuition for the grand-nephew Thomas was raising as a son, a resoundingly clear ethical violation. So Paoletta, predictably, indulged in clumsy misdirection, floating some inane notion about the report amounting to an attack on Thomas and his wife for "caring for" the grand-nephew, claiming the factual report was "malicious." It was "high-tech lynching" all over again. (Paoletta is depicted in the center of an infamous painting of Thomas, Crow, and Leonard Leo, the Federalist Society honcho, smoking cigars at Crow's lodge, and he served as Ginni Thomas's lawyer in her interview with the committee investigating the January 6 insurrection.)

The problem with Paoletta's defense of the indefensible was that its minimal credibility eroded further in the face of ongoing disclosures, and they just kept coming, piling up in a blizzard of damning detail. As *ProPublica* put it in an August 2023 report, Clarence Thomas had accepted from rich donors and again failed to disclose "at least thirty-eight destination vacations, including a previously unreported voyage on a yacht around the Bahamas; twenty-six private jet flights, plus an additional eight by helicopter; a dozen VIP passes to professional and college sporting events, typically perched in the skybox; two stays at luxury resorts in Florida and Jamaica; and one standing invitation to an uber-exclusive golf club overlooking the Atlantic coast." Lots of goodies from Thomas's billionaire patron.

The only way the Paoletta defense made any kind of sense was within a world—where I once lived—in which a conspiracy existed to convince Clarence Thomas, and each other, of the man's greatness, his utter lack of character defect or failing; in short, his near deification. A July 2023 *Washington Post* report revealed just how far this conspiracy had gone, aided by the deep pockets and self-justifying radicalism of Leonard Leo, and his Federalist Society network, the crown jewel of the conservative legal movement, to push a broad pro-Thomas propaganda campaign, starting in 2016, to the tune of more than $1.8 million. That kind of money buys you a lot of hagiography. This was a very sophisticated, coordinated, and secretive effort under Mark Paoletta's leadership featuring state-of-the-art tricks like paying for Google to emphasize links beneficial to Thomas, and pushing pro-Thomas drivel like this on Twitter: "Justice Thomas: The most open & personable of Justices, intimate in sharing his feelings, easily moved to laughter."

Given my firsthand knowledge about what Paoletta—who was paid by Leo to defend Thomas—knew about the truth of the Anita Hill accusations, I was intrigued by the way he pulled out all the stops to try (and fail) to persuade HBO to slant a 2016 film revisiting the Thomas confirmation hearings with actor Wendell Pierce (*The Wire*) playing Thomas and Kerry Washington, nominated for an Emmy, cast as Anita Hill. Paoletta, I know for myself, was well aware he was pushing his own convenient lies in claiming, in a letter to HBO's president and chief executive obtained by *The Washington Post,* that he objected to alleged "distortions, omissions and fabrications in the script" that he said "all appear to be done with the goal of bolstering Anita Hill's credibility and smearing those who debunked her 11th hour allegations."

Smearing? Paoletta knew exactly who had been smeared, and by whom, for he was complicit in those moral crimes if not violations of the law. Even twenty-five years after the Thomas confirmation hearings, the justice and his camp were incredibly insecure about the evident truth of Anita Hill's testimony, since they knew full well that he'd lied to save his nomination. They had to suspect that history, in the end, was going to lay bare the truth of those lies for all to see. Clarence Thomas and his inner circle seemed somehow to know that, even with rich friends like Leonard Leo behind them, they were on borrowed time, or at least that was the nagging fear that galvanized them to action.

Of all the revelations about Thomas in 2023, for all the staggering scale of his corrupt willingness to take millions in gifts from rich extremists seeking influence, one seemingly trivial detail broke through the white noise of unending disclosures in an oddly humanizing, albeit sad, way. That was the story of Thomas and his beloved RV, in which he and his wife, Ginni, would take trips out into the country, visiting various states, making much of their allegedly unpretentious taste in vacations.

Sometimes propaganda is more revealing than its creators realize. Wealthy extremist Harlan Crow, who opened his wallet repeatedly for Thomas, also funded a straight-up propaganda film meant to push a folksy, down-home image of Thomas. This was as subtle and balanced a piece of portraiture as Leni Riefenstahl filming the Nuremberg Rally in the 1930s. The film, soft focus all the way, shows a relaxed, relatable version of Thomas confiding to the camera what a regular guy he is: "I don't have any problem with going to Europe, but I prefer the United States, and I prefer seeing the regular parts of the United States," he says. "I prefer the RV parks. I prefer the Walmart parking lots to the beaches and things like that. There's something normal to me about it.... I come from regular stock, and I prefer that—I prefer being around that."

There was clearly something genuine about Thomas's love of his RV, and that came through. The most effective lies are built on top of a foundation of honesty or truth. In the case of Thomas and his RV, it was almost painful to read about the layers of self-deception and self-delusion the story of Thomas and his RV reveals. About those Walmart parking lots? About those stories Thomas told even his closest friends about how he saved up to buy his RV? *The New York Times* would have something to say about that.

Here was the August 2023 headline: "Clarence Thomas's $267,230 R.V. and the Friend Who Financed It."

And an even more telling accompanying sub-headline: "The Vehicle Is a Key Part of the Justice's Just-Folks Persona. It's Also a Luxury Motor Coach That Was Funded by Someone Else's Money."

The Prevost Le Mirage XL Marathon luxury vehicle that Thomas was able to purchase, used, in 1999 was "superluxury," as a relative of its previous owner put it, a forty-foot-long status symbol. "By that point, the justice had become fixated on owning an R.V., and not just any R.V., but the Rolls-Royce of motor coaches: a custom Prevost Marathon, or as he once put it, a 'condo on wheels,'" the *Times* reported. "Justice Thomas was turned on to the luxury brand by Bernie Little, a fellow Horatio Alger member and the flamboyantly wealthy owner of the Miss Budweiser hydroplane racing boat.... Back in those days, a basic Prevost Marathon sold for about a million dollars, and could fetch far more depending on the bells and whistles. It was a rich man's toy, and the company marketed it that way."

Thomas invited the news program *60 Minutes* aboard his RV in 2007 and talked about his love of visiting friendly red states, away from the "meanness" of Washington, D.C. Left unexplored was the financing of the super-luxury vehicle. "Justice Thomas, who in the ensuing years would tell friends how he had scrimped and saved to afford the motor coach, did not buy it on his own," the *Times* reported. "In fact, the purchase was underwritten, at least in part, by Anthony Welters, a close friend who made his fortune in the health care industry." As recently as July 2023, the *Times* added, Welters—for whatever reason—was still listed as the official lienholder on the vehicle, though Welters had given

Thomas a signed release in 2008, removing him from any further financial obligation, either because Thomas repaid what he borrowed or, more likely, because Welters simply chose to forgive the amount.

For me, and I think even for many Americans who find Thomas a deeply troubling figure, there was something oddly poignant about this man's desperate ongoing effort to present himself as something he is not. In November 1999, soon after first spotting his luxury RV in an Arizona parking lot, Thomas gave a speech to a Goldwater Institute dinner at the Biltmore Hotel in Phoenix that offered some revealing glimpses. First, being in Arizona, Thomas honored his two high court colleagues from Arizona, Associate Justice Sandra Day O'Connor ("both tough, brilliant and gracious") and Chief Justice William Rehnquist. Thomas described telling the chief justice, early in his time on the bench, how odd and out of place he felt on the Supreme Court.

"Clarence, in the first years you wonder how you got here," Rehnquist told him. "After that, you wonder how your colleagues got here."

In honoring Goldwater, Thomas said that for many years he'd been influenced by Goldwater's adage: "Extremism in defense of liberty is no vice." Thomas was saying, yes, he was an extremist, and he didn't care who knew it.

Midway through a speech that was rambling but often oddly affecting, as in his homage to actor Charlton Heston ("Moses!" Thomas exulted), sitting up front near him, Thomas delivered the following line, which he knew would draw laughs: "I can't stand here and tell you all that it was my choice to become a federal judge. Pure and simple, I wanted to be rich."

All he ever wanted was to be rich. The way Thomas said "rich" was like music to the ears of the crowd at the Biltmore. It was taken as a kind of joke, but anyone watching the video of that speech can't help but notice how much more than a throwaway line the words represented. Growing up poor in Georgia, first in the impoverished small town of Pin Point, then in Savannah, living with his demanding grandfather, Clarence Thomas dreamed of escaping from poverty. He dreamed of having the power and freedom from accountability that he saw as going together with being rich. For all his posturing over the years as a deep thinker, a man of principles, the one principle to which he was truly committed from an early age was his own self-enrichment. He would sell whatever he had along the way to win his own freedom from the sting of being dismissed—for being poor or for being Black. He wanted to be rich. He wanted to live the life of a man rich and powerful enough to act with utter impunity.

I can only conclude that Thomas's massive corruption is not some side effect of the dark bargain he made with a highly ideological, highly unethical radical network led by Leonard Leo and his Federalist Society co-conspirators; the graft, corruption, and whole-hog flouting of accountability are a goal unto themselves. When people show you who they are, believe them. Thomas wanted to be rich, and he was fine with being an extremist— since his goal was to try to live in a way where he could convince himself that he did not care what anyone else thought. Of course he racked up platinum miles jetting around with rich individuals seeking to undermine what tiny fragments remained of Thomas's credibility. Of course he let rich friends with agendas buy his goodwill through all manner of gifts, from rebuilding his grandmother's house to paying his grand-nephew's way through expensive private schools to jetting him around in a privately owned 737. This is who Clarence Thomas is.

This context matters in understanding just how unmoored— and how dangerous—the United States Supreme Court has become. Recent years have finally brought growing public awareness of the decisive role that a clandestine network led by Leonard Leo and the Federalist Society has played not only in handpicking President Trump's selections to the Supreme Court, in return for securing the Religious Right voting bloc for Trump (who nevertheless lost the popular vote), but also in installing five extremist justices over thirty years. Each of these five has been indelibly tainted, from Thomas himself, who resorted to multiple instances of perjury in order to win confirmation in 1991, to Samuel Alito (January 2006) to the Trump MAGA selections Neil Gorsuch (April 2017), Brett Kavanaugh (October 2018), and Amy Coney Barrett (October 2020), as I will lay out in careful detail over the course of this account—perjury, a stolen election, a secret pledge by a presidential nominee to special interests who had long sought *Roe*'s demise, and unprecedented and unconstitutional maneuvers by a GOP Senate leader, Mitch McConnell, determined to pack the courts to keep campaign cash flowing from GOP megadonors with interests before them.

Leonard Leo's theocratic project—which seized on an existing Federalist Society scheme to remake the judiciary in its own extremist image and essentially put it on steroids—was developed and undertaken as a natural outgrowth of Leo's friendship with Clarence Thomas, dating back to 1990. When Leo and Thomas first met, Leo was not yet a paid operative for the Federalist Society and Thomas was not yet a Supreme Court justice. Leo had other influential close friends, including Supreme Court Justice Antonin Scalia, but the increasing aggressiveness of the anonymously funded hive he built over the years was encouraged and assisted by Thomas. Seen from the viewpoint of a nonfanatic, the evidence was overwhelming that all five of the extreme justices this right-wing conspiracy had installed blatantly lacked legitimacy, given the lies they had told on the way in, the stunts their confirmations had required, and the deeper underlying truth that their presence on the court amounted to one of the more blatant and dangerous power grabs in U.S. history.

One jarring result of the shift was that Chief Justice John Roberts, confirmed in September 2005, would prove to be a feckless and unreliable brake on the unchecked power this group accumulated, in short, a chief justice in name only. This was the

Thomas Court, created in the image and with the active con-nivance of a judge who had once been on the outer fringes of the court. The power grab was dirty and sleazy, but on its own terms it was effective, culminating in the political earthquake of the Supreme Court's *Dobbs v. Jackson Women's Health* ruling in June 2022 overturning *Roe v. Wade,* stripping women of repro-ductive rights they had enjoyed for over fifty years, and ushering in an entirely new and different political era whose aftershocks will rock—and reshape—the American political landscape for years to come.

At the center of the campaign to pack the court and use it as a weapon in a radical, hard-right ideological and cultural war are the corrupt duo Clarence Thomas and Leonard Leo, the chief operative for the billionaires' scheme, who understood that if you had control of the courts you could change society even over the will of its people, and whose authoritarian machinations and mis-deeds have helped drag down approval ratings for the high court. These two showed no interest in respecting the ideal held by generations of Americans in public life, namely, the importance of an independent and respected judiciary that could function as a disinterested arbiter; they went all in on the logic of mob rule, and its adage that if you have the power, you do whatever you want, including making up the law. The public noticed. By September 2022, Gallup was showing disapproval of the court at an all-time high of 58 percent, compared to a 25 percent disap-proval in June 2001. Majorities of both Democrats and Repub-licans believed that politics guides Supreme Court decisions and that the court should be restructured to reduce political influence.

It matters that the public has lost confidence in the integrity of the high court; over time, the constitutionally mandated role of the judiciary in dispensing impartial justice becomes untenable if a majority of the population sees the court as nakedly politi-cal and untrustworthy. We have moved as a country into very

dangerous, uncharted territory. The current widely acknowledged crisis of public confidence in the high court is the inevitable result of a covert campaign of subversion against America
that brought the calculated ascendance of these five Republican
judges through illegitimate means. The Thomas Court, with
its majority of five, all current or former practicing Catholics,
imposed its will against the views of two-thirds of the American
people—67 percent, according to a March 2023 Marquette University poll—in overturning *Roe v. Wade.*

*Dobbs* was the beginning, not the end. Women of childbearing
age were the first victims of this Christian Nationalist plotting
but they won't be the last. The vagaries of elections aren't supposed to strip people of their constitutionally guaranteed rights.
Thomas and his acolytes throughout the federal judiciary have
it in for such rights as contraception and gay marriage. Yet moving forward, this politicized court is poised to transform America
as we know it, as individual rights and liberties are purposely
taken away from millions of Americans, and corporate interests are systematically advanced against the public interest.
We cannot comprehend this riveting political moment, or the
country's future course as a representative democracy, until the
truth behind these breathtaking plots by secretive groups, like
the Federalist Society and the Opus Dei movement inside the
Catholic Church, is fully revealed through a wide airing of a hidden history of the hijacking of U.S. democracy by a reactionary
elite imposing its own moral and religious vision on the country at large.

"Clarence Thomas is an outlaw and a liar," I wrote in a 2022
*Huffington Post* article arguing for Thomas's impeachment by
House Democrats while they still had the power to do it. "He has
not only misled the Senate, but, importantly, the public. Legal
scholars have noted that the authority and legitimacy of the judicial branch, which is shielded from the whims of voters, depends

on its perceived fairness, impartiality and integrity. On all these counts, Thomas fails the test. He should go."

Clarence Thomas and the other corrupt members of the Thomas Court probably have too much power ever to be toppled. But whether Thomas is ever impeached, as he so richly deserves, may not be the point: As calls for accountability mount, it becomes more challenging to whitewash a record so garishly packed with offenses. The stench will fuel more calls for expanding the Supreme Court, imposing term limits on its members, and the enactment of an actual code of conduct to address the growing sense that members of the high court see themselves as above the law. The pressure will likely lead to some reform, and the more pressure that can be brought to bear, and sustained, the better the chance of meaningful, consequential change.

For me this fight is personal. I was once a young man in whom a combination of ambition and excitement for what I saw as the promise of true conservative ideals, as espoused by Ronald Reagan, led me to lose my way and commit offenses I now regret and lament. I lied for Clarence Thomas and I lied for those around him, like Mark Paoletta. I lied for a cause, a cause I believed in until at last I came to my senses. Only then could I see with painful clarity how misguided my years-long run of destruction and demolition had truly been.

I am sorry for my role in undermining the credibility of Anita Hill, who I know deserved much better. I am sorry for others I smeared as well and I am horrified to see how far the same underhanded tactics and gambits I once aided and abetted have come, and how dangerously close we now are to seeing our fragile democracy—and our fundamental decency as a people—lost to the ash heap of history.

And yet I also nurture a thin, flickering flame of hope. I do not, cannot, believe that there is anything so unique about me. I am no better than anyone, and perhaps also no worse. If I woke up and came to my senses, if I deprogrammed myself from a cult of abject service to a right-wing plot to remake America, then I know for a fact that others can see it as well. If I came to understand how misguided I was in working to twist the public record in service of Clarence Thomas, then others may join the cause of accountability.

To me Clarence Thomas in the end comes across as a tragic, pathetic figure, a shell of a man, disfigured by a bitterness he could never examine enough to understand, an empty vessel ready to be filled by others, so insecure that lavish flattery to this day continues to be remarkably effective. Speaking in Arizona in 1999, Thomas told a fawning audience of self-styled conservatives that he, the man from Pin Point, Georgia, was not unlike Jesus Christ in that he had been chosen. For Thomas, the suggestion was clearly that he had been chosen by God, a sign of a dangerous fanaticism. "Divine Providence is a far better predictor than career planning," Thomas told that Arizona dinner, "and it is only through that Providence that I am here, that indeed I am out of Georgia, and certainly that I am on the Court."

No, Justice Thomas, you were not chosen by God to sit on the Supreme Court. You were chosen as a tool of right-wing interests who knew how useful you could be. They knew, having studied your life, how pliable you were, like clay to be molded. You turned your back on the man who shaped you most, the grandfather who raised you, leaving seminary rather than following through on your promise to him to be a priest. You wore the uniform of the radical Black Panther Party as a student and raged with seething anger. You achieved much through your own work, overcoming your own limitations, to make it to Yale Law School and to graduate, and then played the victim card repeatedly, seeing racial slights anywhere and everywhere. Nothing was ever your fault. Not even the debacle of your Supreme Court hearing. Anita Hill came out of the darkness of your own choices, and so you sought to destroy her, and therefore to destroy the part of yourself that was decent and knew the truth about what you had done. You turned that bulwark of democracy, the nation's highest court, into your own demented psychodrama, and have taken the rest of us along for a ride. I was there in your camp at the beginning, and I hope I have enough years left on this planet to see you meet your rightful end. I hope to be around to see you achieve the lasting ignominy you so richly deserve. I think time is on my side. What do *you* think? What do you have to say for yourself? Your power and your phalanx of sycophants cannot shield you forever.

But the current ethics crisis extends beyond the egregious lapses of Clarence Thomas. The Supreme Court's free-falling legitimacy in the eyes of the public had reached dumpster-fire levels of lurid urgency by 2024—with the potential for far graver long-term damage to the court's legitimacy under the influence of an out-of-control Thomas Court majority seemingly set on radical action far beyond abortion. Even just a few years earlier, questions about the Supreme Court were at most limited to a handful of court watchers in journalism and academia, but the headlines going into 2024 had the general public more focused both on the stain of Supreme Court corruption and the potential for gross dereliction of duty on the part of this court. Once again, the country was warned, as in 2000, that the Supreme Court could very well step in and on the basis of raw power dynamics, not legal precedent, dictate to the American people who their president would be for the next four years. If the court had become a runway fire, it was time to reach for the fire extinguisher.

# PART 1

# THE GENESIS OF THE THOMAS COURT

# CHAPTER 1

# OCTOBER 1973: NIXON'S REVENGE

On Tuesday, April 15, 1969, First Lady Pat Nixon staged a tour de force of endurance at the White House during the seventeenth annual GOP Women's Conference in Washington. Like her husband, Richard Nixon, the onetime red-baiting California congressman elected president in 1968, Pat Nixon had an obsessive commitment to hard work. Born in Ely, Nevada, she paid for her studies at Fullerton State and then USC by working at everything from retail clerk to radiologist. That Tuesday in April 1969, she hosted 4,702 Republican "ladies" at the White House in what *New York Times* reporter Nan Robertson called "the biggest party held there since Andrew Jackson's riotous Inaugural brawl in 1829. They were girdle-to-girdle in the East Room and spilled over into adjoining areas: In the press, one matron fainted and was led out for air." There was even, Robertson added, "some ladylike shoving to see Pat Nixon and cries for 'Tricia, Tricia!'" (Tricia Nixon, one of two first daughters.)

Among the White House visitors the first lady greeted that day was a group of eighty pages led—I'm sure she was leading, even then—by twelve-year-old Virginia Lamp of Omaha, Nebraska. The pages were costumed in—try to picture this—red, white, and blue top hats, and over their white dresses they wore blue sashes emblazoned with the theme of that week's conference: "Forward Together."

Forward together. I get a chill down my spine imagining the future Ginni Thomas, future wife of extreme-right Supreme Court Justice Clarence Thomas, flown to Washington from Omaha the day before on a special charter flight, thrilling to the power of those words. Even then, one can have no doubt, she was vowing to spend her lifetime acting on them—within five years she would be back in Washington as a summer intern, inspiring this prediction in a newspaper: "Don't be surprised if you see Virginia Lamp's name on a ballot someday." At Westside High School in Omaha, young Ginni was pictured as a senior in 1975 working the phones for the Republican Party, and urging other girls to organize for the GOP, this in a post-Watergate era following Nixon's humiliation and resignation when all Republicans carried the whiff of shame. Another yearbook photo captured the future Washington power player as a cheerleader holding a shield and doing the splits with the caption, "Warrior woman: Ginni Lamp." To a normal citizen in a democracy, the words "Forward Together" are an anodyne call to engagement. To an individual predisposed to fanaticism, both capable and willing to bend rules to her will, they are program code calling for a lifelong commitment to imposing her hard-right ideology on the rest of us.

In my lifetime I've watched Nixon go from admired statesman, grinning broadly, if a little too broadly, as he swung his arms wide in 1971 to shake the hand of the leader of Communist China, Zhou Enlai, launching the adage "Only Nixon could go to China"; to a horrifically disgraced outcast, balefully shuffling toward Marine One in August 1974 when he resigned the presidency, rather than attempt to defend himself against the dirty tricks of Watergate and its cover-up; to years as a symbol of lust for power gone wrong, of the age-old truth that absolute power corrupts absolutely, an international outcast whose Christmas bombing of Cambodia during the Vietnam War was increasingly seen as a war crime; to a slow, partial rehabilitation, through penning thoughtful volume after thoughtful volume in his San Clemente mansion in Southern California with its view of the Pacific Ocean; to, most astonishingly, over the past decade or two, something like total erasure, or excision, from U.S. collective memory. Trump henchman Roger Stone, who had a massive and decisive role in plotting the January 6, 2021, attempted short-circuiting of democracy, proudly wears a tattoo of Nixon, a fact too often dismissed as a kind of sick joke, but in fact the joke is on all of us: The legacy of Nixon's willingness to inject a sickness and depravity into the heart of American politics haunts us to this day in ways large and small. The particulars need to be revisited, and need to be retold, as a warning, again and again.

To put the influence of Nixon in context, it's worth focusing on the seminal impact of his so-called Law and Order campaign of 1968, in which the man who lost to John F. Kennedy in 1960, trying to play by the rules, resorted to early dog-whistle politics. Nixon was not subtle in appealing to racists and reactionaries, seeking to make the most of the chaos of the times, including the April 1968 assassination of Martin Luther King Jr., the June 1968 murder of my hero Bobby Kennedy in California, and the August 1968 eruption of crude violence outside of the Democratic National Convention in Chicago, with its memorable footage of police clubbing protesters.

To contemporary readers, the former *Rolling Stone* journalist Hunter S. Thompson is mostly known as a rowdy, self-parodying partier played by Johnny Depp in the film version of his book *Fear and Loathing in Las Vegas.* In the 1960s, Thompson made his name as an acute observer of Nixon. "It is Nixon himself who represents that dark, venal and incurably violent side of the American character that almost every country in the world has learned to fear and despise," Thompson wrote during the Nixon presidency. "Our Barbie-doll President, with his Barbie-doll wife and his boxful of Barbie-doll children, is also America's answer to the monstrous Mr. Hyde. He speaks for the Werewolf in us; the bully, the predatory shyster who turns into something unspeakable, full of claws and bleeding string-warts on nights when the moon comes too close."

Nixon's 1968 election as president represented a broader mobilization of reactionary elements who viewed the progress of the Civil Rights Movement and the social experimentation of the 1960s with the open horror of those who fear that which they do not understand. Nixon was famously square. He was uptight and uncool. And he was fake: His stiff, ingratiating manner bespoke a façade pasted on to convince those willing to be too easily convinced, all in the service of darker motives. Nixon was an avatar of going overboard on pushing back against the perceived freedom of the 1960s counterculture, and not for any good reason, except fear, self-hatred, and unchecked power lust. He helped open the gates to a broader mobilization of reactionary elements, who saw in the 1960s social movements a potential threat to their own privilege and monopoly on power, which required holding others down.

———

When Eugene B. Sydnor Jr. of the U.S. Chamber of Commerce approached his neighbor and friend in Richmond, Virginia, corporate lawyer Lewis F. Powell Jr., with an ambitious request in 1971, during Nixon's first term, it hardly seemed the conditions were ripe for a momentous document that would reshape the American right and with it American politics as a whole. The Chamber of Commerce is not generally thought of as a revolutionary organization, and Powell's career to that point seemed devoted to being a stalwart of the American Bar Association, a civic activist in his local community, and to making a healthy living in corporate law focused on mergers and acquisitions and defending Big Tobacco.

If Americans remember Powell at all, it is likely as a courtly, bespectacled old-school conservative justice of the U.S. Supreme Court, to which he would soon be appointed by Nixon. But first there was an urgent task at hand. The assignment was for Powell to take the substance of conversations Powell and Sydnor had been having and write it all up into a memo, marked "CONFIDENTIAL," outlining an aggressive, some might say radical, plan to mobilize vast resources on behalf of American business interests in response to perceived and actual attacks from the political left. Sydnor likely got more than he bargained for.

Powell's anticommunist, anti–New Deal salvo was blunt about being a sweeping response to the protest movements of the 1960s surrounding women's rights, consumer rights, and the Vietnam War. Powell had been chosen to tour the Soviet Union in 1958 and write up a twenty-four-page report for the American Bar Association on Soviet legal and educational institutions. He seemed to be writing with honest emotion in pushing the paranoid fear of the "destruction" of American free enterprise in the face of growing anticorporate sentiment. "No thoughtful person can question that the American economic system is under broad attack," Powell's thirty-three-page memo began. "We are not dealing with episodic or isolated attacks from a relatively few extremists or even from the minority socialist cadre. Rather the assault on the enterprise system is broadly based and consistently pursued. It is gaining momentum and converts."

Powell's memo identified the ultimate threat to the U.S. way of life not as Soviet Russia, Communist China, or Fidel Castro's Cuba—but Ralph Nader, who, Powell explained had the gall to speak out against corporate executives for, as explained in a *For-*

*tune* magazine article, "defrauding the consumer with shoddy merchandise, poisoning the food supply with chemical additives, and willfully manufacturing unsafe products that will maim or kill the buyer." Also high on Powell's list of villains: Charles Reich of Yale, author of *The Greening of America,* a totem of the 1960s counterculture.

Having identified the enemies, Powell appealed: "The time has come—indeed it is long overdue—for the wisdom, ingenuity and resources of American business to be marshaled against those who would destroy it . . . the enterprise system tolerates, if not participates in, its own destruction." A good deal of the memo spells out Powell's concerns with the liberal tilt of college campuses and national media outlets. Powell recommends "balancing of faculties," "equal time" for conservative speakers, and, more ominously, the monitoring of textbooks and media reports for ideological deviance from the conservative line. "Monitoring," as in censoring.

Powell was going all in. In reaction to the onslaught, he recommended building long-term infrastructure to advance business interests. "Strength lies in organization, in careful long-range planning and implementation, in consistency of action over an indefinite period of years, in the scale of financing available only through united action and national organizations," he wrote. Powell prescribed nothing less than a massive propaganda effort in defense of the interests of the business community and right-wing political forces. The liberal establishment would be challenged, met, and ultimately defeated by a new conservative counter-establishment. On the one hand, Powell argued, the right needed to build and fund its own alternative think tanks, advocacy organizations, media outlets, watchdogs, and academic beachheads to get out the word, while on the other hand infiltrating mainstream elite institutions—academia, media, mainline business organizations—with right-wing propaganda. Confrontation was the watchword.

Powell's sentiments about the judiciary merit special attention. In particular, Powell argued that business's battles should be fought in the courts. In what would become an influential passage under the headline "Neglected Opportunity in the Courts," Powell sounded the alarm that it was time to dramatically step up "exploiting judicial action" for years to come. "Under our constitutional system, the judiciary may be the most important instrument for social, economic and political change," he wrote. "Other organizations and groups, recognizing this, have been far more astute in exploiting judicial action than American business. . . . Labor unions, civil rights groups and now the public interest law firms are extremely active in the judicial arena. Their success, often at business's expense, has not been inconsequential."

Democratic senator Sheldon Whitehouse of Rhode Island, as astute an observer of the courts as there is in American politics, sees Powell's hidden hand in the court-packing scheme of the organized right. As the senator explained in a May 2021 Senate floor speech, "The battle lines were drawn. Indeed, the language in the Powell report is the language of battle: 'attack,' 'frontal assault,' 'rifle shots,' 'warfare.' The recommendations are to end compromise and appeasement. . . . The secret report . . . may have launched the scheme to capture the Court."

The Powell Memo, very much a product of the Nixon years, quietly ushered in a distinctly different era of organizing on behalf of the American right. The memo resonated with its intended audience. Scholars have documented that in the wake of the memo, right-wing funders and business interests stepped up to Powell's challenge and tens of millions of dollars quietly began to flow into such efforts to build infrastructure, independent of the unreliable Republican Party, in a wholesale reorientation of conservative philanthropy. The memo's essentially radical nature, couched in the blandness of its Chamber of Commerce context, would unleash a fervent strain of extremism that, coupled with the allocation of resources to build mostly anonymously funded institutions that could develop ideas and talking points, such as the Heritage Foundation think tank and the Federalist Society, would power the effort to transform the court and with it the character of American life.

It's taken years of prodigious research to identify these core donors. Early funders of the right-wing network—motivated by an antitax, antigovernment ideology—included the Lynde and Harry Bradley Foundation, an electronic parts fortune out of Milwaukee; the Sarah Scaife Foundation, created by the parents of Pittsburgh banker Richard Mellon Scaife; the Searle Freedom Trust, money from the sale of G. D. Searle, the pharmaceutical giant; and the Charles Koch Foundation, established from the personal fortune of Charles Koch of Koch Industries, a multinational conglomerate. For these and other donors on the right, this was less about philanthropy in the traditional sense and more akin to a business proposition. Their self-interested investments—including in the capture of the courts—helped their bottom line.

Two months after the memo was complete, Nixon appointed Powell to the U.S. Supreme Court. Nixon had campaigned on appointing pro-business, law-and-order judges who would strictly interpret the law, and he sought out a white Southerner as part of his Southern Strategy to polarize racial issues and attract white votes. Powell didn't disappoint, becoming a reliable conservative vote on the court led by Chief Justice Warren Burger. Powell ruled in favor of the death penalty, struck down affirmative action programs, and upheld sodomy laws. One deviation from the conservative line came on abortion, as Powell joined the 7–2 majority decision in *Roe,* apparently stemming from an incident during his tenure at his Richmond firm, when the girlfriend of one of Powell's office staff bled to death from an illegal self-induced abortion.

Powell had previously declined a Nixon invitation to join the high court two years earlier, not wanting to take a pay cut from

his lucrative law practice and thinking his background in corporate law ill-prepared him to adjudicate the complex cases that
would come before the court. But in 1971 he agreed, now believing
that taking the post was his public civic duty. What had changed?
Perhaps a newfound sense of purpose and clarity of mission he
felt having articulated his strong feelings in the Chamber memo.
We don't know if Nixon's vetters saw Powell's memo. The Senate
did not. According to a column running in *The Washington Post*
shortly after Powell's confirmation, Jack Anderson, remarking
on the memo's "militant" tone, reported, "Senators, therefore,
never got a chance to ask Powell whether he might use his position on the Supreme Court to put his ideas into practice and to
influence the court on behalf of business interests."

In fact, once on the court, Powell did just that, playing an
important role in paving the way for business interests to fund
political activities. In a series of decisions on money in politics
in the 1970s and 1980s, Powell wrote or joined majority opinions
that chipped away at the government's ability to restrict political
spending, allowing unlimited amounts of unregulated and often
untraceable corporate money to pour into the political system. In
effect, Powell wrote the plan of attack and then paved the way for
its implementation.

As Sheldon Whitehouse connected the dots in a Senate floor
speech decades later:

> In his years on the Court, Lewis Powell made good on the secret
> recommendations that he had made to the U.S. Chamber of
> Commerce five months before joining the Court. He showed
> that "an activist-minded Supreme Court"—his words—could
> be that "important instrument for social, economic and politi-
> cal change"—his words—that he had proposed. He opened
> a lane for unlimited money into politics, enabling what his
> secret report had called "the scale of financing available only
> through joint effort." He bulldozed aside bars on corporate

spending in politics so corporations could deploy, just as his report had urged, "whatever degree of pressure—publicly and privately—may be necessary." And he allowed advocacy organizations to spend their treasuries in politics, opening the way for the "organization," "joint effort," and "united action" he had called for in his report through "national organizations."

The plan of action was apparent. All that was needed was the personnel, the foot soldiers, to push this reactionary movement forward. The Nixon White House, channeling the fervid power of the scheming and devious imagination of the Top Man himself, proved to be a breeding ground for new strains of political perversion, all dressed up as respectable, whose influence and pathology would play out over decades.

———

Flash back to Saturday afternoon, October 20, 1973, when the famous special prosecutor of the day, Archibald Cox, appointed by Attorney General Elliot Richardson to investigate the June 1972 Watergate break-in, stepped in front of TV cameras at the National Press Club in Washington. Cox was there to explain why he was holding his ground in a standoff with President Nixon. The president was resisting a Cox subpoena to surrender nine taped conversations Nixon had made at the White House. Cox announced he would call for a court order to enforce the subpoena.

"I don't feel defiant," Cox said. "In fact, I told my wife this morning I hate a fight. Some things I feel very deeply about are at stake. . . . I am certainly not out to get the President of the United States."

At the White House, Cox's remarks were seen as "insubordination." White House chief of staff Alexander Haig, who would memorably reappear on the national stage when Ronald Reagan was shot, called Richardson and told him to fire Cox.

"Well, I can't do that," Richardson said. "I guess I'd better come over and resign."

That put Deputy Attorney General William Ruckelshaus in charge. He, too, was asked to fire Cox, and resisted on principle. "Your Commander-in-Chief has given you an order!" Haig scolded him. Ruckelshaus was writing out his resignation letter when the White House beat him to the punch and dismissed him.

The two departures meant the next man in line was the solicitor general of the United States, forty-six-year-old Robert Bork, a flamboyantly ideological former Yale Law School professor (whose first appearance in *The New York Times* came in a May 1970 article headlined "Free Enterprise Radicals Score Federal Control"). The White House sent a limousine to fetch Bork and bring him over to be sworn in as acting attorney general, a position he would hold for more than two months.

Bork, highly ambitious but in no way stupid, had an inkling of how bad it would look to be the one to fire Cox after two others had refused. "I was thinking of resigning," Bork insisted in an interview later in 1972, but added, "not out of moral considerations. I did not want to be perceived as a man who did the President's bidding to save my job." Bork, however, did the president's bidding, allowing Nixon to place himself above the law, and fired Cox. "I had some time to think about it since," Bork insisted in 1972. "I think I did the right thing."

Nixon praised Bork as one of the "best" men at the Justice Department and, according to Bork's memoir, offered to appoint him to the Supreme Court as a reward for his loyalty. Nixon, of course, didn't last long enough in office to make good on the promise. Bork soldiered on, working in the Nixon Justice Department with two brilliant lawyers who, along with Bork, would go on to be the key movers behind the Federalist Society, the group that would be founded in 1982 by law students, and whose organizing of right-wing lawyers on college campuses, and later nationally, would move the nation's courts decisively to the right. Bork's compatriots were Harvard Law School graduates Laurence Silberman, who was appointed assistant attorney general by Nixon in 1974, and Antonin Scalia, recruited into the administration by Silberman, who served in the influential Office of Legal Counsel at Justice. Within a decade, all three would be elevated to the federal bench by Ronald Reagan.

When Nixon resigned and Gerald Ford assumed the presidency, the group stayed on, working closely with a former legislative aide to Kentucky senator Marlow Cook: Mitch McConnell. As McConnell tells the story, he watched and learned. "I would have found my job wholly unsatisfying if it weren't for the chance to encounter, above the stacks of paper, some of the nation's best conservative minds—Robert Bork, Laurence Silberman, Antonin Scalia—legal luminaries who were all serving in the department at the time," McConnell gushed in his memoir, *The Long Game.* "We'd hold nearly daily staff meetings, where I'd get a chance to hear them speak. As a younger guy who felt as if I knew nothing about the law, I never opened my mouth. At the time, knowing squat about most legal matters, feeling as if I'd escaped the purgatory of practicing law, I was lucky to be in their presence."

McConnell would emerge four decades later as the most consequential Republican Senate leader in generations. As the legislative partner to the Federalist Society, McConnell would use his position as majority leader to cover up controversies and bend Senate rules like a pretzel to jam through the confirmations of one-third of the current Supreme Court. This, McConnell believed, would be his legacy. Court control would get the organized right the "kind of America *we want,*" McConnell said.

It's fascinating to consider what lessons these appointees—especially the wounded Bork, perhaps less so the impressionable Ford guy, McConnell—were teaching each other about power, how to wield it, how to maintain it. In their later broadsides against the hated liberal establishment that hounded Nixon from office—the Democratic pols, the news media, the legal establishment, academia, Hollywood—one can see a seemingly bottom-less desire to avenge Watergate, and make people forget the shame, by any means possible. Indeed, both Silberman and Bork would play important roles in the 1990s in the right-wing campaign to hound Bill Clinton from office on trumped-up charges. As they somehow convinced themselves, this was tit for tat and poetic justice.

The election of Jimmy Carter to the presidency in 1976, with his earnest promise that he would never lie to the American people, derailed the plans of Nixon's men to advance their careers in the judicial sphere. They all wanted to be federal judges, politicos donning black robes. Bork and Scalia went back to teaching at Yale and the University of Chicago, respectively, where they would bide their time, awaiting a Republican restoration. Silberman decamped for a high position at Crocker National Bank in California, where he began to insinuate himself into the Reagan entourage. And McConnell, for his part, returned to Kentucky to run successfully for local office, beginning his steep climb up the greasy pole of electoral politics.

The Nixon White House looms in history as the crucial breeding ground where a paranoid, self-justifying, and ruthless style of right-wing politics was spawned. To the country at large, the scandal of Watergate was a national embarrassment that led a sitting president to slink out of the White House to a waiting helicopter and resign in shame. "Tricky Dick" Nixon became an archetype of the sleazy, depraved politician, a man whose actual gifts as a geostrategic thinker and statesman were undermined by his sick self-pity. For the nation, shaken deeply by the scandal of Watergate, Nixon's dark side loomed as a kind of wake-up call, a warning to steer away from power-mad schemers; but to his right-wing loyalists, the takeaway from Nixon's demise was the opposite. He was felled not by sleaze, not by ruthless amoral scheming, but by a lack of will to go all in on hardball politics.

# CHAPTER 2

# OCTOBER 1960: RADICAL CATHOLICS

was raised Catholic, a fact about myself that I've gone through most of my life finding utterly irrelevant. Like growing up in New Jersey and then Texas, it seemed a mere data point, somehow isolated and unimportant. Does it mean anything, in looking at the person I would become, to know that as a youth I served as an altar boy? Is there any relevance to my having attended Our Lady of the Assumption Catholic elementary school in suburban New Jersey? Or having been exclusively educated in Catholic school all the way up to tenth grade? I always thought not, but digging into a harder look at the role of extreme Catholics in shaping the Supreme Court over the course of my lifetime, I am not so sure. Maybe my own background, and my own submerged mindsets from my formative years, help in some small way to illuminate the often hidden subtleties of the struggles that helped define the role radical Catholics would play in overpowering the U.S. system of justice.

My father, Raymond, was a radical Catholic. I write that without a trace of hyperbole: He was radical in his belief. He and I were not close, to put it mildly. And when it came time to choose a university, and I left for Berkeley in the fall of 1981 to attend the University of California, I chose "Berzerkely" in part to antagonize, and perhaps punish, my radical-right-wing father. In later years, my father and I somewhat reconciled and I tried to understand his ideological journey. He adhered to a version of Catholicism that was so extreme, he drove fifty miles each weekend to attend a Latin mass in a makeshift church. He hated modernity and wished he could dial it back.

My father was a disciple of ultraconservative French archbishop Marcel Lefebvre, a deeply controversial figure even among conservative Catholics of the time. "In many ways, Archbishop Lefebvre is a man of lost worlds—worlds to which he displays a serene capacity to remain faithful," *The New York Times* reflected in a 1988 article. "He was born on Nov. 29, 1905, in Tourcoing, near the Belgian border, into a family where only French nationalism competed with religious devotion. . . . The family said daily prayers in Latin, and four other children in the family became priests or nuns. The French Seminary in Rome, where Marcel Lefebvre studied for the priesthood, was directed by a sympathizer with Action Française, a right-wing, anti-democratic and anti-Semitic movement led by Charles Maurras that fell from favor in the Vatican and was condemned by Pope Pius XI during the young man's seminary years."

Pope John XXIII decided after being elected to the Holy See in a surprise vote in 1958 that the Catholic Church needed "updating." He called the Second Vatican Council—the first Vatican Council was held from 1869 to 1870—a series of meetings in Rome at which the conservative bloc was led by Archbishop Lefebvre. Pope John XXIII's vision of modernizing the Church, moving away from the Latin mass, for example, also came with an open advocacy of involving the Church in affairs of state, including an Ostpolitik of engaging with Soviet satellite states in Eastern Europe. Leading up to Vatican II, Lefebvre worked for years on the team that drafted traditionalist positions to present to the gathering. In August 1962, he was named superior general of a shadowy traditionalist Catholic faction called the Holy Ghost Fathers, adding to his influence, but his views did not prevail.

"Vatican II was a sound defeat for Lefebvre and for the archconservative group within the council minority," Massimo Faggioli would later write in his study *Vatican II: The Battle for Meaning.* "Lefebvre—who had expressed support in the 1940s for the 'Catholic order' of the authoritarian French Vichy regime (which collaborated with Nazi Germany), for authoritarian governments and military dictatorships in the 1970s (in Spain, Portugal, Chile and Argentina), and for the French far-right party the National Front in the 1980s—added Vatican II as the final link in this chain of 'modern errors.' "

Lefebvre himself, writing in his *Open Letter to Confused Catholics* published in 1986, consciously placed himself at odds with the ideal of the French Revolution, and by extension, the philosophical underpinnings of the U.S. Founding Fathers. "The parallel I have drawn between the crisis in the Church and the French Revolution is not simply a metaphorical one," Lefebvre wrote. "The influence of the philosophies of the eighteenth century, and of the upheaval that they produced in the world, has continued down to our times. Those who injected that poison admit it themselves."

Lefebvre was so militantly opposed to Vatican II's move toward tolerance of other religions, and dialogue with Protestants, Jews, and Muslims, he vehemently denounced Vatican II as the work of "the devil" and "Antichrists." Given such language, it was not altogether surprising, in 1988, that he was excommunicated from the Catholic Church. His 1991 *Times* obituary would explain that

Lefebvre's "defiance of Pope John Paul II caused the first schism in the Roman Catholic Church since 1870."

———

My time in the early 1970s as an altar boy, confused more than anything by the kind of Lefebvre-inspired rants my ultraconservative father unleashed, happened to coincide with clashes within the power structure of the Catholic Church, and its U.S. adherents, that sowed the seeds of much that was to come. Up until the 1960s, no practicing Catholic running for president of the United States could avoid assumptions about somehow being unduly influenced in office by Rome. John F. Kennedy's charisma and eloquence helped override these concerns, but the kind of ultraconservative ideology espoused by Lefebvre and his adherents—including my father—was a brand of fanaticism that would encourage looking for more creative, and more hidden ways of exerting influence.

Consider an often overlooked episode in that 1960 presidential contest between Nixon and Kennedy. That October, three Catholic bishops in Puerto Rico—named a U.S. territory in 1917—issued a pastoral letter, to be read aloud in every Catholic church on the island, directly intervening in U.S. electoral politics by calling on parishioners not to vote for popular incumbent governor Luis Muñoz Marín. His offense? Favoring moderate policies on abortion and contraception.

At San Juan Cathedral, Archbishop James P. Davis, one of the letter's authors, was booed as he read from the text. In the city of Arecibo, a group of fifty led by the governor's wife walked out of San Felipe Cathedral to protest the reading of the letter. "Get out," Father William Crowley taunted the group. "You are not wanted." A United Press International report quoted one churchgoer calling the bold political intervention by Catholic leaders a "sacrilege." The Kennedy campaign, alarmed by the intervention and how it could be used against the Catholic candidate, took immediate notice and issued a statement opposing any such religious intervention in politics.

Bishop James McManus, one of the three who signed the Puerto Rico letter, soon doubled down, announcing that failure to abide by the instructions of the letter would constitute a sin. He was overtly raising Catholic guilt as a tool to win a U.S. election, exactly the sort of scenario Kennedy and his brain trust had assiduously worked to snuff out. Worse, the Vatican put out a statement defending its bishops in Puerto Rico as being within their rights in telling parishioners how to vote. Archbishop Davis, visiting Indiana soon after he and the two others issued a second letter a week after the first, adding a threat of excommunication, defended the bishops' stance by accusing the Puerto Rican government of a "militant" stance.

"Catholic life in Puerto Rico is no longer on the defensive but goes out to meet the foe," Davis told reporters, sounding like a Crusades-era firebrand. "The birth controllers and the social scientists with an itch to remake a culture and a whole people have beset Puerto Rico with not a little help from federal and insular government."

For Kennedy and his advisors, the news out of Puerto Rico amounted to their worst nightmare. The Catholic Church had held too much power for too long not to have tendrils of influence snaking through the West. In 1960 a major story was the rising influence of a secular Catholic organization called Opus Dei, founded in Spain in 1928, which was said to have had ties to Hitler's Germany. Spanish dictator Francisco Franco worked closely with Opus Dei. In January 1960, many saw Opus Dei at work in an apparent rift between Franco and the Spanish royal family relating to the education of the future king of Spain, Juan Carlos, then twenty-two.

"Observers here detect the growing influence of Opus Dei,

the secular Catholic organization, behind the sudden switch," *The New York Times* reported from Madrid that January. "They believe that Opus Dei is now determined to acquire as complete control as possible over the royal family by selecting from its own members the tutors for the young prince. Since Opus Dei has connections in government, finance and education throughout Spain, observers see far-reaching political importance in this. Up to now Opus Dei has benefited through intimate collaboration with Franco. Observers believe that Opus Dei may already, however, be preparing for the day when Franco, who is now sixty-seven, passes from the scene and the monarchy is restored."

Kennedy, running as the first Catholic candidate for president since Al Smith in 1928, could ill afford to have groups like Opus Dei fueling speculation on secret control. He needed to walk a fine line, assuring non-Catholics he was no tool of Rome while avoiding turning off Catholics. Accepting the Democratic Party nomination for president that summer at the Los Angeles Memorial Coliseum, Kennedy had deftly swatted away insinuations that as a Catholic he would be a puppet of Catholic higher-ups and, ultimately, the pope. "My decisions on every public policy will be my own—as an American, a Democrat and a free man," Kennedy declared. Protestant leaders, meeting at the Mayflower Hotel in Washington in September, issued a statement charging that "if a Catholic were elected President, he would be under heavy pressure from the hierarchy of his Church for special favor." It took a strong performance in Houston, where Senator Kennedy firmly reiterated his commitment to "absolute" religious freedom and "separation of church and state," in a speech the campaign circulated widely, for the young senator to put the Catholic issue mostly to rest, at least for the time being.

The Puerto Rico pastoral letter, which inflamed passions once again in the crucial period just before the November election, turned out to have a curious backstory, most likely as a Nixon dirty trick. As Drew Pearson explained in his syndicated column, Bishop McManus was a "close personal friend of Luis A. Ferré, the Republican opponent of Muñoz Marín for Governor." Pearson went on to explain that Ferré, "one of the wealthiest men in Puerto Rico," was a "generous contributor to the bishop's charities," and added, "GOP candidate Ferré is also close to the powers that be in Nixon campaign headquarters and to the brain-trusters of the Republican National Committee." Pearson concluded by noting that "no one remarked on . . . the fact that the Puerto Rican bishops happened to rekindle the religious issue in the United States two weeks before election day."

The established takeaway from Kennedy's victory in 1960 was that his candidacy, in showing that a Catholic could be elected to the White House, removed a national stain of bias against Catholics. Theodore White, in *The Making of the President 1960*, wrote that lieutenants of rival Lyndon B. Johnson—and later, Richard Nixon—"pumped the divisions of religion, insisting that a Catholic could not win, stimulating the deep springs of bigotry that were later to poison the general election campaign." In the end, according to Gallup, 78 percent of Catholics voted for Kennedy.

It's worth revisiting the events of that year with a fresh eye. In our contemporary vernacular, the bishops in Puerto Rico were outliers mostly in saying the quiet part out loud, not for being extremists. John Kennedy in a sense did his job too well. In seeking to quash the idea that as president he would be beholden to the Vatican, he used his glamour and intellectual vigor to such dramatic effect, he overwhelmed concerns that were actually not without some validity. Catholics of extreme viewpoint, like other religious fundamentalists, could in fact exert and manifest undue influence on elected officials and others in government. The lesson of John Kennedy's very public high-wire act as the country's first Catholic president—and only Catholic president, until Joe Biden was elected in 2020—was that Catholics needed to be cunning and secretive in pushing their political agenda.

A *New Yorker* "Letter from Madrid" in November 1960 focused on Opus Dei's stated mission of high-minded public service, but did include this arresting passage: "[S]ince its pursuit of power is relentlessly successful and its silence is absolute, it has, as Spaniards say, 'to be watched with both eyes.' The members of Opus have at least been intelligent enough to see that in Spain a powerful individual in the right place is worth infinitely more than a hundred platforms."

This insight—a belief in the incalculable value of a powerful individual in the right place—would figure prominently in the Opus Dei project in the United States over the coming decades. Its numbers grew rapidly, and so did its influence, though in the United States Catholic hierarchy, many were wary of Opus Dei. That changed with the conservative papacy of John Paul II starting in 1978. "In the early days of his pontificate, John Paul II not only confronted the left in the Church, starting with the Jesuits, but also protected . . . charismatic renewal movements and organizations such as Opus Dei," Deal W. Hudson, a former chair of Catholic outreach for the Republican National Committee, wrote in *Onward, Christian Soldiers: The Growing Political Power of Catholics and Evangelicals in the United States.* "Most of all, John Paul II legitimized the work of pro-life activists who fought abortion directly through legislation and judicial review. . . . As a result, Catholic politicians in the Democratic Party found it more difficult to pretend their pro-abortion stance conformed to Catholic teaching. Reagan's appeal to Catholics in the 1980 campaign, and throughout his terms of office, accelerated the migration of Catholics into the GOP."

The Leonard Leo–driven push toward greater impunity by ultraconservative Catholics in pushing a narrow agenda on the American people has coincided with a gradual shift from the Nixon years in which rank-and-file Catholic voters have been courted—and in turn, radicalized—as reliable Republican voters. Much of this courting has come through the use of coded language and not-so-subtly veiled imagery that appeals to—and stokes—racism and racial hatred, on the one hand, and a broader, more inchoate fear and dread on the other, arising in culturally conservative voters in reaction to the currents in social change unleashed by the upheaval of the 1960s and early 1970s, including *Roe v. Wade.*

The Nixon White House built the template for exploiting these two deeply reactionary impulses, often overlapping, which would prove to be the engine that drove a Catholic-led push to rewrite the rules of how far to take religion in U.S. politics and in remaking our Supreme Court. As with so much that unfolded, this all started with naked fear and wild notions—what amounted to conspiracy theories—of the scope and scale of influence of alternative philosophies and beliefs explored in the 1960s that repulsed conservative Catholic actors like Justice Samuel Alito, the author of *Dobbs.*

———————

Opus Dei, as a secretive organization, has often been overlooked as an important member of the larger coalition of extremist groups that would scheme together to stack the U.S. Supreme Court, but its roots in fascism accurately predicted a strain of extremism that would continue to characterize elements within its ranks. As Robert Hutchison wrote in *Their Kingdom Come: Inside the Secret World of Opus Dei,* "Opus Dei uses the Catholic Church for its own ends which are money and power. . . . They seek to colonize the summits of power. They work with stealth— 'holy discretion'—and practice 'divine deception.'"

Opus Dei member John McCloskey would run the Catholic Information Center of the Archdiocese of Washington, D.C., for many years, where, according to published reports, he recruited various right-wing luminaries to the Opus Dei cause, such as former House speaker Newt Gingrich, Senator Sam Brownback,

Robert Bork, columnists Bob Novak and Larry Kudlow, and Trump attorney general Bill Barr. It's well known that the priests at the Catholic Information Center are Opus Dei members, and expected that the same is true of its shadowy Board of Directors, which has included Leonard Leo.

The spiritual guru McCloskey had extremist views on abortion and homosexuality that were evident in a series of his blog posts. He referred to *Roe v. Wade* as an "ongoing Holocaust" whose main "villains" are the "birth control pill that created the expectation that women could control reproduction . . . eugenics and population control." Pro-choice views are the result of a "distorted mentality and transposed values." Homosexuality, in McCloskey's view, is a "disorder," not genetically or biologically determined, but caused by "weak masculine identity resulting from lack of athletic ability, poor emotional relationship with the father and poor body image." The priest insisted further that "homosexual orientation may, in many cases, be reversed."

McCloskey eventually had to leave Washington because of a sexual misconduct lawsuit, which led to Opus Dei paying the aggrieved woman, a parishioner whom McCloskey was counseling, a $977,000 settlement in 2005.

Journalistic and historical accounts of Opus Dei's influence are scarce. The Catholic Information Center, it turns out, does not provide much information. One exception that seemed to pierce the code of omertà was a March 2001 article, headlined "Washington's Quiet Club," in which *Newsweek* and its respected reporter Evan Thomas named Justices Alito and Thomas as members of Opus Dei and noted the central role played by Antonin Scalia, the Federalist Society advisor and Reagan appointee to the Supreme Court, in the circle of influential right-wing Catholics, a kind of secret underground operating in the nation's capital. "Scalia is regarded as the embodiment of Catholic conservatives," Thomas wrote. "He is careful not to be mixing politics and religion, but his faith clearly influences his work on the high court. While he is not a member of Opus Dei, his wife Maureen has attended Opus Dei 'spiritual functions,' says an Opus Dei member. Scalia's son, Father Paul Scalia, helped convert Clarence Thomas to Catholicism four years ago."

Leo served for some thirty years as executive vice president of the Federalist Society, which portrayed itself as operating outside of politics. But during those years Leo wore several other hats that drew him into the partisan political fray—all revolving around his deep Catholicism. Leo was named national cochairman of Catholic outreach for the Republican National Committee and was the Catholic strategist for the Bush reelection campaign in 2004, a year in which Bush won reelection by running fearmongering antigay ballot initiatives in key swing states.

Leo's dual roles were the embodiment of the connections between conservative antiabortion Catholic constituencies and the campaign to capture the courts. In many ways, Leo was the heir to New Right figures like Paul Weyrich and Phyllis Schlafly, who in the 1970s made the abortion issue political in a successful attempt to oust Jimmy Carter from the White House. The pair found that abortion could motivate voters in a way that the New Right's other priorities—like gutting government regulation and eliminating the separation of church and state—could not. Abortion, moreover, could be made to stand in for inchoate fears in the electorate about the sexual and civil rights revolutions and feminism. Weyrich and Schlafly forged close ties with extremist Catholic intellectuals like Richard John Neuhaus and evangelical preachers like the Reverend Jerry Falwell to form a powerful new Christian right voting bloc that Leo would inherit.

Like his forebears, Leo dedicated himself to the theocratic mission of imposing on society at large the socially regressive dictates of his own extreme brand of Catholicism, which considers abortion infanticide and homosexuality a sin, prohibits sex outside of marriage, and opposes contraception. As a board member of the Catholic Information Center, alongside the disgraced McCloskey, Leo was the connection between the moral vision of that far-right religious sect and the campaign to control the courts. As we will see, three of Leo's handpicked Supreme Court justices—Alito, Kavanaugh, and Barrett—are right-wing Catholics who voted to overturn *Roe*. (A fourth, Neil Gorsuch, is a lapsed Catholic.) The fifth vote was Leo's close Catholic friend, Clarence Thomas, both of whom have received awards that go to religious activists from the far-right Benedict Leadership Institute. "A majority of the Supreme Court and a large number of prominent public officials are faithful mass attending Catholics," Leo noted with satisfaction in a speech accepting an award from the Catholic Information Center at a black-tie Washington gala.

It's worth asking the question of whether and how much these judges bring their conservative religious beliefs into their jurisprudence. For Leo the answer is clear. Opus Dei means "work of God" in Latin. Its followers seek to serve God not only through their spiritual life but in their professional occupations. As Leo explained in that speech, "Each of us is called to seek the kingdom of God by engaging in temporal affairs and orienting them in accordance with God's will. In our particular work, we are supposed to spread the gospel to those we serve and through all that we do." Leo then went on to deny his theocratic mission, while sketching out a paranoid vision of "spiritual warfare" against secularists that seemed to undercut his own denial.

> No question Catholicism faces vile and immoral current day barbarians, secularists and bigots. These barbarians can be known by their signs. They vandalized and burned our churches after the Supreme Court overturned *Roe v. Wade*. They show up at events like this one trying to frighten and muzzle us, from coast to coast they are conducting a coordinated and large scale campaign to drive us from the communities they want to dominate. . . . They seek to have our forums censored or canceled and seek to have us fired from

our jobs or excluded from the public square if we do not swear loyalties to woke ideologies. They're fine with Catholics, as long as we draw the curtains at home and keep it in the pews. Finally there are the current day bigots, the progressive Ku Klux Klan. They spread false and slanderous rhetoric about Catholic apostolates and institutions like the one represented here tonight. They mock our practices and devotions and they repeat the KKK canard that Catholics want this country dominated and controlled by a theocracy.

Of course, most of these words are sheer fantasy. On a mission from God, that's the Manichaean world that Leo lives in.

# CHAPTER 3

# APRIL 1982: THE FEDERALIST
# SOCIETY'S REVOLUTION

Nixon was onto something in understanding that reactionary movements launched out of a deep dread of the 1960s could prove powerful. By the early 1980s, following the election of Ronald Reagan, this movement had unleashed great ferment among conservative and right-wing youth on elite college campuses. Students at Dartmouth, Yale, and Cornell founded their own alternative newspapers, *The Dartmouth Review* foremost among them. These publications, designed to provoke the campus left, often veered into racist, sexist jeremiads and exposés. They were breeding grounds for a future generation of shock-jock pundits like Ann Coulter, Laura Ingraham, and Dinesh D'Souza.

At Yale Law School and the University of Chicago Law School, three friends had a far more subtle idea of how to challenge liberal orthodoxy and promote Reaganite ideology through what Lewis Powell had called "judicial action," although they pretended otherwise. Steven Calabresi of Yale and Chicago students David McIntosh and Lee Liberman Otis decided in 1982 to organize law school chapters of a new conservative group they called the Federalist Society for Law and Public Policy Studies. For advisors the students turned to their favorite law professors: Robert Bork at Yale and Antonin Scalia at Chicago.

Whatever the rhetoric at innumerable Washington banquets and cigar-filled dinners in later years, the student founders could have no idea at the outset that the powerful national networking vehicle they were launching would in time be responsible for dramatically shifting the federal judiciary so far to the right on virtually every issue near and dear to their billionaire backers, from the role of money in politics, to the reach of government in regulating business, consumer protections, voting rights, and abortion. They also sought to roll back the landmark civil rights, privacy rights, and separation of church and state rulings of the liberal Earl Warren Court. And that is just what these three—zealous, blessed with entrepreneurial organizing skills, and backed by some of the biggest donors on the American right—eventually accomplished. Today six of nine Republican-appointed Supreme Court justices are or have been members of the Federalist Society, including all five of the *Dobbs* majority.

(I had my own connection to the Federalist Society for a time in the 1990s. In 1993, following the publication of *The Real Anita Hill,* I was invited to give a speech to a Federalist Society gathering in Washington, D.C., attended by both Ted Olson, a Reagan administration lawyer and major force behind the society in years to come, and Laurence Silberman, among others, and was greeted with the kind of energetic applause with which one honors a conquering hero. That year I was also invited by the Yale Federalist Society to speak and gave a speech at Yale Law School on October 7, 1993, in which I dismissed the avalanche of criticism my book had generated as "hysterical condemnation." As more than a few observers noted, I was using coded language that implied an antifeminist agenda. The speech did not go over well on the liberal campus, but I took that as a badge of honor. I was in effect an honorary member of the Federalist Society, at the time, a fellow traveler, an ally and friend to many of its leading members.)

Perhaps alone among the speakers at the inaugural two-day conference of the Federalist Society at Yale in April 1982, Ted Olson believed that the assembled two hundred students were present at the creation of something special, if not momentous. "I sense that we are at one of those points in history where the pendulum may be beginning to swing in the other direction," he said. "Of course, we do not know now, and no one will really know for many years, whether the 1980 elections have wrought a significant and long-lasting change. But I think that there is an opportunity here; and the organization of this society and this symposium is a cause for optimism and a sign that perhaps something is happening."

When it was Robert Bork's turn to speak, his own words showed that his new doctrine of originalism, which would become the Big Idea behind the judicial power grab, was really a way for its adherents to justify in legalese enacting their own reactionary policy agenda, determining by judicial fiat whose rights needed to be protected and whose did not. Originalism was first conjured by Bork in a 1971 treatise, "Neutral Principles and Some First Amendment Problems," in which he argued that judges should decide cases in accordance with "neutral principles" as reflected in the intentions of the Framers.

Bork and his followers asserted that the law must be interpreted based strictly on their understanding of the Constitution at the time it was written and adopted by the Founders (all white Christian men), as against seeing the Constitution as an ever-evolving document as society inevitably changed. Originalists claim only those rights specifically named in the Constitution are valid. If rights were denied hundreds of years ago, they would be denied in the present day. On this basis, Bork had attacked landmark civil rights laws and privacy rights court rulings.

The bull's-eye was drawn from the beginning: abortion rights, which had been guaranteed with the votes of five Republican-appointed justices. Bork's speech at the Federalist Society's first conference made national news, as an unusually blunt talk from a newly appointed Reagan judge on the D.C. Circuit Court of Appeals. Bork, the AP reported, as published in the *Los Angeles Times,* "said *Roe v. Wade,* the Supreme Court decision that in effect allowed abortion-on-demand, 'is a classic instance' of the court imposing its morality on local jurisdictions. Abortion issues should be decided by local authorities." Bork went on to argue that states should be able to define "acceptable sexual behavior" and he assailed a long line of settled high court decisions on hot-button issues from busing to school prayer, privacy, and contraception. "The problem, he told his audience, is that Justices on the Court are legislating morality based on their own 'middle-class values,'" *The New York Times* reported. Bork here was projecting: He accused liberal judges of bringing personal biases into their jurisprudence, when in fact it was the Federalists, brandishing their cramped legal theories, who were doing this. Originalism was a fraudulent cover for reactionary judges, with a certain moral and Christian religious vision, to trample precedent, block progressive priorities they oppose, and impose antimajoritarian results on the population at large.

Worse still, originalism frequently relies on fake history, and as such it is not a legitimate judicial method. The amateur historians on the court have established a seeming monopoly on divining the real meaning of the Constitution, when in fact there is no unambiguous intent of the Framers. In asserting a bogus authority, originalists are forced to cherry-pick or invent facts to support false arguments. A long line of recent decisions by the Thomas Court, including the *Dobbs* decision itself, were based on bad-faith history, as will be shown later.

Four months after the successful forum, which prompted inquiries from students at several law schools about starting chapters, cofounder Lee Liberman Otis approached the Scaife Foundation for funding. She found a receptive audience. Since the circulation of the militant Powell Memo a decade before, Richard Mellon Scaife, an eccentric billionaire banker based in Pittsburgh, had been the lead funder of a new network of highly effective right-wing institutions like the Heritage Foundation think tank and the American Legislative Exchange Council, which pushed a right-wing policy agenda into the states. Liberman Otis was straightforward in her letter to foundation officer Richard Larry that a key goal of the new group was to reverse liberal dominance in the nation's law schools.

"While there now exist a number of organizations which are beginning to provide a counterweight to the liberal public interest groups, no comparable effort has been made at the law school level," she wrote.

In the proposal one could see the vision taking shape of the society functioning as a kind of job placement agency for those ideologically suitable: "Conservatives have long bemoaned the fact that clerkships to prominent conservative jurists have often gone to people with liberal views. Similarly it has often been contended that far too many legal posts in government offices (even those not controlled by civil service regulations) have been held by liberals under Republican administrations. Finally, it has been generally acknowledged that there is an insufficient number of conservative law school faculty." Unmentioned was perhaps the most important role the society would play during Republican administrations as a seal of approval and turnstile for lifetime appointments of originalists to the federal bench.

All three society founders were soon beneficiaries of their own strategy, each of them taking up legal posts in the Reagan administration, sending "a very powerful message that the terms of advancement associated with political ambition were being turned on their head: clear ideological positioning, not cautiousness, was now an affirmative qualification for appointed office," Steven M. Teles, author of *The Rise of the Legal Movement,* observed.

Despite Bork's outspokenness—or perhaps because of it?—the society's founders decided in the coming months to position the organization to hide its true purpose—revoking liberal gains in the courts in the 1960s and 1970s—from outsiders. The group would do no legal, advocacy, or organizing work, take no positions on issues, and even sometimes dropped the word "conservative" from its narrow mission. It would be pitched on campuses as a "debating society," complete with prominent liberal speakers like First Amendment lawyer Floyd Abrams, in part so that it could more easily attract and convert law students. Membership in the society ostensibly meant nothing other than access to other members, who wore ties depicting James Madison, regarded as the "father of the Constitution"; the ideological commitment would go unstated.

Yet those who knew knew: Belonging to the Federalist Society certified individuals to Republican administrations as suitable true believers for positions throughout the executive branch of government and, increasingly, onto seats on the federal bench. Critically, this stealth strategy would enable originalist nominees for any Senate-confirmed post to deny with a straight face that membership in the organization implied any political or ideological leanings whatsoever. In her Senate confirmation hearing in 2001, Federalist Society member Edith Brown Clement, nominated to be circuit judge for the Fifth Circuit, was asked by Patrick Leahy: "Do you share a judicial philosophy with the Federalist Society?" She replied: "I am unaware of any judicial philosophy articulated by the Federalist Society."

Sounds benign enough, but the answer is insidious. Leo himself is on record stating that the goal of the Federalist Society is nothing less than *to use the law "as a driver, just like the left did, to try to achieve a more just, free society."*

By the late 1980s both student and lawyer chapters were growing. Both funding and prestige soared. President Reagan addressed a Federalist Society conference in 1988. Alan Dershowitz, invited to the same conference as a "token civil libertarian," wrote this account of the president's speech to the Federalists: "Reagan claimed credit for reducing crime by 7 percent and blamed liberals for the continuing problems of violence, drugs and organized crime. He boasted of how tough his judicial appointments—many of whom were selected from the ranks of the Federalist Society itself and other like-minded groups—had been on criminals and on constitutional technicalities." "Constitutional technicalities" was a telling phrase. In practice it meant that the Federalist Society judges would trample constitutional precedent and the rule of law to get the results their rich benefactors wanted.

———

Leonard Leo, born on Long Island in 1965, was always a very serious individual going back to childhood. His father's father had emigrated from Italy at age fourteen and worked his way up at Brooks Brothers, starting as a tailor, later designing clothes and ending up a vice president. More than his own father, a pastry chef who died when Leonard was young, his grandfather was an important role model. For years, he had his picture on prominent display in his Federalist Society office. "My grandfather was a very hard worker," Leo later told the *Washington Examiner*. "He became very successful. He was a very faithful man. He was a good family man, and he was able to thrive in all of those ways because of the freedoms that we have in our country. . . . There's no doubt that my experiences early on with my grandfather helped me to understand why America was exceptional and why the freedom that our Constitution provides is what ultimately leads people to goodness and to their purpose in life."

As far back as fourth grade in New Jersey, where the family moved when his mother remarried, young Leonard told friends he wanted to be a lawyer when he grew up. "When you're that age, you want to be a baseball player or a policeman or a fireman," engineer Snehal Shaw, a childhood friend of Leo's, told WNYC's *On the Media* podcast. "Nobody says they want to be lawyers at nine or ten years old, but he did. If you're different at that age, you're going to get bullied a little bit. . . . Growing up, in elementary school, junior high, high school, he was probably more of an outcast than someone who was popular."

Few high school yearbook predictions look more on target in retrospect than one in the 1983 edition of the Monroe Township High yearbook. Pictured for "Most Likely to Succeed" are Leonard Leo, looking painfully awkward in his usual shirt and tie, though classmates said he made a habit of wearing a tie in high school, and Sally Schroeder. The two are awash in cash, with bills spread on the table in front of them and in their hands. The pair would marry six years later, at St. Augustine of Canterbury Church in Franklin Park, raise a large family together—and rake in the cash by the barrelful.

Leo first wanted to attend Georgetown University in Washington, but ended up at Cornell, where he fell under the spell of Jeremy Rabkin, an outspoken, highly opinionated professor who at the time was codirector of Cornell's Program on Courts and Public Policy. Rabkin, Harvard-trained and brilliant, was by all accounts a gifted educator later named "Cornell's Most Influential Teacher"—twice. He was also a right-wing extremist. As he wrote in 1983, the year Leo arrived on campus, "Ten years after Watergate, liberals are our greatest threat to the rule of law." Even in a serious journal like *The Public Interest*, Rabkin's style sounds more knee-jerk than scholarly, as in the Fall 1983 issue, where he wrote, "Few legal scholars these days believe that constitutional law need have any actual connection with the Constitution.... Yet self-styled defenders of 'civil rights' and 'civil liberties' still march under the banner of the Constitution, as 'public interest' champions invariably denounce President Reagan's regulatory appointees for disregarding 'the law.'" And in 1984, Rabkin, inverting reality, wrote in *The American Spectator*, "Judicial power remains a weapon almost exclusively available to the left, even if it is becoming a less reliable weapon than it once was."

Leo, eager to gain from Rabkin's influence, applied for a position as one of his two research assistants—and was selected, along with another Cornell graduate at the time, Ann Coulter. Working with Rabkin as his advisor, Leo wrote his senior honors thesis on the doctrine of originalism as applied to the free expression of religion. Many years later, the Leo-dominated Supreme Court would take up the issue and adopt his early views, making up the notion of "religious liberty" to justify discrimination as free speech.

His last year as a Cornell undergraduate, Leo spent several months in Washington on a Cornell program and interned for the Senate Judiciary Subcommittee on the Constitution, where he first met Stephen Markman, a future Michigan Supreme Court chief justice. Markman, at the time chief counsel to the committee, introduced Leo to the Federalist Society, taking him to regular lunch meetings at the Golden Palace Restaurant in Chinatown, including one in November 1985 in which Attorney General Ed Meese gave a speech on originalism, as Leo relayed to the *Washington Examiner.*

Meese used all the right code language to hide what the originalists were really doing. "In recent decades many have come to view the Constitution—more accurately, part of the Constitution, provisions of the Bill of Rights and the fourteenth amendment—as a charter for judicial activism on behalf of various constituencies," Meese said. "Those who hold this view often have lacked demonstrable textual or historical support for their conclusions. Instead they have 'grounded' their rulings in appeals to social theories, to moral philosophies, or personal notions of human dignity or to 'penumbras' somehow emanating ghostlike from various provisions identified and not identified in the Bill of Rights. The problem with this approach is that, as John Hart Ely, dean of the Stanford Law School, had observed with respect to one such decision, "is not that it is bad constitutional law, but that it is not constitutional law at all."

From there, Meese concluded, "Recently one of the distinguished judges of one of our federal appeals courts got it about right when he said, 'The truth is that the judge who looks outside the Constitution always looks inside himself and nowhere else.'"

Who was that judge being quoted? Federalist Society founding father Robert Bork.

"That speech had an enormous impact on my thinking and really helped to crystallize my views," Leo told the *Examiner.*

Leo was hooked—and eager to join the Federalist Society network and work for its goals. When he found out Cornell Law School had no Federalist Society chapter, he founded one himself in 1989, and was soon bringing in guest speakers, like Justice Department official William Bradford Reynolds, an architect of the anti–civil rights policies of the Reagan administration, and hosting conferences, including one at which Leo first met Brett Kavanaugh and Alex Azar, respectively the future Supreme Court justice and future Trump cabinet secretary.

In 1989, after finishing his law degree, Leo moved to Washington to clerk for Judge Randall Rader on the U.S. Court of Federal Claims, which led to another clerkship, for Judge A. Raymond Randolph, on the U.S. Circuit Court of Appeals for the D.C. Circuit. Leo was expanding his network quickly, first meeting and befriending Clarence Thomas in September 1990 when he was clerking for Randolph and Thomas sat on the same court.

In 1991, Leo would go to work full-time for the Federalist Society in Washington (as hiring decisions go, this was a ten-strike), assisting his close friend Clarence Thomas in his confirmation hearings, and eventually leading high-profile, expensive advocacy and advertising campaigns for the confirmations of Roberts, Alito, Gorsuch, Kavanaugh, and Barrett. Leo built a powerful network of influential right-wing groups funded by mostly anonymous donors through a labyrinth of dark-money accounts; independent researchers have documented that Leo's network is supported by billionaire industrialist Charles Koch and pro-Trump activist Rebekah Mercer, among others, whose interests in the decisions of the court ran more toward promoting an unfettered business environment with far less regulation. Leo's genius was to fuse the goals of these business conservatives with his own agenda of imposing the values of far-right Catholicism on the nation.

The full force of the Federalist Society came to be felt first in the administration of George H. W. Bush, where those associated with the Federalist Society took up key positions in the White House, the Justice Department, and federal agencies, allowing not only close coordination across the executive branch but also a successful smear campaign that put Clarence Thomas on the high court in 1991. According to one scholar, "every single federal judge appointed in the two Bush presidencies was either a society member or approved by members." One email from inside the Bush White House identified Leo as the "cash machine" behind the operation.

The society had lawyer chapters in every major city and student chapters in every accredited law school. Over time, the work of the society reached far beyond networking and credentialing. The Federalist Society and their backers picked the judges. They also funded academic centers where bought-and-paid-for scholars developed fringe theories later to be adopted by donor-approved judges. They backed litigants to bring cases that could advance their agendas. And they supported an army of right-wing organizations posing as public interest groups that routinely filed amicus curiae (friend of the court) briefs in the cases to signal to the judges how to rule.

It was a veritable conveyor belt of underhanded tactics that, taken in sum, equaled full court control. Amanda Hollis-Brusky, in a 2015 book *Ideas with Consequences: The Federalist Society and the Conservative Counterrevolution,* found that "focusing on key recent decisions on issues like campaign finance, gun control and state sovereignty, as many as two dozen people with Federalist Society connections played some role in crafting the arguments, arguing the cases, clerking for the judges or issuing the rulings."

Here's how it works in practice. One primary goal of the big funders is hobbling the power of government agencies that regulate their ability to pollute. That's what the Thomas court did in narrowing the definition of "water" for purposes of EPA regulation involving the Clean Water Act to exclude wetlands. In that case, among the dozens of groups filing amicus curiae briefs were several—Cato Institute, Claremont Institute, Liberty Justice Center, and the Americans for Prosperity Foundation— funded anonymously by pro-pollution donors to the Leo network. When the court struck down gun restrictions in New York State on the originalist grounds that there was "no tradition" of such regulations in U.S. history, among the amicus curiae were the Cato Institute (again), the Buckeye Institute, the Rutherford Institute, the Claremont Institute (again), and the Independent Women's Law Center. In a campaign finance case, the right-wing majority rejected California's efforts to bring transparency to contributors, in effect creating a new right to dark money. In that case, the amicus curiae were, among others, the Buckeye Institute (again), the Pacific Research Center, Cato Institute (again), Judicial Watch, and Liberty Justice Center (again)—all funded anonymously. You get the idea: These front groups are financed to create the appearance of independence, when in fact they are manufactured and all beholden to the same group of funders, whose interests before the courts are hidden in the scheme. The briefs, often relying on false facts and twisted history, are used to signal to the amenable judges the arguments the big donors want advanced and the outcomes they favor.

Wash, rinse, repeat. Often the front groups find and fund the plaintiffs in the suits as well. Whether weakening organized labor, striking down student debt relief, or gutting consumer protections, the same rigged system comes into play.

———

If Clarence Thomas never became rich stripping away other people's rights, the same cannot be said of Leonard Leo, whom Thomas has called both a "mentor" and "the third most powerful person in the country." Using the credibility of the Federalist Society platform, Leo constructed a web of bare-knuckle political nonprofits to do work the Federalist Society could not do under IRS rules governing charities. The web of front groups was designed in such a way as to conceal the group's activities, tactics, and donors and their interests—to defeat transparency. Foremost among these is the Judicial Crisis Network, essentially the PR arm of the Federalist Society, which takes in tens of millions of dollars from wealthy conservatives, including, prominently, the Koch brothers network, right-wing donors who coordinate their giving, to campaign for Federalist Society judges, with most of the funding hidden from public view. The group was conceived in 2005 at a private Leo-hosted dinner celebrating George W. Bush's reelection. The guests included Antonin Scalia and the California donor Robin Arkley II, the "foreclosure king" of California, who acquires distressed mortgages then forecloses on the owners. According to Sheldon Whitehouse, who has studied the structure of Leo's opaque empire, it has "all the earmarks of a covert operation of the sort run by foreign countries in the intelligence arena, but this is run in America, by Americans, against Americans."

Leo is also a member of the shadowy Council for National Policy, a tight network of social and religious conservatives, alongside his longtime friend Ginni Thomas. The CNP is a kind of who's who directorate of the conservative movement. In 2016, the CNP threw its considerable weight behind Donald Trump's candidacy in exchange for policy concessions and "its choice of federal judges," according to a report by Anne Nelson in *The Washington Spectator.* "Ginni Thomas was known as the not-so-secret weapon of CNP and its allies," the report continued. Before the 2020 election, CNP developed plans to overturn the election if Trump lost. The group was a key player in the January 6 insurrection, with its president, William L. Walton, signing a letter stating, "There is no doubt Donald J. Trump is the lawful winner of the presidential election." As we'll see later, Ginni Thomas was a leading cog in the insurrectionist wheel.

Leo liked to say his judicial advocacy tactics were a mirror of those used by left-wing groups in the campaign to derail Robert Bork's Supreme Court nomination, but this was disingenuous. In fact, the scale of Leo's efforts was utterly without precedent. In 2005 and 2006, JCN took in hundreds of thousands of dollars to run slick confirmation campaigns supporting John Roberts and Samuel Alito, including paid advertisements, telemarketing, polling, and mobilization of conservative grassroots groups. A decade later, with Donald Trump running on an antiabortion platform and promising to appoint Federalist-approved MAGA judges, the special interest funds available to Leo's network ballooned to an unheard-of $250 million in dark money. All together from 2014 through 2022, by my count, Leo's network raised $763 million on its court-packing efforts. Given that big business stood to gain billions from favorable court rulings, the investment was a bargain.

With increased funding, Leo formed an unholy loop: Leo's network funded challenges to laws he opposed, such as President Biden's student loan forgiveness program and affirmative action requirements, and also funneled cash to antigay groups like the Alliance Defending Freedom to challenge antidiscrimination laws. When the cases reached Leo's handpicked judges, he got the political results he and his backers wanted from the compromised judges. (Leo's groups also pushed voter suppression laws in the states in a direct assault on American democracy through a group with the creepy Orwellian name Honest Elections Project. Of course, cheating to elect Republican presidents and senators was an essential element in the court-packing scheme.)

As Leo's coffers filled, he formed a for-profit consulting firm, CRC Advisors, and his nonprofits hired the consulting firm for Leo's services in a circular profit scheme. According to *Politico*, $43 million flowed from Leo's nonprofits into his pockets in just two years. The extraordinary sum attracted the attention of watchdog groups who raised questions about whether Leo was bilking the nonprofits for work he never did. He has also come under investigation by the D.C. attorney general for potentially violating IRS charity rules on personal enrichment. "Since 2016," *Politico* reported, "his recent wealth accumulation has included two new mansions in Maine, four new cars, private school tuition for his children, hundreds of thousands of dollars in donations to Catholic causes and a wine buyer and locker at Morton's steakhouse." (The largesse also created dissension with the Federalist Society itself, according to a society-watcher. Federalist Society president Eugene Meyer makes about $650,000 a year, not bad for nonprofit work, but nothing like the sums siphoned off by Leo.)

Leo's close friend Ginni Thomas was in on the shocking grift. Just days prior to the publishing of the 2010 case *Citizens United v. Federal Election Commission*—which by a 5–4 vote with her husband in the majority loosened federal regulation on political spending and benefited nonprofit groups with anonymous donors—Ginni Thomas filed paperwork to form such a new dark-money group. It was inspired by the Tea Party uprising against President Obama and could take advantage of the new ruling, in which her husband would be a deciding vote. Harlan Crow, the billionaire who gave the Thomases luxury travel and other pricey gifts, gave Ginni Thomas $500,000 in seed money for the new venture she called Liberty Central, whose goal was to tank Obama's health care agenda. Obama was "hard left," leading the nation to "tyranny," according to Thomas. Leo joined the board as the group's moneyman.

After a kerfuffle in the press about the propriety of a Supreme Court justice's wife running a right-wing lobby shop funded by anonymous donors that would advocate for an issue that inevitably would come before the court, Ginni quit Liberty Central. But only days later she set up a firm, Liberty Consulting, to quietly continue her work. This time Thomas tried to present herself as a bridge between the traditional conservative movement and the Tea Party. In an email sent to the offices of freshmen members who had been elected in the GOP wave of 2010, Ginni wrote, "As self-appointed Ambassador to the Freshmen class and an Ambassador to the Tea Party Movement, I am devoted to your individual and corporate success to restore the greatness of this nation and am happy to find ways to be helpful and connect you with resources! I am also committed to the new citizen activists get more and more effective at wielding their power and influence for good, for restoring limited constitutional government, free enterprise, individual liberty and national security!" Along with Ginni's email was a cover note from an assistant, reported here exclusively, who explained, "Ginni knows all the good guys in DC—established conservatives and resources to help connect and ensure success on your priority projects. . . . Ginni has become a great friend of the tea party movement in many areas of the country, as well as can find ways to increase your reputation amongst the right conservatives and beyond and inside the beltway."

Liberty Consulting was propped up financially by Leonard Leo, according to a suspect arrangement unearthed by *Politico*. The money flowed to Ginni from yet another Leo-controlled entity called the Judicial Education Project, funded by a secret donor. It's unclear what actual work Ginni did for the nonprofit, whose work is supposed to be charitable in nature, or whether in fact she did any work at all. With Ginni on the payroll, JEP filed amicus briefs with the Supreme Court supporting one side or the other in hot-button cases, offering legal arguments, and tipping off judges how to rule, for example arguing that provisions of the Obama health care law were unconstitutional, a position adopted by Clarence Thomas in a dissent in the case. JEP also filed a brief contending that the contraception health care requirements of the Obama health law infringed on the religious freedom of the owners of the Hobby Lobby stores. The court adopted JEP's position with Thomas in the majority—an extraordinary conflict of interest that Thomas blithely and typically ignored.

Moving money around and through his nonprofits like a shell game to reward his friends seems to be a Leo pastime. In another shady transaction, Leo directed Trump pollster Kellyanne Conway to bill the JEP and use the money to pay Ginni. Leo told Conway that he wanted her to "give Ginni another 25K," *The Washington Post* reported. Leo underlined that the paperwork should have "No mention of Ginni—of course." Ultimately more than 100K reached Ginni—and her husband—through this pass-through. Undeterred, Ginni Thomas found other venues for antagonizing the Obama administration. She joined the Conservative Action Project to try to derail health care reform and, though she was the wife of a sitting justice, to dirty up Obama's judicial nominees. In 2021, she signed a CAP letter demanding the House Republican Conference remove Liz Cheney and Adam Kinzinger from the conference for their involvement with the "supposedly bipartisan" January 6 House committee investigation. Of course, Ginni herself would later be brought in to testify to Congress about her own election denial activities, but much more about that later.

The full scope of Leo's ambitions is clear. More than simply a political operation to pack the courts, he sits atop an industry that in effect took over control of the courts for special interest donors. Originalist judges are selected with the Federalist Society imprimatur. Groups are funded to bring suits and file amicus briefs before the court, pushing Leo's agenda and signaling to the judges and clerks the desired outcome. And Leo's donors profit from the many Thomas Court decisions that enrich big business. Buying off Clarence and Ginni Thomas has been chump change in the overall scheme.

## CHAPTER 4

# APRIL 1986: WHEN CLARENCE MET GINNI

They met at an affirmative action conference in New York. Clarence Thomas, at the time EEOC chairman in the Reagan administration, had quickly established himself as a lightning rod for criticism, and he was a featured speaker at the April 1986 conference. He took an openly combative approach. "I have watched this debate over quotas, for example, rage for the past four years," Thomas said. "What do you do with people who not only have not been educated for two or three generations, but who can't be educated at this point?"

Thomas, a Missouri assistant attorney general from 1974 to 1977, had earned the notice of movement conservatives in Washington who recognized how useful he could be even before Reagan appointed him to a job in the Department of Education in 1981, when Thomas was working as a legislative assistant for the Senate Commerce Committee. *Conservative Digest* publisher Richard Viguerie lauded Thomas in a December 1980 cover essay in the *Los Angeles Times* Sunday Opinion section as part of "a new breed of Blacks . . . who recognize the destructive cycle of dependency fostered by the liberal program." At a "black alternatives" conference in San Francisco that month organized by the right-wing Institute for Contemporary Studies Thomas had blurted out, "It's really kind of good to be here because someone might agree with me for a change." Thomas's appointment to the top civil rights job in the Education Department that May had civil rights groups "concerned about Thomas," as the *St. Louis Post-Dispatch* put it, "because of his association with a group of conservative blacks who oppose busing and minority-hiring standards."

Among the participants at that April 1986 conference in New York was Virginia Lamp, a labor lawyer for the U.S. Chamber of Commerce who had also established herself as controversial and outspoken. Midge Decter, a leading neoconservative writer and antifeminist, introduced Thomas and Lamp, and the two ended up sharing a cab to the airport. Lamp at the time was in a long-distance relationship, and Thomas, divorced from his first wife and soured by some dating experiences, told friends he planned at the time to remain single.

As the cab made its way toward the airport, Thomas at one point reached into his wallet and pulled out a slip of paper, as he tells the story in *My Grandfather's Son*. Lamp asked the EEOC chairman how he handled being a target of public criticism. Thomas produced a prayer he said he recited daily from St. Francis of Assisi, and the two discussed their shared religious faith. Lamp offered to set Thomas up with a Black woman at the Chamber of Commerce, but Thomas declined the offer. "I thanked her but explained I wasn't interested in dating," he writes. Exiting the cab, Thomas suggested they "do lunch," but did not follow up.

The two had a lot in common beyond religious faith, abundant self-confidence, and a sense of mission; they also shared a similar ideological outlook. Four years earlier, the Supreme Court ruling in *County of Washington v. Gunther* had endorsed the concept of comparable worth, or equal pay for work of equal value. The EEOC under Clarence Thomas had stayed quiet on the issue, but finally in a June 1985 press conference, Thomas announced that the commission had taken a stand in a case involving an Illinois housing authority. As the Associated Press reported, "the commission on a 5–0 vote rejected the use of comparable worth as a means of determining job discrimination. Specifically, the panel said the theory of comparable worth is not recognized under Title VII of the Civil Rights Act of 1964."

The AP quoted Thomas offering this defense of the controversial move: "There was no allegation—and no evidence—that any barriers existed to prevent males and females from moving beyond job categories. . . . We found no evidence that the pay difference was due to sex, and therefore we could not infer that sex was a factor in wage setting."

This was a dodge. The numbers were stark. At the Illinois housing authority involved in the case, administrative staff was 85 percent female, and 88 percent of the maintenance staff was male. Administrative staff was paid less.

The same AP article quoted U.S. Chamber of Commerce labor relations attorney Virginia Lamp cheering on the EEOC position, calling comparable worth "the Trojan Horse of the '80s" and adding: "Rather than using our civil rights laws to identify and address discrimination as it exists in the workplace, comparable worth advocates want to label a social phenomenon—the fact women on average make less than men on average—as 'discrimination' and then use our civil rights laws for purposes for which they were never intended."

In May 1986 a lunch was arranged at the University Club in Washington for Thomas to meet with a dozen business lobbyists and rally support for a second term as EEOC chairman. It was raining that day, and only a few people showed up, Thomas recalled in his book—but among them was Ginni Lamp, whom he'd met a few weeks earlier in New York, now "soaked to the skin" by the downpour outside. This time Thomas did follow up and the two had lunch at Hunan Rose on K Street. He describes it as a "pleasant, professional" conversation.

It was a movie, Thomas relates, that set them in motion as a couple, an early-afternoon screening of *Short Circuit,* no less. For those of you not up on second-tier 1980s films, this was a science-fiction comedy starring Ally Sheedy and Steve Guttenberg, who look after a military robot that has been struck by lightning and turned into an amiable sidekick. Much of the humor in the movie comes from the character of Ben Jabituya, the Indian assistant to the robot's designer, played by Fisher Stevens (not Indian), using a hilariously bad Indian accent to say things like "Did she stick her tongue down your throat?" followed by, "Oh my goodness, I am sporting a tremendous woody right now!"

Thomas loved the movie and laughed uproariously throughout. "I found it hilarious," he writes, "though Virginia seemed more amused by my laughter than the movie."

They may not have shared similar tastes in movies, but they were both highly ambitious culture warriors whose extreme political viewpoints fit like a glove. Small talk about hating equal pay for women might not be the way most couples began a courtship, but for these two, that and related topics could keep them going for hours. They were deeply compatible politically, and the compulsive drive each felt soon fused into a common sense of mission.

———

Growing up poor in Georgia, Clarence Thomas found in Catholicism a respite from the sting of a racist society—and he made a solemn vow to "Daddy," his grandfather, to enroll in seminary and see his studies through to the end. In the small Georgia community of Pin Point, founded after the Civil War by freed slaves, Thomas grew up speaking a dialect called Geechee and later struggled to master standard English. As a boy he had no relationship with his own father, a farmhand who left his wife and kids when Clarence was two, and at age seven he was sent to his grandparents in Savannah. Daddy was a firm believer in hard work who made a living selling heating oil and ice from the back of his truck. "The damn vacation is over!" he told Clarence and his brother, welcoming them to a new life of getting up early, working hard, and keeping quiet.

In April 1968, Thomas was enrolled in Conception Seminary College, a small Roman Catholic seminary in northwest Missouri. Soon after the Reverend Martin Luther King Jr. was murdered, Thomas heard a white student at the seminary say: "That's what they should do to all the n——." Thomas, nineteen years old at the time, thought to himself, "We're supposed to be people of God. If people have that view here, then this is not a place for me to be," as a friend later told *The New York Times*. Thomas lost his faith. He decided to leave seminary, and give up on his dream of being a priest. The move created a rupture in his relationship with his grandfather that never fully healed. Yet he honored his grandfather's influence in the title of his autobiography.

Thomas ended up at College of the Holy Cross, a private Catholic university in Massachusetts, a much different environment than the Missouri seminary he'd fled, and his arrival there was thanks in some degree to the intervention of Rev. John Brooks, a theology scholar who would go on to serve as Holy Cross president. As current Holy Cross president Vincent D. Rougeau wrote in a May 2023 *Boston Globe* article, "During the height of the civil rights movement, at a time when racial integration was sparking controversy on many campuses, [Brooks] drove around the country to personally recruit Black high school students to the college's all-male, primarily white campus in Worcester. The twenty young men he recruited have become an illustrious group, including business leaders, a Pulitzer Prize winner, a Super Bowl champion and Supreme Court Justice Clarence Thomas, class of 1971." Rougeau, a scholar of race who became Holy Cross's first Black president, called Thomas "once the beneficiary of the most overt example of race-based admissions I can imagine."

Thomas, who in later years would rage against affirmative action programs as demeaning and hurtful to Blacks, apparently tried to get around the hypocrisy of both benefiting from and assailing affirmative action programs by contending that Brooks's efforts were not a "program." "I wasn't part of some program to Father Brooks," Thomas is quoted in Diane Brady's book *Fraternity: In 1968, a Visionary Priest Recruited 20 Black Men to the College of Holy Cross and Changed Their Lives and the Course of History*. "We weren't symbols to him. We were just kids."

Soon Thomas was at Holy Cross, his studies financed through a Martin Luther King scholarship. Yet in a 1991 interview with *Business Week* that would have been comical if it was not so serious, Thomas attempted to claim that he was not the beneficiary of affirmative action at Holy Cross.

"That was the creation of politicians, the people with a lot of mouth and nothing to say, and your industry," Thomas insisted. "Everything becomes affirmative action."

Thomas enrolled at Holy Cross in 1968 during a time of roiling cultural currents, especially for a young Black man on campus. He was filled with anger but didn't know how to focus it or channel it. "We were supposed to be revolutionaries," he said later. "We were for anybody who was kind of in your face."

That included the revolutionary Black Panther Party, founded in Oakland, California, a militant, Marxist, Black Power group. At Holy Cross, Thomas "often dressed in the black tam, black leather jacket and black combat boots sported by the Black Panther Party, which preached a mixture of armed revolution and self-sufficiency," *The Atlanta Constitution* reported in 1990. "It was the aspect of self-sufficiency that attracted Mr. Thomas to the Panthers, as well as to Malcolm X and Stokely Carmichael, classmates say." In a 1983 speech, Thomas would refer to Nation of Islam leader Louis Farrakhan, an antiwhite Black suprema- cist, as "a man I have admired." He would, over the years, find a way to twist his sympathy for Black nationalism into an up- by-the-bootstraps justification for opposing programs that help Black people.

Among the points in the Holy Cross Black Student Union man- ifesto, developed with Thomas as secretary-treasurer, were such injunctions as "The Black man does not want or need the white woman. The Black man's history shows that the white woman is the cause of his failure to be the true Black man." Thomas was a hard-liner on the issue, and even composed a poem, "Is you is, or is you ain't, a brother?" in which he pushed the message of what Black men owed Black women. "Looking out of a window at the Hogan Campus Center during one BSU meeting, Thomas spot- ted a particularly attractive Black woman from a nearby school strolling through a parking lot with a white guy," Kevin Merida and Michael Fletcher wrote in their 2007 biography *Supreme Dis- comfort: The Divided Soul of Clarence Thomas.* " 'Do I see a Black woman with a white man?' Thomas said, according to [classmate Gordon] Davis. 'How could that be?' That edgy race conscious- ness was something that friends noticed in Thomas for years."

Later, Thomas would look back and say that it was faith that showed him a way back from hate. "I saw what I had become, lashing out at every single thing. And then I asked God, 'If you take anger out of my heart, I'll never hate again.' And that was the beginning of a slow return to where I started."

That was the story Thomas told, but it does not survive deeper scrutiny. Hate remained central to his being; if you opposed him or his ambitions, he hated you. The story of Thomas's early life is of a man whose passions and self-concept change dramatically depending on whose influence he falls under, from his grandfa- ther to the nuns at school to the priests at seminary and finally his fellow students and professors at Holy Cross and Yale Law School. Thomas was impressionable, ready to be shaped by others. He was not the architect of the plan to work decades to bring about a Thomas Court, religiously motivated ánd willing to dispense with the guardrails, but he was an essential vessel for the plan to move forward.

At Holy Cross, Thomas applied to Yale Law School, which at the time had a program in place to admit 10 percent minority students—and was accepted. As *The New York Times* rather bluntly spelled out the truth of the matter in a 1991 article, "Judge Clarence Thomas, who came to prominence as a fierce black critic of racial preference programs, was admitted to Yale Law School under an explicit affirmative action plan with the goal of having blacks and other minority members make up 10 percent of the entering class, university officials said. Under the program, which was adopted in 1971, the year Judge Thomas applied, blacks and some Hispanic applicants were evaluated differently from whites, the official said."

As civil rights giant Rosa Parks herself said of Thomas in 1996, "I do not consider him a positive role model for blacks. . . . He had all the advantages of affirmative action, and went against it." Longtime Washington columnist Carl Rowan went further in his book on Justice Thurgood Marshall, sharing his conviction that Marshall had been referring to Thomas and figures like him when he ranted to Rowan about "goddamn Black sellouts."

Even Thomas's champions knew the truth of the matter, and no matter what Thomas told himself or others, a simmering resentment remained inexplicably linked to his basic character traits. As Merida and Fletcher report, when Thomas served later in the Reagan administration, at one point William Bradford Reynolds, assistant attorney general for civil rights, "raised a glass to toast Thomas's confirmation to a second term as EEOC chairman and lauded him as 'the epitome of the right kind of affirmative action working the right way.'" Thomas, the authors add, was "mortified."

———

The future Ginni Thomas formed the core of her political identity early. From the time she was young, Virginia Lamp's guiding vision was to emulate her mother, Marjorie Lamp, a right-wing Republican firebrand active in Nebraska state politics going back to the 1960s. In 1964, Marjorie and her husband, Don, an engineer, were staunch backers of Barry Goldwater's conservative campaign for president. In 1967, Marjorie Lamp was so headstrong in supporting anti-feminist icon Phyllis Schlafly in her campaign for president of the National Federation of Republican Women that when Schlafly was defeated, losing by a clear-cut margin of more than 12 percent, Lamp's Omaha Women's Republican Club resigned the group in protest. It was, Lamp insisted to the *Omaha World-Herald* without evidence, a "rigged convention." Kurt Andersen, the future founder of *Spy* magazine, who grew up across the street from the Lamps, told Jane Mayer of *The New Yorker:* "Her parents were the roots of the modern, crazy Republican Party. My parents were Goldwater Republicans, but even *they* thought the Lamp family was nuts."

In November 1968, Marjorie Lamp was a leader of a conservative faction trying to install their candidate as state party chair. The *Omaha World-Herald* reported that one candidate for the office had attended a meeting "at the home of Mrs. Marjorie Lamp, a backer of Ronald Reagan for the Presidency." In September 1970, Marjorie Lamp was reappointed as one of thirty-five women on Governor Norbert Tiemann's Commission on the Status of Women. Then in February 1972, the *Omaha World-Herald* reported that Marjorie Lamp, "long associated with conservative Republicanism," had announced her candidacy for the state legislature. A *Fremont Tribune* article on her race, which described her as "laughingly confident," quoted her calling her key assets in the campaign her husband and four children. "They're right behind me," she said. "I couldn't appreciate it more."

Ginni's mother did not, alas, win office, but she was also a delegate to the 1976 Republican National Convention in Kansas City, where, as a strident Reagan backer, she excoriated incumbent President Gerald Ford as "just not a leader." She warned that if Georgia governor Jimmy Carter were elected, "we'd be heading toward socialism."

These were the reference points around which young Ginni Lamp, the last of the four Lamp children, crafted her political philosophy. In 1980, as a twenty-three-year-old law student at Creighton University, she was on the ballot in Nebraska's 2nd Congressional District as a Ronald Reagan delegate to the 1980 Republican National Convention, and listed her qualifications as "Nebraska College Republicans chairman, member Executive Committee National Federation of Young Republicans," and a recipient of something called the "Outstanding Young Republican Award 1979." Ginni finished second among eight candidates in the voting, with 6,604 votes, trailing only former state Republican chair Anne Batchelder (9,152). That summer she threw herself into the work of volunteering for family friend Hal Daub during his 1980 race for the House, and after he won earned a job on his staff in Washington.

Ginni arrived in Washington at a time when the conservative movement was surging forward. In 1979, Jerry Falwell had founded the Moral Majority, seeking to mobilize the Religious Right to build toward one day overthrowing *Roe v. Wade*. Reagan's election in November 1980, with the support of these evangelicals, brought a flood of ambitious young conservatives to Washington, few more ambitious and conservative than Ginni Lamp. "She was exuberant, enthusiastic and very excited," fellow staffer Mark Mackee told *The Washington Post.* "It was the early Reagan years and she was in the middle of it."

In 1985, Ginni took a job with the Chamber of Commerce, which had unleashed the Powell Memo and its dramatic influence. She was hired by the chamber to be a bulldog, and the role came naturally. She took on the cause of fighting equal pay for women with relish, fronting for the group of male executives in the media. In February 1985 a poll was published that found two-thirds of workers surveyed believed women are not paid fairly in comparison to men, and found that women earn 63 cents to every dollar men make. Ginni Lamp, quoted in a UPI story on the poll, carried on—with no specifics—that "citing such a misleading poll is just one more of the same tactics that comparable worth proponents seem bent on using."

Ginni was honored in the July 1986 issue of *Good Housekeeping* magazine, which published a list of twenty-eight "Young Women of Promise," who, the journal of home etiquette cheerfully hoped, "are blazing trails now and will change our world in the future." That description certainly applied to one of the young women on the list, Virginia Lamp, formerly of Nebraska, identified as a twenty-eight-year-old attorney working with the U.S. Chamber of Commerce, "where she represents the interests of the business community at congressional hearings on such issues as comparable worth and affirmative action." She hopes one day, the article concluded, to go "home to Nebraska and run for Congress. Her biggest obstacle: finding a husband who'll be supportive of a woman in public life."

That turned out not to be a problem. The former Ginni Lamp found, in Clarence Thomas, a husband who would lend her unflagging support as she embarked on a public life that would include collecting hundreds of thousands of dollars in fees to lobby the Supreme Court on which her husband sat and was a key member. It remains to be worked out just how much of an influence her Nixonian, rules-don't-apply-to-me mindset rubbed off on her husband, and how much they were of parallel political disposition from the first days, but their partnership, in all its fiendish energy, would stitch them throughout the vast and expanding network of right-wing influence that would turn the high court into the Thomas Court.

# CHAPTER 5

# OCTOBER 1987: THE DEEPER MEANING OF "BORKING"

It may have been the most important verb in American politics for several decades: to Bork. The use of famous ultraconservative Robert Bork's name in such a manner amounted to an impressive, albeit sinister, act of political jujitsu, in which determined, organized, and well-funded elements of the far right would flex their political muscle to turn the preposterous notion that Bork was somehow a victim into a widely accepted article of faith with the media and even many liberals. Oddly, this exercise in political branding required that everyone pretend not to remember who Bork was, despite the well-established record— Bork stepping in as Nixon's tool during the Saturday Night Massacre, the published clips from his speech in effect launching the Federalist Society as an openly radical organization, which would, soon enough, see the wisdom in refraining from such public explanations of the group's purpose.

Maybe it was a case of Bork's blatant devotion to being a radical activist feeling somehow like an old story, following the rise of Reaganism, with its different set of polestars and its sunny optimism? Reagan made a fateful and likely unintentional decision early in 1981, shortly after his November 1980 election, that preserved abortion rights in America for three decades. Fulfilling a campaign pledge he had made to name the first woman to the high court, Reagan in 1981 nominated Sandra Day O'Connor, a former elected official and judge from Arizona, to fill a seat left open by Potter Stewart's retirement. The antiabortion movement immediately cried foul, viewing the nomination as a direct contradiction of the Reagan 1980 platform and his stated views favoring overturning *Roe v. Wade.* On July 6, 1981, Reagan made the following entry in his diary: "Called Judge O'Connor and told her she was my nominee for the Supreme Court. Already the flak is starting from my own supporters. Right-to-Life people say she is pro-abortion. She declares abortion is personally repugnant to her. I think she will make a good justice." In fact, O'Connor had cast a vote in the Arizona legislature in favor of repealing an antiabortion statute. (O'Connor told Reagan she didn't remember taking that vote.) The right-to-lifers inferred, correctly, that O'Connor would not overturn *Roe v. Wade.* Though she voted during her tenure most frequently with the conservative bloc, O'Connor upheld abortion rights in a landmark opinion in *Planned Parenthood v. Casey* in 1992, a decision that stood until 2022. O'Connor slipped through.

When Chief Justice Warren Burger resigned in 1985, Reagan understandably turned to the reliable senior conservative William Rehnquist to be chief justice. For the seat opened up by Rehnquist's ascension, Reagan considered two pugnacious judges with an intellectual bent whom Reagan had elevated to the federal appeals court for the D.C. Circuit: Robert Bork and Antonin Scalia, longtime co-conspirators since the Nixon days and both advisors to the Federalist Society. Scalia, a principal disciple of Bork's originalism theory, got the nod. Because Scalia's replacement of Rehnquist was not seen as upsetting the ideological balance on the court, the confirmation hearing was not contentious, and Scalia slipped through, too, sailing through the Senate 98–0.

Next up was Bork, who wouldn't slip through. Of all the lies told by and about Robert Bork after his 1987 nomination to the Supreme Court, the biggest was the most obvious: that he was ever a natural fit for the highest court in the land, given his oft-stated extreme views and partisan past. In fact, when Bork served as Nixon's triggerman in the ugly Saturday Night Massacre, firing Archibald Cox, when two other Nixon conservatives recoiled from such a dirty act, he clearly branded himself for life; he was a political operator steeped in the ways of partisan tire-iron fights whose intellect could not make up for his lack of the unimpeachable honor and dignity that, at least heretofore, were seen as prerequisites for sitting on the Supreme Court.

But perhaps that was the point. In 1986, Bork was skipped over for Scalia, whose nomination was made much easier by a Republican-controlled Senate. Now a scandal was raging over Reagan's illegal arms sale to the Islamic theocracy in Iran, despite an arms embargo, and illegal funneling of that money to insurgent right-wing rebels trying to overthrow the socialist Sandinista government in Nicaragua. Democrats had seized control of the Senate in a bad midterm for the GOP, and the administration was on its heels.

Moreover, the open court seat was that of Lewis Powell, who had proven to be a pragmatic conservative in his years on the bench. Bork's nomination would upset that balance, tilting it far right, and Democrats had warned the White House in advance that if Bork got the nod they would fight like hell to stop him. Thus the outspoken Bork, with his long paper trail on every hot-button issue likely to come before the court, was sure to provoke all-out war with the left, just the kind of war Reagan advisors thought they needed to rally his base, especially religious conservatives excited by Bork. From the get-go, Bork could be seen as a useful sacrificial lamb; in defeat, he would become even more useful—as Federalist Society founder Steven Calabresi later admitted, "It was tremendously energizing for conservatives, having a martyr, basically."

About that paper trail: Bork was on record as believing the Civil Rights Act was an unconstitutional violation of the freedom of businesses; he supported poll taxes ("It was a very small tax," the judge noted dryly), literacy tests for voting, mandated school prayer, and he opposed the right to privacy that barred states from outlawing abortion, the use of contraceptives by married couples, and rights protecting homosexual conduct. He had ruled for a company against workers who were forced to be sterilized to keep their jobs. And in 1981, Bork had told Congress that "*Roe* is itself an unconstitutional decision, a serious and wholly unjustified judicial usurpation of state legislative authority."

Less than an hour after Bork's nomination to the Supreme Court was announced, Edward Kennedy of Massachusetts stood on the Senate floor and sketched a stark—and unquestionably accurate, based on Bork's own words—version of how a court dominated by figures like Bork would look.

"Robert Bork's America is a land in which women would be forced into back-alley abortions, blacks would sit at segregated lunch counters, rogue police could break down citizens' doors in midnight raids, schoolchildren could not be taught about evolution, writers and artists could be censored at the whim of the Government, and the doors of the Federal courts would be shut on the fingers of millions of citizens for whom the judiciary is— and is often the only—protector of the individual rights that are the heart of our democracy," Kennedy said. "The damage that President Reagan will do through this nomination, if it is not rejected by the Senate, could live on far beyond the end of his presidential term. President Reagan is still our president. But he should not be able to reach out from the muck of Irangate, reach into the muck of Watergate and impose his reactionary vision of the Constitution on the Supreme Court and the next generation of Americans. No justice would be better than this injustice."

Kennedy's speech kicked off a spirited campaign by a coalition of civil rights and women's groups painting Bork as far outside the judicial mainstream. For the first time in a judicial confirmation, an effort to defeat the nomination with all the trappings of a political campaign—from paid advertisements to the distribution of talking points to allies—was launched by People for the American Way, an advocacy group founded by liberal Hollywood producer Norman Lear as a counterweight to Reaganism. Bork was assailed on the airwaves as a dangerous extremist. One ad with a voice-over by Gregory Peck said, "If Robert Bork wins a seat on the Supreme Court, it'll be for life. His life, and yours."

The White House, seeking to defend its controversial, self-immolating nominee, did nothing. Astonishingly, it fell silent for ten weeks before offering a tepid defense. If the run-up to the hearing was bad, the hearing itself was worse. When asked a softball question about why he wanted to be on the Supreme Court, Bork said it was because such service would be "an intellectual feast." It might have seemed an unremarkable answer coming from someone else, but the hearings were televised nationally, and Bork was coming off as dour, smug, and even callous in his answers. In the words of *The Washington Post,* his comment only "deepened the impression of Bork as an oddly detached legal scholar, an intellectual without feelings." Bork clearly saw a lifelong seat on the Supreme Court, with the unique power and influence the perch would grant him, as his personal entitlement.

In defeat, much was made on the right—then and in the years since—of how the judge had been "Borked," a new coinage, which according to Merriam-Webster means "to attack or defeat (a nominee for public office) unfairly through an organized campaign of harsh public criticism or vilification." Fascinating how "unfairly" crept into the meaning, given the demonstrable untruth of that spin as it related to the Bork case itself. Kennedy's litany of warnings for what Robert Bork's America would look like was, from the standpoint of objective reality, clearly on target. It was also an accurate foreshadowing of the horrors of the Thomas court. "Conservatives frequently invoke Bork's name as a representation of Democratic ruthlessness and partisanship, but the most vicious critiques of Bork were accurate, if uncharitable, and the qualities that liberals found objectionable were precisely those that endeared him to the conservative legal movement," Adam Serwer lucidly summarized in *The Atlantic* in October 2023. "The Bork nomination went down. It was not the first, but the 11th, Supreme Court nomination to fail, and unlike Barack Obama's 2016 nominee, Merrick Garland, Bork actually got a hearing and a vote."

The shell game behind the right-wing power grab to control the courts took an important step forward with the Bork drama. If you don't like reality, try to create your own. Try to create a romance around the fate of Bork the way that the cry of "Remember the Alamo" was raised to fire up an emotional loyalty. It's not that far-fetched a comparison. The actual 1836 battle at the Alamo was a case of a group of more than two hundred revolutionaries seeking independence for Texas from Mexico, knowing full well that a large force of Mexican soldiers was on its way, choosing to deny reality. These men were fools. "One of the great myths," Texas author Bryan Burrough told NPR in 2021, "is the bravery of the Alamo defenders, how they fought to their death and everything. And when you look at the facts, they never made a conscious decision to fight to the death. There was no line in the sand drawn." But the wasted lives were turned into myth. The cry of "Remember the Alamo" was repeated so often, like "Remember Bork," that it took on new meaning. John Wayne made a 1960 movie, *The Alamo,* which he saw as a vehicle to use myth to bolster support for Richard Nixon.

The cry was always "Remember Bork!" No more Borking! There was an element of genuine creativity in the messaging strategy, a breathtaking disconnect with reality. It does not matter if the authors of this strategy themselves believed the fiction they were promulgating, or were cool and detached in manipulating others; what's clear was that a mix of emotionalism, extremism, and imagined victimhood proved a powerful vehicle if it could be coupled to the power to make alternate reality stick. The legacy of Bork, the *Wall Street Journal* editorial page wrote later in an obvious fabrication of myth, was that "character assassination proved an effective tactic," and "special interest groups" discovered "they could demonize judicial nominees based solely on their views."

The *Journal*'s words are unintentionally revealing: Bork's own actual "views," when publicized, amounted to "character assassination"? The dictionary definition notwithstanding, there was nothing unfair about the Bork proceedings. No lies were told about him. The Senate rejected him as having a judicial record that was too far to the right. There were legitimate reasons many Americans wanted to see Bork defeated. Looking back, it seems clear that Bork Borked himself.

But the aggrieved right wing found it useful—and effective—to misrepresent the opposition to Bork as something akin to a liberal conspiracy to smear one of their own. Otherwise they would have to acknowledge the fact that their reactionary challenge to social progress was repugnant to many, if not most, Americans.

Over the coming years, the right would leverage their careful work in building up a mythic alternate history of the Bork defeat by putting forth "stealth" nominees who had less of a paper trail than did Bork for opponents to mine. They would coach their nominees to dissemble under oath about their true (and unpopular) views. And they would raise significant funds from deep-pocketed conservative donors to mount misleading media campaigns to defend their controversial nominees. The false notion of "Borking" by the left would provide a convenient excuse for their own misrepresentations. In later battles, over

Clarence Thomas and Brett Kavanaugh, the same playbook would be used, viewing the airing of facts as somehow below the belt, adopting the deeply arrogant notion that entitlement to power made any challenge unfair and somehow sleazy. The "Remember Bork" cries would drown out any reasonable discussion, weaponized to inoculate extreme-right-wing nominees from fair scrutiny, falsely presenting the guilty as victims of slander.

But that all lay in the future. For now, chastened by the reaction to Bork, Reagan turned to Anthony Kennedy, a Republican California judge unaffiliated with the Federalist Society, to fill the open seat, and he was confirmed with ninety-nine Senate votes. Like Sandra Day O'Connor, Kennedy would become a classic swing vote on the court, disappointing conservatives with rulings in favor of abortion rights and gay marriage, but notably freeing a tide of money for Leonard Leo's vast project with his vote in *Citizens United* (2010), which opened the floodgates to corporate and anonymous money in politics.

Kennedy turned out to be a Federalist Society project. He was wobbly, that was clear to all, and the Federalist Society decided to help him wobble some more by implanting strident conservatives as his law clerks—including, from 1993 to 1994, Brett Kavanaugh and Neil Gorsuch, who had known each other since high school, both attending Georgetown Prep in North Bethesda, Maryland.

"Justice Kennedy, appointed by President Reagan after the Senate had spurned the arch-conservative Robert Bork, was already a figure of ridicule and scorn," David Margolick would write in a deeply reported *Vanity Fair* article in October 2002, based on extensive conversations with Supreme Court clerks. "Kennedy, they felt, was pompous and grandiloquent. His inner office was filled with the trappings of power—an elaborate chandelier and a carpet with a giant red star—and his writing, too, was loaded with grandstanding flourishes. The clerks saw his public persona—the very public way in which he boasted of often agonizing over decisions—as a kind of shtick, a very conspicuous attempt to exude fairness and appear moderate, even when he'd already made up his mind."

Margolick went on to offer the startling revelation that the Federalist Society mobilized to manipulate the weak-willed justice. "Convinced he'd strayed on abortion under the pernicious influence of a liberal law clerk," one who had studied with liberal Laurence Tribe at Harvard Law School, "they took steps to prevent any reoccurrences. Applicants for Kennedy clerkships were now screened by a panel of right-wing stalwarts. 'The premise is that he can't think by himself, and that he can be manipulated by someone in his second year of law school,' one liberal clerk explains." Added another clerk, speaking of Kennedy, "He had four very conservative, Federalist Society white guys."

## CHAPTER 6

# JULY 1991: CLARENCE THOMAS, REVEALED

If you'd asked me in the 1990s about the one moment when Clarence Thomas most unmistakably revealed himself to the world, for all to see, I'd have focused on the obvious example. I'd have pointed to the sequence in his confirmation hearings before the Senate Judiciary Committee when he complained, full of righteous indignation, about being the victim of a "high-tech lynching." Even as someone who at the time found himself in Thomas's circle, there was something crude and depressing and shocking about the sad spectacle of a would-be Supreme Court Justice so nakedly turning showman. Was his self-justifying ambition and hunger for acceptance truly so insatiable and urgent that it required steering an ostensibly solemn proceeding toward emotional theatrics with such obviously loaded language as "uppity blacks"? The shock factor worked well for Thomas. It was like someone shouting at the top of his lungs in the middle of a staid social gathering. Everyone else shuts up and looks uneasily around the room, unsure what to do next. Eventually, the rattled guests start talking again, but no one wants to bring up the deep awkwardness they're trying to push out of mind.

I now see this mawkish moment as the beginning, not the end, of the crucial sequence in which the Thomas Court would stabilize its foundation over the critical years that followed—or fail to do so. An epic battle would play out over the coming years to shape collective memory on what Thomas said and what it meant, a battle in which I was both sniper and cannon fodder. The battle turned into a rout, one side raging forward with such giddy abandon that it cast aside all vestiges of restraint or respect for existing institutions. It was cheap and sordid for a man of Clarence Thomas's intellectual pretensions and high-arching pride to indulge in so base a case of victim playing, knowing full well how absurd it was—and yet, the move was extraordinarily effective.

The ranks and coffers of the Federalist Society swelled dramatically and a willingness to use the language of victimization fell quickly into vogue, proving a powerful political weapon.

Thomas had been chosen precisely so he could play the victim if it turned out to be necessary. He might as well have had a thick backpack—decorated with a big V for Victim—stuffed with a parachute, reading "Pull in case of emergency." He could always float down to safety, cushioned by the certainty that guilty white liberals would cower in horror at the idea that an African American, chosen *because* he was an African American, might actually say out loud that racism was his trump card.

Having been privy in those years to intimate details of Thomas's life, shared by his closest friends, I'm well aware that Thomas was fiercely proud of his own up-from-the-bootstraps story. I was also aware that work associates and others who knew Thomas found graceful ways to point out that his intellectual powers were not always what one might call dazzling. This was cited as a way to burnish rather than detract from extolling his virtues. He had cleared various hurdles in his path, including Yale Law School, which could not have been easy, and to do so he relied more on dogged determination than intellectual spark. Having never met the man personally, I cannot attest to his intellectual agility or lack thereof, but I can report from personal experience that it was widely understood in his own inner circle that such considerations were completely beside the point. This was a blunt power play.

Given Clarence Thomas's long record of opposing programs to advance Blacks, the fact that he was chosen specifically because he was Black must have been a bitter pill for the prideful Thomas to swallow. He was caught up in a cynical White House strategy to win confirmation of a true believer by earning the votes of Democratic senators from the South who had large Black constituencies—Howell Heflin of Georgia and Fritz Hollings of South Carolina among them—and by splitting the liberal civil rights community by appealing to racial loyalties. The Federalist Society denizens in the White House counsel's office— C. Boyden Gray, a patrician heir to the Reynolds tobacco fortune, Lee Liberman Otis, the Federalist founder with thick coke-bottle glasses, and Mark Paoletta—had their own Southern Strategy using Thomas as their pawn. They'd learned from their own past missteps and were determined to play to win this time.

The plan to capture the courts had suffered a setback, which had the effect of radicalizing the agents of change further, a process accelerated in 1990 when President George H. W. Bush had his first Supreme Court opening to fill. Senator Warren Rudman, a moderate Republican when there was such a thing, assured White House chief of staff John Sununu that a judge named David Souter, from their home state of New Hampshire, was the kind of conservative the White House was looking for. Word had gone out from the Oval Office that the president did not want a fight with the Democrats over his first Supreme Court pick. Souter, a longtime state judge, had never ruled on matters of federal law, so his record was in effect a blank slate, which would grease the skids toward confirmation. Rudman, in his memoir, crowed that he misled Sununu, having known all along that his friend Souter was the kind of old-school conservative who respected judicial precedents, even liberal ones. Decisions like *Roe* would be safe on his watch. Sununu convinced Bush to go along, and once on the court, Souter often voted with the liberals, just as Rudman had expected. When the next vacancy came up, the chagrined Federalist Society operatives who stocked the Bush White House counsel's office were desperate to put the plot back in motion.

———

The contrast with Thomas's predecessor, Thurgood Marshall, was almost cruelly revealing of Thomas's limitations. Before Marshall became the first African American on the Supreme Court, the man had argued thirty-two cases before the Supreme Court—and won an astonishing twenty-nine of them, including the landmark *Brown v. Board of Education* in 1954. Marshall's brilliance and courage were widely recognized, even by many Republicans, and upon his death in 1993, he was celebrated on the front page of *The New York Times* as a "major figure in American life for a half-century . . . a figure of history well before he began his twenty-four-year service on the Supreme Court on Oct. 2, 1967."

"There is mourning throughout the land for the first African-American justice," wrote *Louisville Courier-Journal* columnist Betty Winston Bayé.

> Thurgood Marshall fought for Black people in days when many of us quaked in our boots and bare feet, too cowardly, too accommodating, too afraid of losing our jobs, or our status as accepted colored folk, to fight for ourselves. Thurgood Marshall was enraged about how Black people were treated in America, and he used his rage constructively. During his eighty-four years, his mind stayed fixed on freedom, his eyes stayed on the prize. It took audacity and courage for a young

Negro lawyer to go about America in the scary-for-Black people days of the 1930s, 1940s and 1950s speaking out against
lynchings, poll taxes, segregated schools and housing and piling up victories in Jim Crow courts.

From Marshall to Thomas, the highest court in the land had
gone from a man eloquently speaking out against real lynchings
of African Americans to one so invested in his own advancement
at whatever cost that he summoned an imaginary "lynching"—
though in fact the only violation was of the lies Thomas told and
asked others to tell for him. Given Marshall's stature, it was
degrading, and a figurative stick in the eye, when Bush picked
Thomas, a Black Bork without his brains, to replace him. (Thomas
had his intellectual pretensions, citing as influences Ayn Rand,
who through her celebrated novels and subsequent works of
nonfiction promoted laissez-faire capitalism and opposed stat-
ism in all forms, and the right-wing academic Thomas Sowell,
best known to the public for his frequent appearances on the
Rush Limbaugh show, where he argued that government programs hurt those they actually benefited.)

Give Thomas credit for one thing: He was alert and honest
enough to have "felt sick" when looking ahead to what he knew
would be a protracted nomination fight. And that was with or
without any public airing of Thomas's fondness for Long Dong
Silver videos and explicit-porn pinups, or his habit of proposi-
tioning his employees.

Thomas was chosen precisely because he was bluntly, even
crudely controversial. In a 1984 interview, Thomas asserted that
Black leaders were "watching the destruction of our own race"
as they "bitch, bitch, bitch" about Reagan while refusing to work
with the administration to alleviate teen pregnancy, unemploy-
ment, and illiteracy, even though Reagan had no programs to
address any of these ills. Thus it was no surprise when a coalition
of civil rights and women's groups actively opposed the Thomas

nomination. The *Washington Post* article announcing his nomination took only until its third paragraph to point out: "Conservatives were delighted by the nomination of a longtime favorite, while some Democrats expressed fears that Thomas, whose views on abortion are not publicly known, would help overturn *Roe v. Wade,* the 1973 decision that established a constitutional right to abortion."

The civil rights leaders were also concerned that in his post at the Education Department and then as chairman of the Equal Employment Opportunity Commission, Thomas was an outspoken voice against affirmative action, preaching a doctrine of self-reliance for Blacks, and against equal pay for women. At the EEOC, he worked under the tutelage of the vice chair of the commission, Ricky Silberman, the wife of Judge Laurence Silberman, who sat on the U.S. Court of Appeals for the D.C. Circuit, where he was, similarly, a paternalistic mentor. Ricky Silberman was an ardent antifeminist and when Thomas was announced for the court she spearheaded a noisy group she called Women for Judge Thomas. Her handiwork with a black Sharpie could frequently be seen in Thomas's acerbic speeches.

Thomas's actual record, if it was allowed to be the central focus of confirmation hearings, was unlikely to withstand scrutiny, so the Bush White House team shepherding the nomination embarked on a strategy of playing up what they saw as an inspiring biography. Thomas was coached by his handlers to dodge any honest reckoning with his firm beliefs and instead lean into his compelling personal life story: The man from Pin Point.

Among the Thomas advisors who keenly understood the necessity of this play was the most important Thomas advisor of all, his "best friend" and wife, Ginni. When Bush summoned Thomas to the family compound in Kennebunkport, Maine, the last weekend of June 1991 to ask Thomas some questions face-to-face before he announced him as his Supreme Court pick, Ginni had some instructions for her husband—"advice," they would call it, but clearly these were instructions. First, Ginni directed, her husband needed to spend his time on an Air Force jet, en route to Maine, writing out an acceptance speech, just in case. This assignment was detailed. He needed to explore in his speech the theme of "only in America," highlighting his hardscrabble childhood. Thomas aced this assignment, doing just what Ginni wanted. "As a child I could not dare dream that I would ever see the Supreme Court, not to mention be nominated to it," he said. "Only in America could this have been possible."

The following day in Maine, when Bush made the offer formal and Thomas accepted, he immediately tried calling Ginni, but was unable to reach her. She was busy that day at the Labor Department, where her role was to continue to undermine the policy of comparable pay for comparable work for women, the issue over which she had first bonded with Thomas. He tried again, minutes before stepping before the cameras with President Bush for the announcement, and reached her in time to pass on the news.

Standing behind the president at the Walker's Point compound as Bush announced his nomination, Thomas looked notably uncomfortable, as many observers remarked at the time. The president was warm in his remarks, even if he hit heights of silliness. It was not enough to praise the nominee's "wonderful sense of humor"—which, as fans of *Short Circuit* can agree, was clearly first-rate—but Bush also prattled on about Thomas's "excellent legal mind."

Thomas was understandably a little overwhelmed. He tried to thank his grandparents, but faltered and had to pause several seconds—then tried again, and was again overcome by emotion, shaking his head. He soon thanked his "wonderful wife," and added, "Only in America could this be possible," emphasizing the very words Ginni had directed him to say that day.

Clarence Thomas was hardly the first public figure whose engaged wife took an outsized role in crafting his public image;

one thinks for example of explorer/blunderer/statesman John Frémont and his daughter-of-a-senator wife, Jessie Benton, so richly explored by Steve Inskeep in *Imperfect Union: How Jessie and John Frémont Mapped the West, Invented Celebrity, and Helped Cause the Civil War.* As with Jessie Benton and John Frémont, once the mythmaking got going, it was hard to stop—and no one seemed to want to.

Thomas and his network would go to great lengths to take his high-stakes theater-of-victimization performance during his confirmation hearings and enshrine it as if Thomas were a hero in some critical U.S. military battle, raising the flag at Iwo Jima, perhaps, or among the first few insanely brave individuals to hit Omaha Beach. At the time of the Thomas hearings, I thought there were elements of political maneuvering in the sleight of hand that went into taking a massive negative—all the baggage from the accusations of Hill and Wright and the others and the widespread assumption that where there's smoke there is surely fire—and somehow turning it into a positive, a brave, me-against-the-world kind of defiance.

Decades after I did so much to help Thomas and his circle smear his critics, I see with increasing clarity that Clarence Thomas's psychological reaction in the months and years after his confirmation hearings says more about him even than the "high-tech lynching" posturing. His closest friends knew he was guilty. He himself clearly knew he was guilty. Yet Thomas has spent years—decades—building an elaborate and escalating series of self-justifying lies and fictions to shield himself from having to confront the painful reality of his own guilt. Like many drunk on their own power, Thomas wobbled steadily downhill in his epic and public self-abasement over the years with the help of a powerful enabler, his wife, Ginni. Together they created a cosmology in which they were virtuous and righteous in whatever they might choose to do, from sexual harassment to lying to pocketing gaudy gifts, and in which anyone who stood in their

way represented some shade of evil, of biblical dark forces blocking their divine right to do whatever the hell they felt like doing.

The signs of Clarence and Ginni Thomas being seriously,
deliriously drunk on power are all too numerous and unmistakable. Perhaps most bizarrely, immediately after the hearings
concluded, the pair invited *People* magazine into their home
for a November 1991 cover story and self-serving photo spread,
complete with obligatory shot of the couple lovingly entangled
on a sofa, each with a hand on the Bible. The magazine of fluff
gave Ginni a forum to rail bizarrely, calling Anita Hill's testimony
a case of "spiritual warfare" and "good vs. evil," a formulation
neatly demonstrating her deep wells of fanaticism. Ginni went
on to push passive-aggressive character assassination against
Hill, claiming to believe that Hill's testimony reminded her "of
the movie *Fatal Attraction,* or in her case, what I call the fatal
assistant. In my heart I always believed she was probably someone in love with my husband and never got what she wanted."
(Adding to the undercurrent of plutonium-powered nuttiness
running through these remarks was the odd footnote of Ginni
Thomas, in 2010, nearly two decades after the confirmation hearings, phoning Anita Hill and leaving her a creepy voicemail asking her to apologize to her husband—a bizarre twist that made
me shudder, having received my own creepy Ginni Thomas
voicemail. As I broke ranks with conservatives, Ginni left a voice
message saying she understood that I was being blackmailed "by
the left" to betray my former friends, which I took as a reference
to being gay.)

The *People* magazine charm offensive, if that's what it was, left
many perplexed—and some outraged. *Washington Post* columnist
Richard Cohen was excoriating: "You would think that having
gone through such a public ordeal—I am referring to questions
regarding sexual harassment—Mr. Justice Thomas would want
to lie low for a while. You would think that having been elevated
to the court by a mere two votes, Thomas might want to issue

an opinion or two before inviting photographers into his home. If you thought that, you would be just plain wrong. Clarence Thomas is the complete Washington figure: He is all image."

Ginni Thomas also told the magazine: "Clarence will give everyone a fair day in court. But I feel that he doesn't owe any of the groups who opposed him anything."

Retorted Cohen: "Maybe for the first time in American history we have the wife of a Supreme Court justice saying—in what can only be considered an authorized text—that her husband is entitled to certain grudges.... Anita Hill's charges raised questions about Clarence Thomas' character. Thomas and his wife, though, have raised some important questions on their own. One has to do with fairness and the other with taste. After reading the *People* article, it's not clear Thomas is capable of either."

Everyone from Leonard Leo to President Bush understood full well that Thomas and his wife were, politically and otherwise, extensions of each other. If there was any daylight between them on anything, it was trivial; on all fundamental matters, they were in lockstep. Ginni Thomas was an antiabortion activist of the extreme variety, and her views clearly offered reliable insights into those of her husband.

Ginni Thomas's ardent antiabortion advocacy has been well established. Documents unearthed by *The New York Times* showed that while she was working with the Council for National Policy and its affiliates, Ginni Thomas co-moderated a panel called "The Pro-Life Movement on Offense." Ginni was also a key player in a secretive group called Groundswell, a right-wing coalition dedicated to a "30 front war seeking to fundamentally transform the nation," according to documents obtained by *Mother Jones*. Groundswell "zeroes in on contentious issues that come before the high court, including voting rights, abortion and gay marriage," the magazine found. The Eagle Forum, which opposes abortion rights, has honored Ginni Thomas with an award, and Clarence Thomas has twice headlined the group's annual conference. In September 2022, an analysis by the non-partisan research group *Advance Democracy Inc.* found that 51 percent of the parties who filed amicus briefs—written legal arguments used to lobby justices—calling for an end to federal abortion rights had political ties to Ginni Thomas.

Before giving their sworn testimony, Supreme Court justices are put through murder boards, a committee of tough questioners, to help prepare for the ordeal of answering senators' questions. The team grilling Thomas—Gray, Lee Liberman, Paoletta, and other Federalist Society lawyers from the Justice Department—was determined not to have a repeat of the Bork hearings, where the nominee killed himself with honest answers. If it took lying to earn confirmation, then lying would be the order of the day. This time, the embattled nominee would brazen it out by simply dissembling. Thomas was the first of a long line of Republican nominees who—under oath—hid their views from the Senate and the public, and later voted to overturn *Roe.*

In his Senate confirmation hearing in 1991, Thomas said he supported the right to privacy, which undergirds *Roe,* and that he had no personal biases in approaching the abortion issue. Thomas testified: "I believe the Constitution protects the right to privacy. And I have no reason to prejudge or to predispose to rule one way or the other on abortion, which is a difficult issue." In 1987 Thomas had signed on to a White House working group report that criticized the right to privacy as "fatally flawed." Thomas told the committee he never read the report and believed in the right to privacy. Yet given these statements and his and his wife's longstanding ties to the antiabortion movement, this sworn testimony was nonsense. Thomas was only confirmed through the illegitimate means that seemed to be second-nature to the nominee.

# PART 2

# A REACTIONARY MOVEMENT BUILDS

---

## CHAPTER 7

# JANUARY 1993: THE RIGHT SETS OUT TO GET BILL CLINTON

K en Starr—or "Judge Starr" as he insisted on being addressed—was bitter even before Bill Clinton was elected in 1992. Up until two years earlier, Starr openly coveted a seat on the Supreme Court and had every reason to believe he would not be disappointed. In 1989, reporting on Starr's nomination as solicitor general, *The New York Times* wrote, "Judge Starr, forty-two years old, is seen in Washington legal circles as a possible candidate for a Supreme Court vacancy in the Bush Administration, and today's announcement seemed to strengthen his chances of being selected for the High Court." Sure enough, when Justice William Brennan retired, Starr was considered the leading candidate to replace him. He was, it was said, on the shortest of short lists. But Deputy Attorney General Bill Barr, charged by Attorney General Dick Thornburgh with whittling down the list, deep-sixed Starr. Along with another Thornburgh lieutenant, J. Michael Luttig, Barr sneered at Starr, whom he considered "soft and bookish in appearance," as author Jan Crawford

Greenburg described it in *Supreme Conflict: The Inside Story of the Struggle for Control of the United States Supreme Court.* Barr and Luttig, resentful of Starr for not having adopted their extreme view of presidential power in a previous dispute, soured Thornburgh on Starr, and the next day the attorney general told President Bush, "Starr is unacceptable." Instead David Souter, also squishy soft in the eyes of many right-wingers, as it turned out, would get the nod. Starr, who never stopped smarting over the knife in the back, resolved that he would find ways to shed his reputation for caution and show he could be as much of a fire-breathing extremist as any of them.

When Clinton was elected in November 1992, the Federalist Society and the right wing of the GOP assessed the threat he represented to their long-term objectives and settled on a strategy of attempting to discredit and smear Clinton. Starr and others in the Federalist Society, virtually from the moment Clinton took office, embarked on a plan to undermine him through all possible means, up to and including impeachment, on whatever pretext they could find.

No fewer than six Federalist Society members played key roles in the hunting of the president: Judge Silberman of the D.C. Circuit, whose curdled ambition after being passed over three times for the Supreme Court was now palpable; Ted Olson, a pillar of the D.C. legal establishment about to descend into the mud; embittered Robert Bork, who came out of retirement for a disgraceful encore performance; Judge David Sentelle of the U.S. Court of Appeals for the D.C. Circuit; and Ken Starr, the pious Whitewater independent counsel who would become a kind of Inspector Javert in his relentless pursuit of the Clintons, along with his savage young deputy, Brett Kavanaugh, who would be rewarded for his all-out devotion to the anti-Clinton cause with a future Supreme Court seat.

For all the tortured rationalizations offered then and later, the reality was that for these six men this was all about power:

Clinton's victory ended twelve years of GOP rule, during which the conservative legal movement had been able to advance its campaign to seize control of the nation's courts, under both Ronald Reagan (Scalia) and George H. W. Bush (Thomas). Now that effort had stalled—and along with it, thwarted Supreme Court ambitions would be left to fester and turn rancid.

The Arkansas Project, funded fully by Pittsburgh banker Richard Mellon Scaife, the billionaire hard-right activist who was also a conspiracy theory buff, sought to uncover stories tying Bill and Hillary Clinton to murders and drug smuggling as well as adultery. In the early 1970s, Scaife had run afoul of the law himself in making shady campaign contributions to Richard Nixon, earning unwanted headlines when it emerged that he had donated $1 million to the Nixon reelection campaign. An early funder of the Federalist Society, Scaife learned to get more creative with his subterfuge and began quietly channeling funds outside direct electoral politics and into right-wing think tanks, militant advocacy organizations, and fringe alternative media outlets like *The Spectator,* which he had supported for two decades before Clinton came on the scene. It was all part of the post-Powell-Memo mobilization.

Super-lawyer Ted Olson joined the magazine's board of directors, and his legal bills and the scandalmongering stories he shepherded into print were underwritten by Scaife. At one point, Olson secretly helped prepare the attorneys for Paula Jones, who brought a dubious sexual harassment case against Clinton stemming from a scurrilous report in *The American Spectator* retelling stories of Clinton's alleged infidelities by his state trooper security guards. (The article was by this author. Nervous about publishing such a salacious exposé, I was strongly urged on by Silberman, a sitting federal judge. "It would be the most devastating piece ever published about a sitting president," Silberman told me, licking his chops. I took in what I saw as sage counsel and faithfully went forward. I learned later that the troopers were paid by a conservative donor to talk to me and that their stories were greatly embellished.)

The Arkansas Project employed a group of eccentric "investigators" including a rough-hewn former cop and an Arkansas bait-shop owner obsessed with bringing down Bill Clinton. In the end, this screwball crew turned up nothing, yet created a debilitating atmosphere of scandal. (The *Spectator* also succeeded in destroying itself; in 2000, government investigations of the Arkansas Project caused the sale of the magazine to conservative venture capitalist George Gilder, who drove it into the ground after a series of financial setbacks.)

No one was more feverish in scheming against Clinton than my boss at the *Spectator,* R. Emmett Tyrrell Jr., editor-in-chief of the magazine, which he founded on the campus of Indiana University Bloomington in 1967 as a conservative reaction to the liberal activism of the 1960s. During the Reagan administration, Tyrrell moved the *Spectator* from Indiana to the Washington, D.C., area and set his sights on becoming the next William F. Buckley, the venerable founding editor of *National Review,* whom no one could accuse of being a lightweight. A sometimes gifted satirist, Tyrrell was out of his depth in the capital. His efforts to reinvent himself as an investigative journalist during the Clinton years made a mockery of the form.

Nevertheless, he persevered. In 1997, he published a thin, glossy book with Regnery, known for making money by putting out fact-free right-wing tracts that were widely promoted on talk radio. The title was *The Impeachment of William Jefferson Clinton: A Political Docu-Drama,* and Tyrrell's coauthor on the book, listed as "Anonymous," was none other than Ted Olson, or that at least was the widespread assumption inside the magazine.

To push the book, Tyrrell called in Robert Bork, making the most of the not insubstantial gravitas he still retained in conservative circles at that point. In an August 1997 "review" in the pages of the *Spectator* in August 1997—six months before anyone had heard of former White House intern Monica Lewinsky or her involvement with a president, setting in motion impeachment proceedings—Bork made the case for Bill Clinton's impeachment.

"If Nixon deserved impeachment, Clinton certainly does," Bork began his review. In summoning the ghosts of Watergate, the intent of Nixon's onetime accomplice seemed to be as much about dry-cleaning Nixon's crimes for a new generation as it was about indicting Bill Clinton. "The real charge, as Tyrrell and Anonymous make clear, is abuse of power," Bork continued. "Of that there is ample evidence—enough to make the Nixon administration seem merely, almost mildly, errant by comparison." By turns comic, tragic, and frightening, Bork's argument in the end was that impeachment is not about evidence—he dutifully ran through a farrago of nonsensical allegations—but about political might. Republicans should impeach Bill Clinton because they could.

Ken Starr pursued another, more lethal avenue of wrecking the Clintons. Barr and Luttig had not been wrong about Starr. There was something choirboy soft and milk-fed about how he came across. He did not look like someone you wanted guarding your back in a scuffle, put it that way. He was the son of a Church of Christ minister, and was a Democrat in college who escaped having to go to Vietnam and fight because he had psoriasis.

Laurence Silberman, who had once threatened to punch another judge in the nose over a dispute about affirmative action, told me that he and others in the right-wing legal establishment saw Starr as a weak, unprincipled opportunist who was more interested in advancing his own ambitions than in conservative ideology. Silberman, who had served with Starr on the D.C. Circuit Court, also said Starr was thought to be politically clumsy and naïve. We would all soon see that assessment was correct.

When he was profiled as a high school senior in 1963 by his hometown paper, the *San Antonio Express-News,* the headline was "Future Politician." "Starr, president of the senior class at Sam

Houston High School, wants to continue holding office after completing his education," the article explained. "He hopes to be a politician." Added Kenneth: "This field has fascinated me greatly, and I believe my interests and abilities lie in this direction." However, the short article held other clues to Starr's future. Besides coming in second in a persuasive-speaking contest—persuasive, but not that persuasive—he was sports editor of the school paper and also secretary-treasurer of the Creative Writing Club. Creative writing—that was a skill that would aid him in authoring the Starr Report with the help of his hotspur protégé Kavanaugh.

Before Starr would ever get his shot at lasting historic infamy, first the right would have to target Republican Robert Fiske, the honorable centrist attorney general Janet Reno appointed as special prosecutor in January 1994 to investigate Whitewater, a failed real estate investment made by the Clintons in Arkansas. A former U.S. attorney for the Southern District of New York, Fiske "brings the middle-of-the-road political credentials that Reno clearly found desirable," as Timothy Clifford wrote at the time in the *New York Daily News*. Even Republican senator Bob Dole acknowledged "people who know him think he is extremely well-qualified, is independent." That turned out to be the problem.

One clear challenge for Fiske was going to be investigating the death of Deputy White House Counsel Vince Foster, whose July 1993 suicide had illustrated the deadly consequences of the attack politics that the right wing was increasingly adopting. No one had more to be ashamed of in the death of Vince Foster than the Whitewater-obsessed Robert Bartley and the *Wall Street Journal* editorial page he oversaw. I don't write those words lightly. It pains me a little to make that acknowledgment, since I once had great respect for the *Journal* editorial page as an institution and was proud to see my byline there. But as with so many others, Bartley let Clinton hatred turn him into someone else.

Foster was brilliant, but it was also known in political circles that he had a sensitive temperament.

On June 17, 1993, Bartley's *Journal* editorial page published a hit piece headlined "Who Is Vincent Foster?"—one in a series of what former *New Republic* editor Michael Kinsley called "a series of viciously unfair editorials." It was all just innuendo and bombast, suggesting there was anything unusual about the Clinton administration relying on attorneys from Hillary's Rose Law Firm in Arkansas, the state's top firm, although all administrations bring in top legal talent from the home states of presidents. But for Foster, the attacks hurt. What was "most disturbing," Bartley and the *Journal* harrumphed, was the Clinton administration's "carelessness about following the law," a wild charge backed up, if at all, with weak complaints about the White House being slow to produce computer records—from a previous administration.

On July 20, 1993, five weeks after the *Journal* plumbed the depths with its attack editorial on Foster, he parked his car in Fort Marcy Park in Virginia, held a .38 up to his head, and killed himself. There is no need to speculate on what drove Foster to suicide. His suicide note made clear he had been traumatized by the wild, unrelenting attacks of Bartley and *The Wall Street Journal*. His note mentioned "WSJ editors [who] lie without consequence."

Bartley could have responded to this tragedy with remorse. He could have asked himself hard questions about the harm he caused. Instead, like so many cogs in the right-wing machine that gained momentum in those years, he focused mostly on covering his own ass and preserving his own power: Incredibly, he went on the attack. Seeking to deflect attention from the sinister, sordid role the *Journal* editorial page had played in Foster's death, a damning indictment indeed, Bartley and the *Journal* lent weight to the absurd story that Foster had been murdered as part of a Whitewater cover-up. Weirdly pretending to be well acquainted with those close to Foster, the *Journal* wrote, "Those who knew him consider him an unlikely suicide." And—falsely—added, "We're told he had no history of depression." Bartley sought to amplify the conspiracy theory mumbo-jumbo of Christopher Ruddy, a *New York Post* provocateur who would go on to partner with Richard Mellon Scaife to found Newsmax in 1998. He disingenuously concluded, "Until the Foster death is seriously studied, a Banquo's ghost will stalk . . . the Clinton administration."

It was fiction writing as political commentary. Bartley knew better. He'd been awarded a Pulitzer Prize for editorial writing in 1980 and was fully aware of what he was doing. But he didn't want the rest of the world to catch on and start asking more questions about the *Journal*'s appalling role in helping drive Foster to suicide. So when Robert Fiske, working industriously, debunked the fervid conspiracy theories about Foster's death and concluded this was a clear-cut case of a distraught man taking his own life, a suicide that was the result of undiagnosed and untreated depression—the *Journal* was ready to use its wide influence in certain Republican circles to get Fiske's head on a platter.

In going after Fiske, Bartley had nothing, so he pretended as if he did. He pounded away with a lonely but sustained attack on the ethics of the widely respected Fiske in editorials with headlines such as "Fiske: Too Much Baggage" and "The Fiske Cover-Up" and the like. The fix was in. The *Journal* might as well have published an editorial, "Will No One Rid Me of This Meddlesome Attorney?"

Word got out, to people like North Carolina senator Lauch Faircloth, who was also out to get Fiske—and had complained about his findings on the Vince Foster case. Faircloth was pushing for Fiske to be replaced, and he made his case at a lunch meeting with Federalist Society judge David Sentelle, a North Carolina crony of his. Chief Justice Rehnquist had appointed Sentelle to head a three-judge panel that was about to make the shocking move to oust Fiske, and replace him with none other than Ken Starr, a case of Republicans turning the get-Clinton movement into a witch hunt with the Federalist Society's fingerprints all over it.

"The change came as a complete surprise," *The New York Times* reported at the time. "Mr. Starr, forty-eight, a conservative Republican in private law practice, is untested as a prosecutor. His background contrasts sharply with that of Mr. Fiske, a Wall Street lawyer, a former United States Attorney and a political moderate. . . . The assignment was seen as the capstone to the career of Mr. Fiske, who is sixty-three. His reputation for even-handedness dates from 1976, when, even though he had been appointed United States Attorney in Manhattan by President Gerald R. Ford, he was kept on by President Jimmy Carter. Mr. Starr, by contrast, is a darling of conservative law groups."

# CHAPTER 8

# AUGUST 1991: THE CITIZENS UNITED FILTH FACTORY

Here's something to keep in mind about the mushrooming anti-Clinton industry that sprang up in the early 1990s: It was extremely lucrative for a lot of people. Even if you had a vantage point at the center of that bizarre feeding frenzy—as I, oddly enough, did at the time—it was hard to know how much the mad gleam in the eye and demented energy of so many people attracted to the cause was primarily driven by actual hatred of the Clintons and what they represented, and how much by the age-old stimulant of waving fresh C-notes in the air and shouting, "Come and GET it!" If that sounds crass, I'm sorry, but that was the reality. For all the performative moral superiority in that crowd, self-enrichment was not a goal to be dismissed.

Take the odd career of Floyd Brown, a big, bumptious, rabble-rousing former operative for Senator Bob Dole and others known for the verve with which he pursued the dark art of the crude political smear. Brown was the one to give us the infamous, racist Willie Horton ad that helped the Bush campaign bury former Massachusetts governor Michael Dukakis in 1988. If you chart out Brown's various schemes in the decades since, many in tandem with his son, Patrick, for all their true believer hot air and bombast, they seem at least as devoted to chasing dollars as inflicting actual harm on the opposition—making me think maybe that was the point all along.

The early years of the Clinton presidency were a time of unprecedented weaponization of innuendo, gossip, and out-and-out fabrication—and Brown and I were both key players in this appalling break with the basic standards of decency and decorum that had for decades provided a brake on such low attacks. Even before Bill Clinton was elected in November 1992, Floyd Brown had founded a nonprofit called Citizens United that would attempt to skirt the spirit of federal nonprofit law by registering as a "social welfare organization," that is, a 501(c)(4) nonprofit. This was a category requiring that "an organization must not be organized for profit and must be operated exclusively to promote social welfare." None of those words seems particularly ambiguous to me, or I think to any half-honest person considering the question. The tax-exempt status comes because of the commitment to "social welfare." Just what "social welfare" work Citizens United ever pursued remains dubious. This was a group set up to smear opponents, often maliciously—and get a tax break for doing so! Only in America!

Floyd Brown's story about the Willie Horton spot, for what it's worth, was that it started with his own, honest trauma. Brown told a *Washington Times* reporter in 1992 that when he read a July 1988 *Reader's Digest* article, "Getting Away with Murder," about a convicted murderer in Massachusetts, William R. Horton, who attacked a man and raped a woman while out on a weekend furlough, he felt triggered; the incident "reopened an old family wound," he told the *Times*. "When Floyd Brown was in the fourth grade, his twenty-two-year-old aunt, a recent nursing school graduate and newlywed, was robbed and murdered. Though her killer was caught, convicted and imprisoned, he eventually was released."

A gruesome story, one that might even have some basis in fact. But the low-budget Willie Horton ad Brown produced, working with TV ad maker Larry McCarthy, was straight political smear, crude in its racism and invocation of fear. "What crossed the line was not that he was raising the issue of crime itself because crime was a big issue, and that's fair game," *Republic of Spin* author David Greenberg told *The New York Times* in 2018. "But to use the image of this threatening black man—people call it a dog whistle; it was a pretty clear whistle."

Go-for-the-jugular Bush operative Lee Atwater would insist on his deathbed that he regretted fixating on Willie Horton during the 1988 campaign. This is a man who at the time actually said, "If I can make Willie Horton a household name, we'll win the election." Atwater even called Horton "Dukakis' running mate," pure sleaze, basically. Roger Ailes, then a Bush strategist, later the founder of Fox News, said: "The only question is whether we depict Willie Horton with a knife in his hand or without one."

———

Three years later, in September 1991, Floyd Brown was functioning as the angry id of the Bush administration in the days before the Clarence Thomas confirmation hearings had even opened, putting out a crude attack-ad smear-job on Democratic senators daring to stand up to the debased Thomas—and overtly threatening them with more trash if they did not cease and desist. It was a coarse enough display that both President Bush and Clarence Thomas himself denounced the ad. Were the denunciations just theater? Their way of working the good-cop, bad-cop two-step? Hard to know for sure, but the episode says everything about the fevered mentality of Citizens United.

Senator Ted Kennedy could hardly have been surprised to

be bludgeoned for his opposition to Clarence Thomas, but he was one of many in Washington startled by the starkly personal nature of the attacks, with a narrator asking whether Kennedy and Biden were fit to judge Thomas, because Kennedy had been "suspended from Harvard for cheating, left the scene of the accident at Chappaquiddick where Mary Jo Kopechne died." The ad recycled unfair criticism Biden had faced for plagiarism four years earlier, when in a Democratic presidential debate Biden left out the usual acknowledgment he gave U.K. Labour leader Neil Kinnock for a passage of his he routinely summoned in his stump speech.

"The sponsors of the commercial say they hope to show these and other lawmakers what would be in store for them if they engaged in what the conservative groups termed the 'character assassination' of Judge Thomas during confirmation hearings scheduled for next week," *The New York Times* reported. Note the "next week." This was preemptive.

"We have what we need to turn ads around very quickly," Floyd Brown, "chairman of Citizens United," told the *Times.* "I can produce an ad tomorrow if I have to."

For the man who gave the world the Willie Horton ad, that was a vivid threat indeed, but Brown overplayed his hand, sounding a little ridiculous. He and his partner on the ads, Brent Bozell, founder of a right-wing media watchdog, next tried to leverage their threats. The two, having just been denounced by the president of the United States and a Supreme Court nominee, "issued a statement saying that if opponents of Judge Thomas stopped all campaigning against him, including petition drives, fundraising and public relations efforts, the two conservative organizations would 'hold off any further activity,'" the *Times* reported.

They sounded like dime store cowboys, and their threats were dismissed. "These guys ought to grow up," said Arthur Kropp of People for the American Way. "I don't think they're taking this whole process very seriously."

But Floyd Brown knew what game he was playing. Bush, speaking to reporters just before a meeting of his cabinet, called the ad "offensive"—but the *Times* revealed that the White House had advance knowledge, reporting, "Mr. Brown, Mr. Bozell and Judy Smith, the White House deputy press secretary, all said the Bush Administration was aware that a commercial sharply critical of the three Senators was being prepared." So much for plausible deniability.

All it took was a low-budget ad—$15,000 to $20,000—and a $40,000 ad buy to air the spot briefly, and Brown knew the controversy would take off—and Kennedy and Biden and the other senators and their staffs would get the message. "The latest advertisement shares another common feature of the Willie Horton commercial," the *Times* reported. "In both cases, the sponsors have been able to cause a sensation with the advertisements, prompting news organizations to give prominent coverage and thereby vastly increasing the audience for the groups' messages at no additional cost. 'We've leveraged our money well,' Mr. Brown said."

It's tempting to dismiss the whole episode as mostly farce, since it certainly played out as one. One day later, Brown and Bozell told reporters they refused to back down, even after a direct appeal from White House chief of staff John Sununu. The writing of the statement Brown and Bozell issued to the press had the mawkish tone of grievance I associated with some of the lesser talents drawn to campus right-wing rags in that era, practically shedding crocodile tears with its lament: "Unfortunately, the administration has no desire to confront the radical left."

Revisiting the whole ugly contretemps from my perspective now, thirty years later, Brown's work as a no-holds-barred disrupter looks much more like a sign of things to come, a willingness to push the limits of dirty politics, all under a banner of righteous indignation that not everyone accepted the precepts or alleged beliefs of the far right. Brown admitted at the time his own rationalization for engaging in such disgusting personal attacks: Robert Bork. In the world of right-wing movement opportunists at that time, propagating the fantasy that the Nixon-serving ideologue Bork had been treated in his confirmation hearings with outrageous, below-the-belt unfairness was like a rite of passage. Endless empty talk, all aimed at riling each other up, started and ended with the legend of Bork—for that is what it was, a legend, a creation. The week before the Clarence Thomas hearings, as the fuss over the attack ads percolated, Brown—"chairman of Citizens United"—told the *Times:* "What people don't understand is how bitter conservatives are about Bork."

It's an age-old syndrome: Complain loud and often enough about how you've allegedly been wronged by others and you can justify most anything—and if the money is there, why not push the limits?

At the time this was my world. I only recall meeting Floyd Brown once, at some point in the months before the November 1992 election, and the circumstances of that meeting are I think quite revealing of how this sordid ecosystem worked. My beat at the time was digging up dirt on Bill Clinton, which *The American Spectator* would then inject into the media and give Rush Limbaugh more to rant about. One of the individuals helping fund my activities for the *Spectator* was a Chicago financier named Peter Smith, who was finance chair of Newt Gingrich's PAC. Smith made a small grant to the *Spectator* to cover costs as I followed up leads on Clinton's personal life that had been splashed across tabloid covers—and it was Smith who set up my meeting with Floyd Brown.

Why was I there in Brown's small, nondescript office off Capitol Hill, just the two of us and one young male associate of Brown's, who I assume must have been his one aide at the time, David Bossie? What did I hope to gain? I was looking for dirt, and clearly Brown had dirt. He had published a "book" that year— really more of a pamphlet, a 192-page paperback with a poorly reproduced photograph on the cover—entitled *Slick Willie: Why America Cannot Trust Bill Clinton*. It wasn't much of a book—with chapters like "First Feminist: Hillary Rodham Clinton," opening, "Hillary Clinton was not always a liberal." But Brown had talked to people in Arkansas, and I knew he would be happy to share some gossip with me, which was just what he proceeded to do. Nothing he told me led to any immediate breakthrough in my reporting, that much I know—since my ongoing investigation of Clinton in Arkansas for the *Spectator* that year proved fruitless.

Not until the following year would I publish the "Troopergate" story, in which Arkansas state troopers made the dubious claims that they had helped facilitate affairs by the then governor. The article led Paula Jones to come forward and charge Clinton with sexual harassment in a case that, thanks to Ken Starr and Brett Kavanaugh, who expanded their moribund Whitewater investigation into the salacious terrain of Clinton's private life, led to the president's impeachment. The partisan impeachment effort by the GOP failed, but it helped set the stage for a successful Republican campaign on restoring "honesty and integrity" to the White House in 2000—and a Federalist Society comeback under President George W. Bush. According to exit polls, it worked.

## CHAPTER 9

# SEPTEMBER 1994: KEN STARR'S SIDEKICK

I t was the night of Bill Clinton's 1997 State of the Union address, and I'd been invited to a desultory viewing party hosted by Laura Ingraham, a close friend, drinking buddy, and confidante in those years. The mood that February evening in Laura's Woodley Park townhouse was grim. The people gathered around the television, nursing both high-end cocktails and a sallow sense of grievance at having to endure Clinton's reelection the previous November, seemed oddly out of place, given the fake-cheerful mood evoked by the Southwestern décor Laura had chosen. I scanned the room, and saw a friend of mine at the time, ambitious young lawyer Brett Kavanaugh, sitting across from me. Kavanaugh and I were never especially tight, but we often attended the same events in those years and conversed occasionally, though never memorably. In September 1994, Kavanaugh—and another friend of mine at the time, Alex Azar, whom I knew to be notably witless—had been named as deputies to Ken Starr in his Whitewater investigation. Starr and his sidekick Kavanaugh were working hard to dredge up some scrap of something, anything to lend legitimacy to their witch hunt. I'd known before then that this was all part of a broader, well-funded right-wing effort to smear Bill Clinton, whose popularity and evident political gifts threatened to sideline Republicans for a generation, but I didn't fully grasp how personal—and unhinged—the Starr circle had made its anti-Clinton crusade until that night at Laura's.

I think it was just before the president started his speech, the camera panned over to the first lady, Hillary Rodham Clinton, and I saw Kavanaugh, sitting across from me, contort his face into an ugly sneer and then angrily mouth, "That bitch!" I should not have been surprised, or unsettled, by the violence of Kavanaugh's reaction, but I was. So much so, in fact, that I excused myself and sat alone in Laura's pine-scented dining room, smoking and ruminating on what I increasingly saw as a sickness leading otherwise sane people to lose their minds—and jettison any standards of decency or perspective—all in the name of sticking it to the Clintons.

My own role in this larger effort was, at that point, ambiguous. I'd parlayed the success of *The Real Anita Hill* into a contract to write a book on Hillary Clinton that promised to do to her what I'd done to Anita Hill. Something went wrong along the way. I couldn't be the monster my "friends" in the "conservative" movement wanted me to be, and I couldn't drop an Oppenheimer-sized mushroom cloud on Hillary.

Published the month before the 1996 presidential election in which Clinton would easily be reelected, my book *The Seduction of Hillary Rodham* landed with a thud, having failed to do what was expected. Author James B. Stewart was tart but accurate in summing up in his *New York Times* review:

> Mr. Brock is best known for *The Real Anita Hill,* his best-selling exposé of Clarence Thomas's accuser, and his lurid account

of Bill Clinton's sexual escapades in *The American Spectator.*
He has been lionized by many conservatives as an antidote
to the allegedly liberal national media, and his new book has
been eagerly awaited by anti-Clinton zealots still looking for
the elusive silver bullet that might halt the White House reelection juggernaut. They are in for a shock. They will not
only be disappointed; they will be infuriated. While almost
perfunctorily placing his story within the lines of conservative politics, Mr. Brock seems to have found in "St. Hillary" a
means to attempt his own redemption as a journalist. In substance and style, he distances himself from the polemicist of
*The Real Anita Hill.* He has tried to do his subject justice in the
broadest sense.

Stewart went on to quibble over points I'd made in the book
on which history would more than redeem me, from the inside-
the-Beltway fuss over personnel changes at the White House
travel office, to the absurdity of the Whitewater land-deal hulla-
baloo itself. However, Stewart was pretty on target in concluding:
"Given his own constituency, it has no doubt taken courage for
him to reach the conclusions he does. While it might seem ironic
coming from the writer who once called Anita Hill 'a bit nutty,
and a bit slutty,' Mr. Brock is right that Hillary Clinton has been
demonized at times by misogynists and right-wing fanatics."

The misogynists and right-wing fanatics in question, from
Brett Kavanaugh to my former friends at *The American Spectator,*
were not pleased. My attendance at Laura Ingraham's State of
the Union gathering was an outlier, an exception to the broader
pattern of my exclusion—sometimes I was actively disinvited—
from the social gatherings that had for years filled my schedule.
For a right-wing movement that was all about power and relationships, far more than content or ideas, these cocktail parties,
receptions, and lunches were an essential element of maintain-

ing relevance within the hive. And that hive which was gearing up to make an even stronger push—expanding their extreme and illegitimate means—to bring down Bill Clinton.

The role of Brett Kavanaugh stood out in particular for its naked partisanship powered by a seething hatred and resentment. I really hadn't seen much of this side of Kavanaugh personally. He drank, but then so did we all, and he could get loud in conversation, but not much more than anyone else. Much later, we would all find out much more about Kavanaugh's long history of mixing his hair-trigger temper with binge drinking and resentment of women in a volatile cocktail.

A Yale friend of his, basketball player Charles Ludington, explained: "He was definitely a big partier, and over time it became pretty clear he was aggressive as he partied. And certainly he brought a lot of, how should we say, high-school attitudes towards women that I think a lot of us were shedding at that time." The drinking led to more displays of anger, much of it directed at women, Ludington says, and remembers being put off by Kavanaugh's "particularly aggressive style of misogyny," and an "aggressive masculinity that was constantly relying on demeaning others in order to make himself feel good about himself."

Kavanaugh's work for Starr clearly provided an outlet for these impulses. As the O.J. Simpson Ford Bronco chase provided a template for decades of cable news spectacle coverage, the Starr investigation provided the model for right-wing disinformation campaigns through official Washington organs of government for years to come. One notable feature of such investigations was how little they were based on. These were head fakes, nothing more, which should have been ignored or severely downplayed in respectable media coverage, but instead were blown out of proportion as voluminously as Hillary's emails later would be.

I'm sorry to be blunt, but it remains a very good question

about the pseudo-scandal Starr and Kavanaugh were pursuing:
How did so many smart and able reporters go along with such a
bullshit story? If a two-bit land deal gone bad—and at a loss!—
disqualified one from public office or moral leadership, then basically the whole of official Washington could pack it in and go take
jobs in the private sector. What reporters were really covering,
under the amorphous and ever-changing rubric of "Whitewater,"
was in effect a reality TV show. It was somehow deemed intriguing that enemies of the Clintons were going all out. But why? And
why not find a way to introduce into coverage an undercurrent
of skepticism with some real heft? Instead, the reality TV show
was played AS a reality TV show. As if there were anything particularly arduous about deflecting asinine questions about a land
deal in Arkansas that had nothing to do with anything.

Yet when First Lady Hillary Clinton arrived at a federal courthouse in Washington, D.C., to answer questions before a grand
jury on January 26, 1996, even old pros like Pete Yost of the Associated Press went a little breathless. "Today's grilling by Whitewater prosecutors before a twenty-three-member grand jury
will occur behind closed doors," Yost wrote. Flinging of spitballs
might have been just as accurate. And speaking of accuracy, Yost
and the AP—representing the safe middle of Washington political conventional wisdom—also opened by somewhat insidiously
seeking to undermine Hillary's credibility. You judge for yourself:
"Her veracity under attack in the Whitewater affair, Hillary Rodham Clinton says her unprecedented grand jury appearance is
not a first she's particularly pleased about."

See what he did there? Snuck in the reference to her veracity,
as if a disinterested observer, in the Walter Lippmann tradition,
should grant any credibility whatsoever to dubious attacks made
with clear malice and a disregard for facts. The factual justification allegedly leading to this grand drama was the unremarkable
matter of billing records showing that Hillary, through Rose Law

Firm in Little Rock, had done legal work for a troubled savings and loan owned by her partner in the Whitewater investment— sixty hours over more than a year.

Amid the circus of badgering the Clintons, who should show up, but none other than attack-dog-in-training Brett Kavanaugh. Yost's account moved on from observing that Hillary was "testifying today in the same U.S. Courthouse where grand juries investigated the Iran-Contra and Watergate scandals" to noting the arrival on the third floor of the courthouse that day at mid-morning of "Whitewater associate independent counsel Brett Kavanaugh."

I'll leave Gail Sheehy–type character studies to other authors. I'm not a big believer in thinking we can peer into the human psyche with complete clarity. We can't know what exactly motivated Brett Kavanaugh. He himself may not be able to untangle all those threads. Clearly he was ambitious and willing to get when the getting was good. Did he really hate Hillary? When I think of the way his face looked, calling her a bitch, at that party I also attended, I'm inclined to think so. What's very clear is that he *smelled* power. He knew there was rich opportunity for him in aiding the right-wing effort, through any and all means, to tarnish the Clintons with whatever combination of exaggeration and outright concoction proved necessary.

Consider the strange story of the one case attorney Brett Kavanaugh argued before the court on which he would one day, implausibly enough, sit. Kavanaugh helped write the thirty-page legal brief on which the case was based, working with John Deacon Bates, who would also go on to serve as a judge, though of a less openly ideological bent than Kavanaugh. Here the two young hotshots were, chasing after a dead guy they could smear, and apparently unbothered at this ambulance-chaser-on-steroids approach to the law.

It's actually hard to believe such a case even made it to the Supreme Court: Kavanaugh and his boss Ken Starr, who had long since gone beyond the pale in obsessing over their lurid imaginations, thought they could get the court to break attorney-client privilege for them. Seriously. That was the case. Kavanaugh argued a case that, if he had prevailed, would have hobbled a cornerstone of U.S. jurisprudence. Even curmudgeonly old men on the court who thought of themselves as "conservative" found this argument somewhere between offensive and wackadoodle.

Specifically, Kavanaugh wanted to plunder the death of Vince Foster for possible Kompromat on Hillary, but it was a reach. A big reach. As Starr's deputy, a desperate Kavanaugh—egged on by House Speaker Newt Gingrich—had insisted on opening a new investigation into Foster's death, investing federal money into magnifying a partisan conspiracy theory. After three years, the investigation would determine, yet again, that Foster had committed suicide; there was no foul play.

Look, it's hard to explain how anyone could have gone along with the whopper that some staffing decisions in the White House travel office were some kind of scandal, but, yes, some reporters pretended that was actually a story. And in so pretending, they gave cover to the likes of Kavanaugh to bray about it. And Kavanaugh went all the way to the Supreme Court with the hilariously weak argument that, as Kavanaugh argued before the court, his voice no doubt cracking for effect, that Foster "would have been an important, indeed critical witness" in looking at the staffing question related to the travel office, so therefore the Supreme Court should give Kavanaugh and his hound dogs access to Foster's private papers, despite attorney-client privilege. Got that? No, I didn't think so.

Foster's lawyer, James Hamilton, had previously told an appeals court hearing, "I am totally certain of one thing. If I had not assured Vince Foster that our conversation was a privileged conversation, we would not have had that conversation, and there would have been no notes that are the subject of this situation today."

If you're an ambitious attorney going before the Supreme Court to argue the merits of a case, you probably want to *have* a case. Kavanaugh had none. And, to be blunt, he must have known just how weak that case was.

On June 8, 1998, at 10:38 a.m., Kavanaugh appeared before the Supreme Court to make oral arguments in *Swidler & Berlin v. United States,* on behalf of the respondent. The first words out of his mouth, the first Brett Kavanaugh words ever in the Supreme Court, amounted to the judicial equivalent of stepping on a whoopee cushion. It is truly a shame that we don't have a video of this unbelievable moment.

"Mr. Kavanaugh, we'll hear from you," said Chief Justice William Rehnquist.

"Thank you, Mr. Chief Justice, and may it please the Court," Kavanaugh began. "In light of what petitioner has stated, let me state at the outset there can be no mistake about the pernicious consequences of petitioner's theory, taken to its logical extreme. By permanently walling off a critical category of evidence from the criminal process, petitioner's theory will lead to extreme injustice. Not our words, the words of Mueller & Kirkpatrick. That will mean that innocent people—"

And here, mid-drone, young Kavanaugh was interrupted. Seventy-six words into his debut before the court, he was slapped down.

"Who are Mueller and Kirkpatrick?" Rehnquist demanded.

What important legal references was he invoking?

"They are two commentators on the law of evidence," Kavanaugh replied.

"Oh," Rehnquist replied, not able to hide his clear derision.

"That will mean that—" Kavanaugh, digging himself deeper, attempted.

And at that point the official Supreme Court transcript reads: "(Laughter)."

They laughed at Kavanaugh, the first and only time he tried to argue a case before the Supreme Court.

"They're not quite as well-known as Professor [John Henry] Wigmore and the like," Justice Stevens said, rubbing it in a little by citing the universally respected author of *Wigmore on Evidence.*

Among those in the press gallery was syndicated "Covering the Courts" columnist James J. Kilpatrick, who wrote at the time: "Brett M. Kavanaugh argued the case on behalf of independent counsel Starr. Unfortunately he did not argue it well. He got off to a bad start by telling the court that Mueller and Kirkpatrick support his view that the privilege terminates with death. Chief Justice Rehnquist rose like a big bass to a fat fly. 'Who?' the Chief demanded."

Later on in Kavanaugh's awkward attempt at a credible showing, John Paul Stevens, a Republican appointed to the high court by Republican president Gerald Ford, drew more laughter with a question—or really, an observation—that sounded incredulous.

"You want us both to say what the law now is and change it," Stevens scolded Kavanaugh, and again the transcript shows laughter.

"We don't know what the law—we don't know what the law is, Justice Stevens," Kavanaugh said.

This one was not going to be close. As David Savage wrote the next morning in the *Los Angeles Times,* under the headline "Justices Skeptical of Effort by Starr to Waive Privilege," Kavanaugh's arguments "did not appear to sway the justices, most of whom spent parts of their careers as lawyers representing clients. For generations, the 'understanding of the profession' has been that a conversation between a lawyer and a client is private, said Justice David H. Souter." Added Stephen Labaton in *The New York Times,* "When Kavanaugh told the justices that they could presume that most people would not object to their conversations with lawyers being made public after death because of a civic obligation to be truthful with grand juries, Justice David Souter did not buy it."

Later that month came the ruling: By a solid 6–3, the Supreme Court swatted down Kavanaugh's arguments on behalf of Starr. "In a sharp defeat for independent counsel Kenneth W. Starr," wrote Aaron Epstein on the front page of *The Philadelphia Inquirer*, "the Supreme Court blocked him yesterday from obtaining a lawyer's notes that Starr said he needed for his criminal investigation of Hillary Rodham Clinton."

The humiliating smackdown does not seem to have slowed Kavanaugh down much, but the press was easy on him, all things considered. Why was that? Kavanaugh knew how to play the Washington game. All along, Kavanaugh was widely known to have been involved in strategic leaks to the press to dirty up the Clintons, including quite possibly of grand jury secrets, a violation of law. A judge identified twenty-four news reports that she said contained evidence of violations of grand jury rules on secrecy and appointed a special master to investigate Starr's office.

"He was a go-to source for journalists and authors," *The Washington Post* reported on Kavanaugh in 2018, part of a network that sprang up to funnel garbage from Starr and other sources to the odd constellation of grifters, operatives, and scandalmongers who were working to get in on the action any way they could. The *Post* itself was a beneficiary of many of these leaks. An analysis shows that from late 1997 through 1999, the *Post* cited sources from the independent counsel's office in eleven major stories. The lead reporter for the *Post* at this time was named Sue Schmidt— "steno Sue" to close observers of her work.

In Kavanaugh's Senate confirmation hearing, Sheldon Whitehouse laid out the accusation: "Now let us look at where you fit in. A Republican operative your whole career who has never tried a case. You made your political bones helping the salacious prosecution of President Clinton and leaking prosecution information to the press." In a colloquy with Whitehouse, Kavanaugh admitted that he had in fact frequently briefed the press on prosecutorial matters at the direction of Starr, but denied improper disclosures. Challenged by Whitehouse to release the press from their off-the-record agreement to provide clarity, Kavanaugh refused.

A report by the special master appointed by the judge to investigate leaks from Starr's office admonished Starr's deputies for talking off the record with reporters but could not reach the conclusion that those conversations included grand jury material. No matter: Kavanaugh's leaking earned him chits with a scandal-crazed press corps desperate for scoops. The relationships would pay off when many in that same press corps treated Kavanaugh with kid gloves when his confirmation hearings blew up.

The Starr investigation, with unmistakable undertones of misogyny, moved on to try to frame Hillary Clinton for crimes she didn't commit as first lady. After breaching legal ethics by secretly counseling the Paula Jones lawyers, Starr sought and received authority to conduct additional investigations into the Jones lawsuit and possible perjury and obstruction of justice to cover up Bill Clinton's affair with a White House intern, Monica Lewinsky, which had been unearthed in the course of the Jones case. Starr had been given secretly made tapes of Lewinsky talking about the affair with Clinton.

In seeking broad authority to investigate Clinton's personal life, Starr crossed far over the line that separated prosecutor from political hitman. At his side was Kavanaugh, who urged Starr to ask sexually graphic questions of Clinton in a deposition—a move they clearly planned as a perjury trap. Kavanaugh was also the principal author of a report from the independent counsel alleging that Clinton lied about the Lewinsky affair in that deposition, which led to Clinton's impeachment in the House. The Starr Report provided extensive and explicit descriptions of each of Clinton's sexual encounters with Lewinsky, a despicable effort to humiliate the president, many of them authored by Kavanaugh himself, reading like a bad pulp novel: "She unbuttoned her jacket; either she unhooked her bra or he lifted her bra up; and he touched her breasts with his hands and mouth."

Clinton was acquitted in a Senate trial. For the moment, the Clintons won the Clinton Wars. In the 1998 midterm elections, the public decisively rejected the unconstitutional and partisan Republican impeachment, delivering a big win for Clinton's party and leading to the resignation of Speaker Gingrich, when reports resurfaced from a decade earlier about how he left his first wife, while on her deathbed, for another woman, exposing his rank hypocrisy.

Ken Starr ended his career in ignominy. Following an investigation into his mishandling, as university president, of sexual assaults at the school, including a gang rape by football players, the board of regents fired him. Starr later joined Trump's legal team during his first impeachment trial, and also joined the team defending Palm Beach billionaire Jeffrey Epstein, accused of the statutory rape of numerous high school students. Starr's representation, involving a brutal smear of a female prosecutor, allowed Epstein to evade justice for years.

Like his deputy, it turned out Starr, too, had a dirty mind; and the old judge acted on it. In 2021, Judi Hershman, his former public relations advisor during the Clinton impeachment, came forward to admit she'd had an extramarital affair with Starr during the investigation, revealing Starr's bogus religiosity and also highlighting Brett Kavanaugh's "uncontrollable temper." Hershman pinpointed the blatant hypocrisy of Starr, noting that his "1998 pursuit of former President Clinton over his sexual relationship with a White House intern . . . was bookended by his recent impeachment foray, this time defending an adulterous president, who lies about so much more than that." Starr, he of such pious pretensions in his pursuit of Clinton's sex life, had taken her hand while she was his employee and "placed it on his crotch."

In his 2018 memoir, *Contempt,* Starr wrote: "I deeply regret that I took on the Lewinsky phase of the investigation, but there was no practical alternative." Starr was aware that his Supreme Court dreams had gone up in smoke. But Kavanaugh's star in the conservative firmament kept rising.

## CHAPTER 10

# JUNE 1997: JOHN EASTMAN AND THE GROWING THOMAS NETWORK

S upreme Court law clerks as a group are smart, ambitious, and highly loyal to their benefactors. That is a general rule of access to power—and all the ways it propels former clerks in their supercharged path forward in life, post-clerkship—that was in no way unique to the constellation of clerks and former clerks that grew around Clarence Thomas in his early years on the high court. Ginni and Clarence Thomas just pushed the cult-ish aspects of in-group loyalty to new extremes, as is their wont. The pitch was both simple and potent: Stand with us, against our enemies, real and imagined, and you can share in unfathomable power. It was in effect a pyramid scheme, and neither Thomas was especially subtle about the sales pitch, which may be why it attracted individuals like former Thomas clerk John Eastman, whose efforts to undermine the rule of law in advising Trump on his January 6 scheme led to his being indicted as a Trump co-conspirator in Georgia and to another court ruling stating that

Eastman "more likely than not" committed a crime in scheming with Trump to defraud voters.

"You're going to be future leaders!" Thomas would tell his clerks, according to no less a source than his wife. "It's coming your way. You're going to be next."

As Eastman's case shows, the words were more true than anyone could have known, as in, leaders of attempted coups. If that sounds shocking, it shouldn't, given the kind of us-against-the-world extremism considered a badge of honor in this circle. Thomas made a ritual of his clerks sitting down to watch one of his favorite movies, *The Fountainhead* from 1949, based on an Ayn Rand novel, starring Gary Cooper in a black-and-white paean to arrogant individualism. As film critic David Thomson put it, "*The Fountainhead* is like a comic strip bursting to be God's mural in the sky . . . delirious and dangerous, maybe." This is a movie about a proud architect who doesn't get his way so he blows up a skyscraper—not metaphorically, but with high explosives.

"My law clerks are my kids," Clarence Thomas said at a 2008 event at Pepperdine University. "I hire them knowing that I want them to be part of my family. They *are* my family."

What that really means, of course, is they can be counted on to take his side, as Thomas made clear in the same talk, engaging once again in his lifelong song of self-pity, one of the most powerful men in the world who likes to complain that "the whole world's against you."

In a 2022 book, *Created Equal*, Ginni Thomas expanded on her appreciation of having all those former clerks as loyal co-conspirators: "It's a joy for us to have hundreds of young people and now middle-aged people, all former clerks, sprinkled around the country who are doing amazing things, both personally and professionally—judges, and teachers, and lawyers, and even housewives who are spending their time with their children. It's really exciting to watch what they're doing."

That would be one way to put it: exciting. Among the former clerks was John Eastman, a friend of Clarence Thomas's going back to the 1980s. Eastman's history with Thomas provides a cautionary tale in the private networks of influence, post–Powell Memo.

The bond that formed between John Eastman and Clarence Thomas in 1980s Washington had in part to do with their mutual interest in the attempt by a Southern California think tank called the Claremont Institute to dress up familiar right-wing ideas with the trappings of high intellectual gloss. "Claremont is among the most influential California think tanks," the *Los Angeles Times* wrote in 1996.

> Its staff includes former television commentator Bruce Herschensohn, hired after his failed run for U.S. Senate in 1992. Its major donors include Los Angeles industrialist Henry Salvatori, who was part of President Reagan's kitchen cabinet, conservative foundations and corporations such as Philip Morris and Union Petroleum. . . . Through position papers and books, Claremont advocates applying the nation's founding principles to current problems. Claremont papers conclude the state would be better off with free-market economics, fewer government restrictions on business and lower taxes. Its tracts also oppose gay rights, pornography and abortion.

Eastman, who grew up in Texas and studied economics and politics at the University of Dallas, earned his PhD at the Claremont Graduate School east of Los Angeles. His thesis advisor, Bill Allen, later told *The Washington Post* about Eastman: "He was a political animal from his undergraduate days."

Allen, a member of President Reagan's Black Economic Council at the time, decided to run for the Republican nomination for U.S. senator from California, hoping to challenge incumbent Democrat Alan Cranston. Eastman, identified as Allen's "campaign coordinator," told the *San Bernardino County Sun* in January 1986 that Allen would contrast himself with other Black candidates who pushed "watered-down liberalism" on African Americans. "Bill's focus is not on race at all," Eastman said. "The focus is going to be to ignore race and politics and go straight to the issues, no matter what groups we're talking to."

Allen's candidacy did not exactly take off. That June, he finished eleventh out of thirteen Republican primary candidates, gaining all of 12,990 votes (.65 percent), but the following April Reagan appointed him to the U.S. Civil Rights Commission, created by the Civil Rights Act of 1957. Before long Eastman moved to Washington to work with Allen as a spokesman and congressional liaison for the bipartisan Civil Rights Commission—and also, of course, to network.

"In Washington, he was a gregarious go-getter and was well-connected in Republican circles, according to Melvin Jenkins, who served as acting staff director for the commission," *The Washington Post* later reported. "Jenkins recalled that Eastman introduced him to Thomas in 1989 or 1990, by which time Eastman and Thomas seemed to already know one another well."

Eastman would later talk of "many fond dinners" with Thomas in this period, and their discussion often turned to the ideas being espoused by right-wing conservatives at the Claremont Institute, which Eastman had embraced and Thomas was curious about. So curious, in fact, that he started hiring Claremont-affiliated scholars, including Ken Masugi and John Marini. Claremont—now infamous for its active support of Trumpism—was known at the time principally for its adherence to the ideas of Harry Jaffa, a conservative political philosopher credited with supplying Goldwater with his 1964 statement: "I would remind you that extremism in the defense of liberty is no vice. And let me remind you also that moderation in pursuit of justice is no virtue."

Thomas, a man whose ambition impelled him toward conservative notions, but who himself lacked the intellectual firepower to develop his own ideas, asked the Claremont scholars to tell him what he believed. "In a period that Thomas was later to recall as one of 'great intellectual development,'" *The New York Times* later reported, "they spent hours discussing Jaffa's teachings on natural law and an interpretation of the Constitution, based on the principles of the Declaration of Independence, which Thomas began to cite." (In a speech at the Heritage Foundation, Thomas later praised an article that made the argument that natural law protects the right-to-life. In his confirmation hearing Thomas attempted to minimize the import of his endorsement, claiming it was a "throwaway line.")

Eastman completed his law degree at the University of Chicago, and in a 2008 post at *The New York Times,* he was surprisingly generous in his assessment of the course offered at the time by Barack Obama, which Eastman himself had not taken. "I am not surprised to see the intellectual diversity for which Chicago is famous reflected in then-Professor Obama's course syllabi and examinations," Eastman wrote. "The syllabus from the 1994 'Current Issues in Racism and the Law' course is particularly instructive. While at many law schools, such courses are frequently taught by critical race theorists who focus largely on one side of a complex legal and policy debate, then-Professor Obama's course included, quite appropriately in my view, readings from across the ideological spectrum, from Derrick Bell and Malcolm X to Chuck Cooper and Lino Graglia."

Law professor Garrett Epps, writing at *Washington Monthly* in 2023, also reflected on this intellectually generous, open orientation of Eastman for many years. "As professor and eventually dean of Chapman University School of Law, he was respected by people on both sides of the philosophical divide," Epps wrote. "Most important to me, of all the Federalists whom I have (for my sins) debated over three decades, John was the only one who ever publicly said, 'You know, you raise an interesting point—I am going to have to think about that.' Today, the strange career of John Eastman raises questions about whether any of those values—civil discourse, careful analysis, mutual respect, the entire small-l liberal intellectual project—have any substance at all, or are just fairy tales that disguise the grim reality that law, and everything else in American politics, is nothing more noble than a knife fight in the dark."

Well put. Clarence Thomas rewarded his friend Eastman, his conduit to the Claremont crowd and his eager interlocutor for wide-ranging bull sessions, when he was elevated to the Supreme Court, naming him one of his clerks starting in July 1996. Earlier, Eastman had also clerked for J. Michael Luttig—who would later speak out against Eastman's role in the January 6 attempt to short-circuit democracy.

Eastman for many years chaired the Federalist Society's federalism and separation of powers practice group and could reliably be depended on to flog Federalist Society talking points. Eastman, by all accounts a creative thinker, was also, as his mentor had said, "always a political animal." In 1990, two years after working on the California campaign of a Republican seeking to challenge entrenched incumbent Democratic congressman Esteban Torres, Eastman decided to have a go at Torres himself. He finished well back, with 36,024 votes to 55,646, but learned enough to want to run again.

Eastman's big chance came in 2010 in one of the great "What might have been?" races in recent U.S. political history. Sound like an overstatement? Not at all. Eastman threw his name in the hat in the 2010 race for attorney general of California, vying with State Senator Tom Harman and Los Angeles District Attorney Steve Cooley for the Republican nomination. Over on the Democratic side, the candidates included Ted Lieu, then a state assemblyman, Chris Kelly of Facebook, State Assemblyman Alberto Torrico, and San Francisco district attorney Kamala Harris.

Eastman ended up finishing second to Cooley, and Harris won in November—but many in California politics think Eastman might have run a stronger race against Harris than Cooley, her fellow D.A. "I think I would've beaten our now Vice President had I won the nomination," Eastman later told *Washington Monthly*.

"Just think about that, how our lives would be different today if we'd had John Eastman as Attorney General, not Kamala Harris," recalls Republican consultant Wayne C. Johnson, who ran Harman's campaign that year. "The reason he ran as well as he did was he was all over talk radio, and he nailed down the right flank. Tom Harman was a conservative, but not on the hard right."

Eastman struck Wayne Johnson as a "great legal mind" with a lot of energy—who liked to kick around new ideas. "If he's in the room, he's talking," Johnson says now, laughing. "He has a lot to say. He was very much a political animal." He remembers him as "brilliant," someone who was always thinking "What if?" and liked to indulge in the theoretical and look for the limits— qualities that would later get him in trouble.

Among the contributors to Eastman's California attorney general race that year: Ginni Thomas, Leonard Leo, Robert Bork, Texas senator Ted Cruz, talk show host Hugh Hewitt, Federalist Society founder Lee Otis, Federalist Society lawyers Erik Jaffe, Walter Weber, and Dean Reuter, and Scalia law clerk Glen Summers. Eastman ran a serious race and the *Los Angeles Times* editorial board gave consideration to giving him their endorsement in the Republican primary. Eastman, the *Times* wrote, "brings intriguing credentials. He is an original thinker and constitutional scholar. He presents new ideas for how to organize and direct the attorney general's office, and he amassed an impressive record as Chapman's dean."

Eastman would finish with 737,025 votes, or 34.5 percent, in the Republican primary, second to Cooley's total of more than a million. Eastman later explained that it was largely one issue that pulled him into the AG race, same-sex marriage, and he was a vocal supporter of California Proposition 8 seeking to amend the California Constitution to ban same-sex marriage—ultimately thrown out as unconstitutional.

In September 2011, Eastman was named chairman of the National Organization for Marriage, an anti-same-sex-marriage group. The role seemed to ease Eastman further along in his gradual evolution from tolerant man of ideas to mean-spirited zealot. As a former Supreme Court law clerk, it was highly unusual for him to aggressively attack Chief Justice John Roberts, but that was exactly what he did in October 2014 when the chief justice resisted taking up the issue before the Supreme Court. "You've got state constitutional amendments being struck down by lower federal courts . . . and the Supreme Court just lets it stand," Eastman, speaking in his role as chairman of the National Organization for Marriage, told *USA Today.* "He's not doing his job in enforcing the Constitution as written."

Even for a man as self-assured as John Eastman, lecturing the chief justice of the United States on what constituted doing his job and what did not must have represented crossing the Rubicon. There was only one interpretation: Eastman, a former Clarence Thomas clerk, well understood that this was not, in any sense, the Roberts Court. It was the Thomas Court, and when it came to bizarre, insecure projections on the "sanctity" of the institution of marriage, Eastman knew both Clarence and Ginni Thomas stood shoulder to shoulder with him. Eastman, trying to lobby swing vote Anthony Kennedy in the press, knew he spoke with his Thomas association giving his words added weight, even when he sounded pious, as in a 2012 quote to the *Los Angeles Times:* "I know some people say Justice Kennedy will ask: Should we stop progress now? I think Justice Kennedy will ask: Do we want to put a stake in the heart of an institution, marriage, that has done so much for society?" Despite Eastman's pressure tactics, in June 2015, the Supreme Court ruled, 5–4, enshrining a right to same-sex marriage as the law of the land in an opinion written by Kennedy.

By December 2020, Eastman found himself at the heart of the Trumpist plot to rob the American people of their rightful choice for president of the United States, lending his prestige to the sinister effort. It says something that the coup-plotting lawyers apparently believed they could enlist Thomas in their scheme.

Looking for some argument that could keep Trump in power, despite his repudiation by voters, Trump lawyer Kenneth Chesebro emailed the Trump team of lawyers that month that the goal should be to "frame things" so that Justice Thomas "could be the one to issue some sort of stay or other circuit justice opinion saying Georgia is in legitimate doubt." To this fevered, arguably treasonous suggestion, John Eastman replied: "I think I agree with this," and suggested such a move from Thomas, who as a justice oversees the appellate court that covers Georgia, would "kick the Georgia legislature into gear." Eastman, architect of the legal rationale behind the outrageous scheme to invalidate votes, was also in regular email contact with Ginni Thomas, at the same time Eastman was writing, in December 2020, "So the odds are not based on the legal merits but an assessment of the justices' spines, and I understand that there is a heated fight underway." And how might he know about that heated fight? Yes, Clarence Thomas said it best, he and Ginni and his former law clerks were indeed all "family."

## CHAPTER 11

# DECEMBER 2000: THE SUPREME COURT STEALS AN ELECTION

On election night 2000, Al Gore won the popular vote over former Texas governor George W. Bush by more than three million votes, but the vote was tight in the Electoral College, with the outcome hanging on Florida's twenty-five electoral votes. Just before 8 p.m. East Coast time on election night, CNN, FOX, ABC, CBS, and NBC all called Florida for Gore, seeming to give him the presidency. However, over the next two hours, the networks started retracting their early verdict on Florida and moved the state back into the "Undecided" column. It was bedlam. As the vote counting continued after midnight, the networks then announced that Bush had won Florida—but the tally was so close, a mandatory recount was triggered.

With Bush leading by only 1,784 votes, Miami-Dade County sought to recount 10,750 ballots that the machines had been unable to tally. Fearful that a recount would reverse the result and give Al Gore the presidency, Republican campaign operatives, many of them congressional staffers, disrupted the recount at a critical juncture, shutting it down entirely. The stakes were so high, Republicans had taken to the streets. Sometimes referred to as "the Brooks Brothers riot," the violent protest—Democrats were trampled, punched, and kicked—was set off by Representative John Sweeney of New York, who directed an aide to "shut it down." (Bush rewarded him with the nickname "Congressman Kick-Ass.") Right in the middle of fomenting chaos once again was Roger Stone, the self-described "Republican hit man" who would play a key role in organizing the January 6 assault on democracy as the main conduit between Trump and groups like the Proud Boys, who shared with the Brooks Brothers rioters a commitment to the kind of thuggery and raw physical intimidation as a political tool that the National Socialists in 1930s Germany used to legally take over the government and turn it into an autocracy.

The standoff over the 2000 Florida recount went all the way to the Supreme Court, where Bush was represented by Federalist Society founder Ted Olson and a legal team stacked with the society's rising stars. Five Republican appointees voted to countermand the Florida Supreme Court and halt the recount of ballots, allowing a previous certification of the vote to stand for Bush, who thereby won Florida's electoral votes. That gave Bush 271 electoral votes, one more than the 270 required to claim the presidency. Rather than petition the Florida Supreme Court, Gore decided to accept the high court's decision, unite the nation, and concede the election to Bush.

The Supreme Court's majority decision was nakedly political, an egregious performance, wrong on both the facts and the law. There was nothing "conservative" about this intervention. The five right-wing justices ruled in a way that was inconsistent with their prior jurisprudence, deciding to involve the federal judiciary in a matter that should have been left to the states. It is clear that Republican judges only believe in "state's rights" when the states agree with their stance. One sentence in the majority opinion indicated that its logic only applied to "the present circumstances," and therefore was intended to set no future precedent. This was the tell that the majority realized its holding was untenable—but didn't care, since this was a move all about power; they had the votes, so they used them.

Scalia, in on the scam but too proud in his independence of mind not to call bullshit when he smelled bullshit, actually told a colleague at the time, referring to the legal reasoning behind *Bush v. Gore,* "as we say in Brooklyn, a piece of shit." Specifically, Scalia was referencing the attempt to justify the move to stop the Florida recount on the argument that variations in the sets of standards different Florida counties used to determine how to count ballots amounted to a violation of the Equal Protection Clause of the Fourteenth Amendment of the Constitution, from 1868, which held, "nor shall any State . . . deny to any person within its jurisdiction the equal protection of the laws." (The clause, seeking to bolster the Civil Rights Act of 1866, was used to form the basis for more liberal Supreme Court decisions such as *Brown v. Board of Education* in 1954, finding racial segregation in schools unconstitutional. It wasn't a conservative favorite.)

Scalia was not the only justice to find this argument, pushed by Kennedy, absurd; apparently, Kennedy believed it somehow made a monstrous ruling—and usurpation of the legitimacy of a U.S. president—seem more "fair." The fix was in and everyone knew it, even if most Republicans shut up about it. A prominent exception was Republican senator Chuck Hagel, who admitted in a November 2000 appearance on *Hardball with Chris Matthews* on MSNBC, "It may well be . . . the only way you're going to resolve this in a fair way, in a way that's perceived as being fair by both sides, is recount all sixty-seven counties in Florida." Hagel was right. A clean and thorough recount was the only way to make the unruly process fair. But Republicans did not care about fair—and the Federalist Society and its network, hungry to replace Bill Clinton with a Republican who could appoint legions of Federalist Society judges, cared not at all about fairness, only about getting the result they wanted.

As one Supreme Court law clerk at the time told *Vanity Fair* in 2004, emphasizing how unthinkable it was to clerks that the court would involve itself in the Florida recount, "It was just inconceivable to us that the Court would want to lose its credibility in such a patently political way. That would be the end of the Court."

David Margolick, who interviewed former clerks for *Vanity Fair* in 2004, summed up their sentiments about what happened this way: "Now out in the working world, the two clerks, along with most of their colleagues who worked for the four liberal justices and the occasional conservative justice, remain angered, haunted, shaken, and disillusioned by what they saw. After all, they were idealists. They'd learned in their elite law schools that the law was just and that judges resolved legal disputes by nonpartisan analysis of neutral principles. But *Bush* v. *Gore,* as seen from the inside, convinced them they'd been sold a bill of goods. They'd left their clerkships disheartened and disgusted."

Just as the Republican forces mobilized in Florida to work on behalf of the Bush cause outmaneuvered and outmuscled the Democrats, under the leadership of former secretary of state James Baker, a tough political street fighter matched up against wan, punchless, dithering Warren Christopher, so, too, did the conservative Supreme Court justices and their enablers outmaneuver their opposite numbers on the court on *Bush* v. *Gore.* As one former clerk explained to Margolick, "They gave just enough cover to the five justices and their defenders in the press and academia so that it was impossible to rile up the American people about these five conservative ideologues stealing the election."

The insidious nature of the Federalist Society's key role in stealing an election runs much deeper simply than the role of Olson and a vast legal team that included future Supreme Court justices John Roberts, Brett Kavanaugh, and Amy Coney Barrett, each of whom chipped in on the frantic legal wrangling and strategizing unfolding behind the scenes and establishing bona fides for their futures.

Federalist Society clerks also played an important role in seeking to keep Kennedy in the majority. As Evan Thomas wrote in his biography of Sandra Day O'Connor, during the frantic maneuvering on the case, "For a moment, Kennedy seemed to waver and tip into the liberal camp." The case would be sent back to the Florida court for fixing; the recount would continue. What brought Kennedy back? According to law clerks at the time, Kennedy's clerks were plugged into the Federalist Society network working to install Bush. "We assumed that his clerks were coordinating with Scalia's clerks and trying to push him to stay with the majority," explained one clerk.

Several of the justices in the majority had partisan and personal motives to rule as they did. As Clarence Thomas was deciding who would be the next president, Ginni was intimately involved in the Bush campaign, working for the right-wing Heritage Foundation to draw up lists of potential Bush appointees to be forwarded to the White House. But the swing vote belonged to O'Connor, who despite voting to protect abortion rights and generally demonstrating a streak of independence in her past opinions, was still first and foremost a lifelong Republican. Acting more like the Republican State Senate leader she once was in Arizona than a judge, O'Connor was hell-bent on stopping the recount, period, full stop. Law clerks later leaked that O'Connor had circulated a draft opinion the night before the decision that used entirely different logic to reach her preferred result than what the final opinion reflected. This would be a partisan, unprincipled decision, a political result looking for a legal rationale.

In his book *Too Close to Call: The Thirty-Six-Day Battle to Decide the 2000 Election,* Jeffrey Toobin reported that O'Connor looked stricken at an election night party in November when the networks initially called Florida for Gore. O'Connor's husband told guests at the party that the justice was angry because the couple wanted to retire to Phoenix, and she did not want a Democratic president to name her successor. Thus, according to O'Connor's husband, a Gore win would have meant four more years in Washington. Chief Justice Rehnquist had also reportedly told associates of his desire to retire sooner rather than later.

"The decision in the Florida election case may be ranked as the single most corrupt decision in Supreme Court history," wrote Harvard Law professor Alan Dershowitz, "because it is the only one that I know of where the majority of justices decided as they did because of their personal identity and political affiliation of the litigants. This was cheating, and a violation of the judicial oath."

Polls showed that by substantial margins the public believed personal politics influenced the decision of the justices and that faith in the integrity of elections had declined. A year after the election, the nonpartisan Florida Ballots Project concluded that if the dispute over the validity of all ballots in question had been consistently resolved and uniform standards for counting ballots applied, Gore would have won the election. In other words, Gore *had* won the election, the American people *had* elected him president, but that victory was stolen. Concerned about the stench surrounding the decision—call it a demonstration of consciousness of guilt—no Republican justice retired during Bush's first term. Still, the stolen election denied Al Gore the possibility of appointing justices to the bench, and it set the stage for a Federalist comeback later in the 2000s.

## CHAPTER 12

# OCTOBER 2005: THE FEDERALISTS SHOOT DOWN BUSH'S CHOICE

When Sandra Day O'Connor retired in October 2005—at long last getting that retirement in Arizona's Valley of the Sun that she had long craved—the Bush administration surprised many by putting forward White House counsel Harriet Miers, who had headed up the administration's search committee to fill the seat, inspiring cries of "Harriet who?"

It made sense for Bush to select a woman to replace the first woman to sit on the Supreme Court, and because Miers had no prior experience as a judge and thus had no paper trail for potential foes to scrutinize, she was in some ways the perfect pick for the post-Bork era. Miers was a throwback choice: She would be the first justice who would not have any judicial experience since 1972.

Born in Dallas, Miers had spent most of her life in Texas until moving to Washington at the start of the Bush administration, after having served as Bush's personal lawyer and counsel to the campaign. Prior to that, Miers had been the first woman to serve as president of the Texas State Bar Association, was the managing partner of a major law firm, and had served as a local Republican elected official after switching parties. When Bush named her White House counsel in November 2004, *The New York Times* published an article, "Low-Profile Woman, High-Powered Job," describing Miers as "hardly known in Washington," adding, "she has rarely, if ever, talked to reporters since arriving in Washington in 2001." Bush referred to her as a "pit bull in size 6 shoes."

Miers was a rock-ribbed conservative and evangelical Christian but her lack of a judicial record cut both ways: She would be hard for the left to attack, yes, but also hard for the right to support. To the right-wing legal movement, she was an unknown. She didn't wear the Federalist Society James Madison tie (or pin). Right out of the gate, Robert Bork, now licking his wounds in a conservative think tank, declared the nomination a "disaster on every level" and a "slap in the face to the conservatives who've been building up a conservative legal movement for the last twenty years." Bork might as well have come right out and said: We want activists who will do our bidding, not judges!

Eugene Delgaudio, president of the right-wing grassroots organization Public Advocate, was also excoriating, calling the nomination "a betrayal of the conservative, pro-family voters whose support put Bush in the White House in both the 2000 and 2004 elections and who were promised Supreme Court appointments in the mold of Thomas and Scalia. . . . When there are so many proven judges in the mix, it is unacceptable this president has appointed a political crony with no conservative credentials." Miers also drew staunch opposition immediately from radio host Rush Limbaugh, and syndicated columnists Pat Buchanan and Ann Coulter. Senate Sam Brownback speculated that if confirmed Miers might end up being a "Souter-type" judge, referring to the George H. W. Bush nominee David Souter, who had so bitterly disappointed the right.

Abortion was the central issue in the fight as Miers was to replace O'Connor, who had voted to overturn a number of state restrictions on abortion, often in narrowly decided 5–4 decisions. When running for the Dallas City Council in 1989, Miers had indicated that she favored a Human Life Amendment for the state of Texas in a questionnaire circulated by Texas United for Life. On the same survey, however, she indicated support for affirmative action and gay rights. Then it leaked that in a meeting with GOP senator Arlen Specter, who supported abortion rights, Miers told Specter she recognized a right to privacy, the major underpinning of *Roe*. Bush officials frantically spun to party activists that Miers opposed abortion rights, but nobody believed it.

Miers's nomination caused a rare split in the Federalist Society with figures like Bork irate over Leonard Leo's support of her, even if he had taken a leave to curry favor and work with the administration on confirmation. Other nodes in the campaign to capture the courts were also livid. "Roger Pilon, vice president for legal affairs at the Cato Institute, a libertarian think tank, was fuming in his Washington office when the Miers nomination was announced," *The Wall Street Journal* reported. "When he saw Mr. Leo on television, defending the nominee and identified as a Federalist Society officer, Mr. Pilon picked up the telephone and complained to the society's president, Eugene Meyer." This wasn't what the dark-money donors to the Federalist Society and the Cato Institute wanted.

In the end, after an intense flurry of controversy, the administration withdrew the nomination, casting the move as an irreconcilable dispute over the Senate's access to executive branch privileged documents that might have revealed Miers's position on some legal issue. In fact, as everyone knew, Miers went down because of the influence of right-wing conservatives, who wanted a scalp and got one, emboldening them in the judicial wars moving forward. As Federalist Society expert Ann Southworth, a law professor at the University of California at Irvine, later told *The New Yorker,* "What tanked her is that she was not seen as having come up through the conservative legal movement."

As Federalist founder Steven Calabresi later told *The New York Times,* in an interesting kind of code, "It was a striking example of the grass roots having strong opinions that ran counter to the party leaders about what was attainable." By the "grass roots" Calabresi was of course referencing the Federalist Society network, more numerous, more influential, and better funded with each passing year, and determined to enforce its own model of power on old Republican Party structures.

"The radical, unrelenting right wing of the Republican Party killed the Harriet Miers nomination," Democrat Harry Reid, Senate minority leader, said at the time. "Apparently, Ms. Miers did not satisfy those who want to pack the Supreme Court with rigid ideologues."

Charlie Savage of *The Boston Globe* ran through options on whom Bush might nominate next: "Bush may want to reward the few conservatives who stuck with him during the Miers fight by giving the nod to either of two highly conservative appeals court judges, J. Michael Luttig and Samuel Alito. Both of the men, who are white, are favorites of the influential Federalist Society, whose executive vice president, Leonard Leo, was a key Miers supporter."

Most liberals cheered when Miers's nomination was withdrawn, seeing this as a case of a win is a win, and many viewed her as woefully unqualified for the position anyway. But that reaction missed the point: This fight was about *Roe v. Wade.* Hidden donors had clearly been involved in inflaming the right against Miers.

With the Federalist Society split, a crucial role was played by the Heritage Foundation, which had pushed hard against Miers, led by Cuban-born conservative Catholic lawyer Manuel Miranda. A flamboyant self-promoter and former Senate Judiciary Committee staffer working for Orrin Hatch credited with crafting a "Miranda Plan" of attack on judicial confirmation fights, Miranda employed scorched-earth tactics, even against a fellow Republican who might not toe the Heritage line. Miranda rallied other conservative movement players, getting wide credit for leading the drive to sink the nomination. When Miers was withdrawn, Miranda crowed to *The Washington Post:* "This is an enormously significant event for conservatives, no doubt about that. It will be stamped across our foreheads for years: Which side were you on in the Miers fight?" Working alongside Miranda in that fight, the Heritage Foundation's liaison with the Bush White House at the time: Ginni Thomas. That's right: The wife of a justice was working for an organization leading the charge to torpedo a court nominee.

The episode, seen in retrospect, offers useful lessons on the nature of Federalist Society–organized power. The heavy breathing over "Borking" was always about having the power to enforce your narrative, if not broadly, then at least broadly enough to have energetic allies pretending along with you. Was Miers Borked? No, she was "Miered."

The Associated Press posed the question in October 2005: "Is 'miered' the new 'borked'? . . . Now there is talk online about whether Harriet Miers' withdrawal of her nomination to the high court will give rise to the term 'miered.' While liberals led to the opposition to Bork, it was conservatives who brought down Miers' nomination."

# CHAPTER 13

# JANUARY 2006: SCALITO

The Bush administration followed up its botched Miers move by nominating Samuel Alito in October 2005, a choice the Federalist Society and right-wing religious conservatives loved—and one they would push through in what might count as their first strong-arm maneuver in the long project to stack the courts. Leonard Leo, ever the apple polisher, had dissented from the right-wing line and supported Miers out of loyalty to Bush. Now Bush returned the favor. Leo's prize was Samuel Alito, a conservative Catholic with purported Opus Dei ties who grew up near Trenton, New Jersey, and struck many as bland enough for his extremism not to jump out at them. Nicknamed Scalito for his reputation as a clone of Antonin Scalia, he was not going to Bork himself—and Leo and his legions were not going to let him be Borked.

Alito had been a good enough student at Steinert High in Hamilton Township to move on to Princeton, where he was later described by classmates as low-key and serious. He supported

Barry Goldwater's run for president in 1964, and was an avid reader of William F. Buckley's *National Review,* but he kept his politics quiet. He focused on studying and declined to join any campus political clubs, although apparently Alito thought nothing of joining a sexist campus organization called Concerned Alumni of Princeton, which opposed the admission of women.

The antiwar protests of the 1960s left Alito cold. He was put off by the events of spring 1970 when Interior Secretary Walter Hickel visited the campus to give a talk, to a couple of thousand gathered in a gymnasium, on the topic of "Ecology and Politics in America's Environmental Crisis," and a group of students loudly heckled him, chanting, "Talk about the war!" That spring, thousands turned out to protest the U.S. bombing of Cambodia, an expansion of the war in Vietnam, and many students boycotted the last day of classes, a mode of protest said to have discomfited young Sam Alito. He was one of only twelve members of his class at Princeton to receive a military commission through the ROTC program.

A formative experience came in spring 1971, Alito's junior year, when he joined the campus Whig-Cliosophic Society, founded in 1765, for a visit to Washington, D.C. The students hoped to meet with legal titans Justice Thurgood Marshall or Justice Hugo Black, but instead settled for a meeting with Justice John Marshall Harlan II, a Princeton grad whose grandfather had also been a Supreme Court Justice.

Harlan, a conservative on the Warren Court often called the Great Dissenter, would retire later that year and be dead of cancer by December. Young Sam Alito was a Harlan fan and asked him to expound on the "law of the case" doctrine, which the justice enthusiastically did, as fellow student George Pieler later recalled to the *Princeton Alumni Weekly,* explaining, as Pieler remembered it, "the duty of the judge to decide the case at hand, not promulgate new rules of conduct for society as a whole."

Alito was ambitious and full of himself enough to write a

dense senior's thesis on Italian law, for which he made a research trip to Italy. Trying for a terribly droll tone, dry humor for the type of student whose idea of naughty was a tipple of sherry, Alito wrote a self-description for the *Nassau Herald* recalling that he researched his thesis "in various sidewalk cafes in Rome and Bologna during the summer of 1971" and concluded: "Sam intends to go to law school and eventually to warm a seat on the Supreme Court."

At Yale Law School, Alito hoped to study with his intellectual hero Alexander Bickel, a vocal Warren Court opponent, but did not get the class—and seethed with jealousy when a friend of his wound up studying with another renowned right-wing professor, none other than Bork. "In one of the worst pairings of student and professor in course-scheduling history, Alito ended up with Charles Reich, the eccentric counterculture guru who had written the best-selling manifesto *The Greening of America*," Margaret Talbot wrote in *The New Yorker*. "Alito, having read the book, formally requested to switch out of the class, but he was told no. Reich loved flower-child sensibilities as much as Alito hated them—he saw even bell-bottoms as a form of rebellion worth validating." Years later, in 2008, speaking at an *American Spectator* event, Alito would draw puzzled stares with his continuing obsession with the 1960s, evoking a Country Joe and the Fish song no one remembered and positing—dubiously—that "for the past forty years there have been places in this country, sort of like the island in *Jurassic Park*, where it's always been 1967." If so, probably better than places in the country where it's always been 1862.

Working in the Reagan administration in the 1980s, Alito was less reticent about expressing his political views. In a 1985 application to be deputy attorney general in the Reagan administration under Attorney General Ed Meese, after serving in a lesser position in the Reagan Justice Department, Alito came right out and espoused deeply conservative views in a letter to Meese, declaring, "I am and always have been a conservative." He told Meese that he opposed *Roe v. Wade* and took particular pride in helping the administration argue before the Supreme Court that "racial and ethnic quotas should not be allowed and that the Constitution does not protect a right to an abortion." And lest anyone later wonder if he was merely arguing on behalf of the administration, at odds with his personal beliefs, these were his own, deeply held convictions. "I personally believe very strongly," he stated outright, with no room for spin.

In 1990, Bush nominated Alito to the U.S. Court of Appeals for the Third Circuit, and Leonard Leo shepherded his confirmation through the Senate. Having been known mostly for his work going after white-collar criminals, he was approved unanimously. But when Alito was nominated to the Supreme Court, Democrats opposed him, recognizing him as a hard-right conservative in the mold of Bork, Clarence Thomas, and Scalia. In the midst of the confirmation fight, his ninety-year-old mother, Rose Alito, told reporters, "He is against abortion—we both are."

Scalia's 1985 letter to Meese struck many Democrats as a potent weapon with which to go after him. After all, he not only had staked out an extreme stand on racial quotas and abortion, he'd emphasized he "very strongly" believed in these personal convictions. Some Democratic staffers gained a sense of false hope. "It was a done deal," one staffer told *The New York Times*. "This was the most evidence we have ever had about a Supreme Court nominee's true beliefs." All the more reason for the Federalist Society network to get to work—for example, organizing Italian American groups to speak out, claiming to be offended at the nickname "Scalito," arguing—preposterously, it went without saying—that it amounted to a slur against Italian Americans. Alito was saved because Republicans controlled the Senate and there would not be the votes for a Democratic-led filibuster.

Alito was also carefully coached to reassure the committee he would respect the *Roe* precedent. "*Roe v. Wade* is an important precedent of the Supreme Court," Alito said. "It was decided in 1973, so it has been on the books for a long time. It is a precedent that has now been on the books for several decades. It has been challenged. It has been reaffirmed. But it is an issue that is involved in litigation now at all levels." Referring to a subsequent decision to *Roe* that preserved abortion rights, he told Arlen Specter, "I agree with the underlying thought that, when a precedent is reaffirmed, that strengthens the precedent." And he dismissed the Meese memos as "What I thought in 1985, from my vantage point in 1985."

This testimony was dishonest. On *Dobbs,* despite the posturing, Alito wrote the majority opinion overturning the precedent of *Roe v. Wade,* with which he had disagreed all along.

Like Thomas, who lied under oath to win his seat and the power that came with it, Alito was also clearly illegitimate, both because he misled the Senate and the public itself to win confirmation, and also because the president who appointed him came to power through a stolen election.

---

In his time on the bench, Alito became known as a highly partisan political player who twisted the "original meaning" of words in the Constitution to reach his preferred political result. An *Axios* analysis of the 2022–2023 Supreme Court term found Alito was furthest right among his eight colleagues. That was the term that the court, with Alito in the majority, overturned longstanding court precedent on affirmative action; ruled that a private business owner could discriminate against an LGBT customer on "religious liberty" grounds; and weakened the Environmental Protection Agency, a boon for big business. Alito has also led the charge on requiring states to subsidize religious schools, weakening the Affordable Care Act, and expanding the right to carry firearms in public.

Far from the mild-mannered student he once was, on the court Alito seems to relish his brash partisanship. In 2020, he gave a blunt speech to the Federalist Society in which he discussed several issues before the court—an unprecedented breach of judicial norms. Along with plugs for "religious liberty" and loosening gun laws, Alito said this about gay marriage: "You can't say that marriage is a union between a man and a woman. Until very recently, that is what the vast majority of Americans thought. Now it's considered bigotry."

Like Clarence Thomas, Alito has been dogged by ethics problems. In Alito's case, *ProPublica* broke the news that he failed to follow the law and publicly disclose a fishing trip in 2008 with hedge fund billionaire Paul Singer, flying to the location on Singer's private plane (valued at $100,000). The trip was organized by none other than Leonard Leo, who also arranged the plane. Singer is a donor to an array of organizations that have conservative ideological interests in the outcome of court decisions, and he has heavily supported the Leo network. Three nights of luxury lodging was paid by yet another donor who supports Leo, Robin Arkley II.

In 2014, Alito ruled in a 7–1 case that gave Singer's companies $2.4 billion from the government of Argentina. Georgetown law professor Abbe Smith told *ProPublica* that if she had a case where a judge had received a gift from the opposing party, "she would immediately move for recusal." Alito did not do so.

The night before the *ProPublica* article published, Alito took the extraordinary step of answering the reporters in print, preemptively. This was a familiar damage-control maneuver in politics, but unheard-of from judicial chambers. Under the headline "ProPublica Misleads Its Readers," Alito took to the op-ed pages of *The Wall Street Journal*—a frequent Federalist Society billboard—in a hair-splitting, disingenuous piece in which Alito declared himself innocent as charged. He contended that he was not required to recuse in the Singer case because Singer's name was not connected to his companies in the briefs (even though this was an easily discernible fact) and that the trip did not have to be disclosed because he understood he was following "standard practice" (which was exactly the problem!) and, seriously, that if wine was served, it was inexpensive. He failed to address the federal law on gifts he violated. The law has a "personal hospitality" exemption for "food, lodging and entertainment" but clearly covers gifts of transportation like private jet flights. Alito laughably claimed the gift didn't matter because the seat on the plane would have stayed empty if he hadn't filled it.

In the wake of revelations about expensive vacations taken by both Thomas and Alito, Democrats have called for tighter ethics rules, along the lines of rules followed by all lower court judges but not Supreme Court justices, but legislation to enact them is stalled in the Senate for lack of Republican votes. Lost in all the discussion about ethics codes was the fact that there already is a law on the books, the Ethics in Government Act, that Alito ran afoul of.

Apparently not concerned about the political nature of his opinion writing, after the *ProPublica* article Alito again appeared on the *Wall Street Journal* op-ed page, this time in a two-part interview conducted by sympathetic partisan players. He made big news when he told the *Journal,* "I know this is a controversial view, but I'm willing to say it. No provisions of the Constitution gives them [Congress] the authority to regulate the Supreme Court—period." A cottage industry of op-ed writers quickly sprang up to fault Alito, most with headlines like "Alito Is Wrong." Congressional expert Norm Ornstein wrote in *The New Republic* that the Framers "left it to Congress to define the broader architecture of the judiciary and the role of courts in particular." He went on to point out that Congress has the power to impose ethics rules on the court because the Congress can impeach justices, reject nominees, and add and subtract members of the court—so it clearly had the power to impose ethics rules on the third branch.

To Democratic senator Sheldon Whitehouse, Alito's opining about congressional power was itself an ethics violation because the matter of an ethics code could well come before the court. Whitehouse lodged an ethics complaint against Alito with Chief Justice Roberts and asked him to investigate. But given the arrogant attitude of this court, it's likely that Whitehouse's complaint ended up in Roberts's circular file. Whitehouse might have had better luck if he had the support of fellow Democrats, some of whom are skittish about demanding accountability for ethical breaches. Whitehouse has privately complained that Senator Dick Durbin, Chairman of the Judiciary Committee, stymied efforts to compel Leonard Leo and Harlan Crow to testify about their relationship with Clarence Thomas, although the committee eventually did so. When the powerful believe they can't be held accountable and act that way, this is not only a political but a large moral problem in a democracy. Clearly, nothing will change without Democrats acting in concert to demand it.

The outcry over the revelations that two flags expressing sympathy for the January 6 insurrection put the pre-existing concerns about a rogue, lawless high court in sharp relief. Outside the Alito home in Virginia, an American flag was flown upside down just days after the 6th. The flag was adopted by supporters of the "Stop the Steal" movement that perpetuated the Big Lie that the 2020 election was stolen from Trump. A different flag, "Appeal to Heaven"—embraced by Christian nationalists who want a theocratic form of government in the United States and also carried by January 6 rioters—was flown over the Alito's New Jersey shore vacation home in the summer of 2023. Taken together, the flags confirmed that Alito was not an impartial finder of fact, the traditional role of judges, but rather a hard right Republican conservative hack. He is a bad actor on the court.

The flag embroglio reignited frustrating discussions about "what be can be done" to address the crisis of the court. For many Democrats the answer was "nothing"—a form of learned helplessness in the face of a once-august institution that polices itself. But that was the wrong answer. Certainly Alito, under subpoena, if necessary, should be hauled in front of Congress to explain the circumstances around the flying of the flags and whether in fact Alito aligned himself with domestic terrorists, in the description of the FBI director. Given his stance that Congress has no power over the court, Alito would likely defy a subpoena, leaving an impeachment inquiry as the only means to get to the bottom of events.

Certainly, such an inquiry is justified in this egregious case, but the only chance of that happening would be a takeover of the House by Democrats. This is where the courts come into play as an issue for voters who want to see the Supreme Court held acceptable. That will never happen as long as Republicans control Congress.

A broad consensus emerged that, at the very least, Alito must recuse himself from two January 6 cases before the high court. Anything short of that would be unfathomable, as the recusal statute standard is not limited to actual bias—it also includes the appearance of bias. The first case involves a claim by Trump that former presidents enjoy presidential immunity from criminal prosecution for official acts while in office. By taking this case and then slow-walking it, the court had already given Trump the win he wanted—likely delaying the case until after the November election.

The second case involves a claim that prosecutors stretched federal law that charged January 6 rioters with "obstruction" of an official proceeding. The ruling could negate hundreds of prosecutions, and as Trump is charged under the same logic, he would also get a get-out-of-jail-free card. In oral arguments, the conservative bloc seemed sympathetic to Trump's argument.

The decision to recuse is up to the justice himself. If Alito decides to flout the law that requires recusal, he could be criminally prosecuted by the Justice Department. As a convicted felon, perhaps he will share a cell with his convicted colleague, Clarence Thomas.

## CHAPTER 14

# THE THREE AMIGAS: GINNI, CLETA, AND CONNIE

I f for many on the left, and especially for many African Americans, the November 2008 election of Barack Obama as the first Black president of the United States represented a watershed moment, that was also true for wide swaths of the far right. Nothing unleashed the energy of right-wing operatives like happy Democrats. From the Leonard Leo network to garden-variety racists and scoundrels looking to whip up the racial hatred of reactionaries and bigots, Obama's election would prove to be a potent catalyst. The massive post–Powell Memo project of funneling resources into building a new radical-religious-right power structure was far from complete, and the star power of Obama led some on the right to falter. These were not by and large visionaries, not independent thinkers, but a network of insecure, power-hungry opportunists who badly needed to be bucked up by those with more conviction and more brass. This world needed stars, it needed a center, and a trio of conservative women in Washington were happy to fill the void. The three of them, Ginni Thomas, Connie Hair, and Cleta Mitchell, were all happy warriors with a demented brand of true-believer conservatism, each in her own way full of herself but effective, the best of buddies in the let's-tear-down-America-and-call-it-"Conservatism" funhouse-mirror nuthouse. Former Virginia congressman Denver Riggleman, senior technical advisor to the January 6th Committee and the man whose team identified the Ginni Thomas texts to Mark Meadows, put it this way: "I would say that Cleta, Ginni and Connie are sort of like the three amigas."

Cleta Mitchell had the distinction of being named second, behind only Donald Trump, in the Georgia grand jury report that would lead to Trump's indictment for seeking to overturn the 2020 election—but she would also, unaccountably, escape indictment. As *The Intercept* wrote in September 2023, "Mitchell is arguably the most central player in the attempt to steal the election who isn't facing prison time."

Talking to the January 6th Committee, Ginni Thomas said, "I *love* Connie Hair.... I talk to her a lot. She comes to my Thanksgiving." Added Riggleman: "Ginni is *very* good friends with Connie Hair."

Riggleman and his data team were the ones to scrutinize the Ginni Thomas texts within the huge volume of digital material former Trump White House chief of staff Mark Meadows voluntarily handed over to the January 6th Committee, apparently believing the identities of those he was in touch with could not be confirmed. Ginni Thomas not only pushed Meadows hard to try to overturn the results of the November 2020 election, calling that effort "a fight of good versus evil," she also referenced talking to her husband the Supreme Court justice "just now," clearly meaning about the texts to Meadows. That same month, Ginni Thomas forwarded to Meadows an email from Hair, at the time chief of staff to Freedom Caucus congressman Louie Gohmert of Texas, reading, "the most important thing you can realize right now is that there are no rules in war." It was, as Riggleman and others would note, elements of all three branches of government working together on an attempted coup.

Hair, a key cog in this network, came to holier-than-thou politics from an unlikely background. She grew up in Louisiana and moved out to California, where she actually had small parts in a few forgettable films. Her breakthrough, if that's the word, came in a 1982 Pia Zadora vehicle called *Fake-Out,* with a cast also featuring Telly Savalas of *Kojak* fame. The Zadora character is in a women's prison for protective custody, which naturally—fifteen minutes in—leads to a scene in which Zadora, naked in the shower, is set upon by a group of several tall, naked inmates, looking to scare her. What follows is nothing shocking if you're into lesbian rape fantasies, but a little odd in a future "conservative" Washington heavy. Connie Hair plays Roberta, one of the tall, menacing—naked—women in the shower who converge on Zadora.

"Don't let them make you do this, Roberta," Zadora says.

Connie Hair as Roberta, admittedly, does a highly effective job of smiling in a creepy way that makes her look crazy and dangerous. She takes a step toward the Zadora character, menacingly places her hand on the shower wall just behind her, and says, "Relax. Enjoy it." Then she leans in for a slow kiss on the lips, and when after a few seconds the Zadora character does not respond, Connie Hair takes a swing and slaps her hard across the cheek. The next shot is of Connie Hair moving in again on Zadora, this time taking her kisses lower.

There were other film roles, including in *Death Wish 4* with Charles Bronson, but Hair found her true calling when she moved to Washington and came into her own as part of the anti-Clinton mob. She started working with a rabidly anti-Clinton group called Free Republic and spoke at a so-called March for Justice rally in Washington the group organized in 1998. Like Ginni Thomas, Connie Hair sprang very much from the Happy

Warrior tradition, smiling and laughing and very comfortable in her own skin even as her words reveal her to be a political extremist filled with hate.

Introducing Clinton-hating former FBI agent Gary Aldrich, Hair grinned as she described him as a "friend and supporter" of Linda Tripp, the values-challenged former White House employee who secretly recorded conversations with Monica Lewinsky, and "a fan of" Ken Starr and Congressman Bob Barr, a leader of the effort to get Clinton. The raucous little crowd at the event cheered loudly for Aldrich, who stands looking bemused. Then Connie Hair, moving easily on the stage in black high heels, came back—more Happy Warrior—to tell the crowd, "Could I ask for some people to lower their signs? You're blocking the CNN cameras."

After Aldrich and Barr aired their grievances, Hair came back to fire up the small crowd. Giddy and bouncy, she led cheers. "Are you guys ready to rumble? Let's rock and roll. Yeahh!!!!! Yeahh! How about some impeach?? Impeach! Impeach! Indict! Indict!" And finally, "Throw the bum out!" which she followed with a dirty laugh.

Among the speakers that day was Alan Keyes, a low-level official in the Reagan administration known for studying with *Closing of the American Mind* author Allan Bloom at Cornell and rooming with William Kristol at Harvard. When Keyes first ran for president, in 1996, Connie Hair was his spokesperson, a role she reprised when he ran again for president four years later— and again when Republicans drafted him to run for an Illinois U.S. seat against a state senator named Barack Obama—even though Keyes had already lost Senate races in Maryland in 1988 and 1992 and had never lived in Illinois. During that Senate race, Keyes created a flurry of controversy when he did an interview with Michelangelo Signorile, a well-known gay radio host, and launched an antigay attack, ranting about "selfish hedonism."

Asked if Vice President Cheney's lesbian daughter, Mary Cheney, was a "selfish hedonist," Keyes said, "Of course she is. That goes by definition."

An indefensible outburst, it went without saying, but here was the Happy Warrior Connie Hair—whose Hollywood debut came in a naked lesbian prison rape sequence—stepping up to back her candidate in an antigay slur. As reported in *The Southern Illinoisan,* "Connie Hair, another spokesperson for Keyes, said if an apology should be issued to the Cheney family, it is not the responsibility of Keyes. 'He never personally attacks people,' Hair said. 'As he said today, if anyone owes Mary Cheney an apology it is the press because they started this firestorm and this radio outlet since they are the ones that brought her into this.'"

Next up for the Happy Warrior was a gig working with the Minutemen in Arizona, the group of armed vigilantes who decided to patrol the state looking for anyone crossing the border illegally. When the group's efforts in the Southwest earned it widespread notoriety—and a hero's welcome—it made a widely mocked decision to expand its efforts to the U.S.-Canada border, and there was Connie Hair, telling the Toronto *Globe and Mail* in August 2005 that the Minutemen were looking for volunteers in eight Canadian provinces. By April 2006 the Minutemen were riding a wave of interest in their alleged plan to Build a Wall. "Volunteer offers are flooding in to a border watch group that said it will build a fence on the Mexican border unless President Bush militarizes the border and adds new security fencing," the Associated Press reported that month.

"We've certainly struck a chord and a nerve with the American people on this one," founder Chris Simcox told the Associated Press.

"Minuteman spokeswoman Connie Hair called the response to the fence proposal unbelievable—'people wanting to donate, to help build a fence, people wanting a fence on their land.'"

How did the group take off so dramatically? Here was how the

Southern Poverty Law Center assessed the sequence of events in a hate-activity-monitoring report at the time. The "paramilitary vigilante effort to seal off the Arizona border," SPLC wrote, "may not have accomplished much in terms of stopping illegal immigration. But it was a remarkable media success, sparking upbeat coverage and the creation of some forty similar groups in ensuing months. It soon became apparent the project had metastasized from the one-man operation started by Chris Simcox as the Tombstone Militia into a movement that was sweeping the nation. With that—and with the $50 application fees that thousands of people began sending in to join his Minuteman Civil Defense Corps—Simcox knew it was time to professionalize. Flush with cash, Simcox hired the exceedingly professional Connie Hair as the Minutemen's official media spokesman. It was Hair who got Simcox onto Fox News Channel's *Hannity & Colmes* in August, banking on her long friendship with Sean Hannity. It paid off—Hannity did several broadcasts direct from the Texas border, where he strolled along the Rio Grande side by side with Simcox and tossed stones into Mexico. She also managed to regularly serve up worrying sound bites like this one: "If you're from the Middle East, it only makes sense you might be in a Middle Eastern terror cell."

It was in effect Trumpism before Trump came down the escalator, and not just because of the whole Build a Wall fantasy: The Minutemen, for any grifter on the make looking for ideas, offered a mother lode. This was how you did it! You shopped a paranoid fantasy in a way that seemed fun and cowboy-like, found the right professional Washington crazy—ideally one of the Three Amigas—to tap you into the right network and then, whoosh, you rode the gravy train. All it took was a little flair and some vague willingness to pretend you were on a mission. If with the Amigas' help you could load up your outrage with an actual idea or two, so much the better.

For another example of the Amigas' influence, consider the

frantic chumming of highly visible curmudgeon George F. Will, whose syndicated column in late March 2001—fully a decade before the *Citizens United* ruling—carried the following headline: "Campaign Reform Seeks to Muzzle Free Speech." Will, framing his argument around "limiting political speech," openly advocated the system we now have in which billions of dollars in right-wing dark money has overwhelmed the checks and balances of democracy to put us on the brink, in more ways than one, heading into the November 2024 election cycle. Will cited a *New York Times* formulation that seems coolly reasonable to those not gripped by a political fever. "Congress is unable to deal objectively with any issue, from a patients' bill of rights to taxes to energy policy, if its members are receiving vast open-ended donations from the industries and people affected," the *Times* wrote. Well yes, obviously. There can be no intellectually honest argument against that proposition. So Will resorted to the in-print version of making a sour face, retorting, "Oh, if only people affected by government would stop trying to affect the government."

Will's column turned for help to attorney Cleta Mitchell and a pamphlet she had written on *Who's Buying Campaign Finance "Reform"?* for the American Conservative Union Foundation. That "study," as Mitchell liked to term it, represented a fascinating case of turning the world into a place analogous to that depicted in the famous Saul Steinberg 1976 cover for *The New Yorker,* showing a New Yorker's "View of the World" looking west, in which the world basically consists of New York City with a tiny backdrop of everything else out there. To ideologues like Cleta and Ginni living in this self-reinforcing mindset, their extreme politics represented the "mainstream" of America, despite decades of public opinion polls demonstrating how fraudulent a notion that was, and anyone of reasonable, centrist views was denounced as a "liberal" or "ultra-liberal."

Chapter 3 of Mitchell's 2001 pamphlet, so warmly cited by Will, opens: "It's amazing that there could be in America funding sources that are willing to finance anti–free speech fighters to the tune of millions of dollars per year. And that doesn't even count all the free media enjoyed by the campaign finance reform movement at the hands of the liberal media nationwide." In other words, to follow the fevered reasoning here: Any attempt to reform out-of-control campaign spending must by definition be suspect and probably "ultra-liberal." The "anti–free speech fighters" referenced by Mitchell would be: the campaign finance reform movement.

The object of Mitchell's gimlet eye, it's worth pointing out, was none other than the Bipartisan Campaign Reform Act of 2002, which regulated how political campaigns were financed by amending the Federal Election Campaign Act of 1971. BCRA banned so-called soft money—unlimited donations to political parties from individuals or organizations. It was truly bipartisan, with Republican maverick John McCain of Arizona one cosponsor and the other Senator Russ Feingold of Wisconsin, a Democrat. McCain and Feingold had worked closely together on the legislation for years, starting in 1995 with an op-ed they wrote together. "The McCain-Feingold bill became perhaps the best-known legislation Congress has passed since the mid-1980s," *USA Today* wrote in 2002. "Feingold marveled at the long odds he and his allies had overcome: 'There is one way to pass a bill and 1,000 ways to kill it. It's almost impossible to pass a bill that goes against special interests.'"

Mitchell brought a formidable legal mind to the chore of muddying the waters with an odd slurry of random facts, willfully misinterpreted, and borderline hallucinatory leaps of deduction and pure free association. As often turns out to be the case with such writing, more a bludgeon to bring down on the heads of any and all opponents than any attempt at clarity, dishonesty jumps off the page. But the point of view of the argument is clear in the following lines: "The campaign finance reform movement is also funded by the same sources as the movement for abortion rights. The National Right to Life Committee clearly understands that the campaign finance bell tolls for them—which is why it is so important to anti-abortion activists to fight the campaign finance reformers at every step. Those who champion 'reform' have a substantive, liberal political agenda of their own. Their proposed rule changes are designed to tilt the playing field in favor of candidates who will enact a liberal agenda at every level of government."

Or how about this astonishing acknowledgment? "In other words, the campaign finance reform movement is undeniably a liberal plot to silence the less than vast right wing conspiracy," the pamphlet reads. "Sound paranoid? Probably. But as the saying goes, just because we're paranoid doesn't mean they're not out to get us."

Or maybe you're just paranoid—and off your rocker. Mitchell had by that time charted an unlikely journey. Born Cleta Deatherage in Oklahoma City, she was always a serious, brainy child. A photo of her at age fifteen in her high school yearbook shows her carrying a huge pile of books and smiling apologetically as she and another studious girl "plead" with two boys "to get up so they may sit and study." Just missing out on a competition to be named Oklahoma City's first "Junior Miss" in December 1967, Cleta, first runner-up, said she was looking at a career in journalism.

Her politics back then were standard-issue campus liberal, not even remotely conservative. At the University of Oklahoma in 1971, she was coordinator for a national "teach-in" on the war in Indochina, for which classes were canceled. She ran that year for student body president—and lost. She was known then as an outspoken feminist. *The Daily Oklahoman,* in a December 1992 article looking back on her generation of campus activists, wrote: "Cleta Mitchell's outspokenness and tendency to agitate for change were also present twenty years ago. She sued the university because it had different curfews for men and women, she wore jeans to class—which at that time was a barrier-breaking act—and she formed a women's political group to campaign for the Equal Rights Amendment."

But in her run for student body president, she was ridiculed by opponents for being too serious. "Cleta put out an eight- or ten- or twenty-page position paper, so we put out an eight- or ten-page paper that dealt with horoscopes and nice things to eat," one rival recalled. "We didn't exactly mock her. We were kind of just saying: 'Lighten up!'"

Running as a Democrat, Cleta Deatheridge was still in her twenties when she was elected to the Oklahoma House of Representatives in 1976, and became head of the powerful Appropriations Committee. She was a Democrat for many years, including in 1986 when she ran unsuccessfully for lieutenant governor—but after that, her politics shifted rightward, in part because she was bitter that a teachers group did not endorse her, despite her extensive work on education issues.

"After I left the legislature, I began to realize a government big enough to take care of everyone is big enough to destroy anyone it chooses any time it decides to do that," she told *The Norman Transcript*, expressing the importance to her personal political evolution of a book by Myron Magnet, *The Dream and the Nightmare: The Sixties' Legacy to the Underclass*. "All that really started my change of heart. I thought, 'I got to rethink all of this.'"

The Myron Magnet book she mentioned, cited by many conservatives as a strong influence, including future President George W. Bush, served to put in black-and-white the right-wing argument that pretty much everything bad in the world could be blamed on the 1960s counterculture. The sexual revolution, Magnet opined, held "the poor back from advancement by robbing them of responsibility for their fate and thus further squelching their initiative and energy." Who were his primary culprits?

Books by Ann Beattie and Bret Easton Ellis. And respect for African Americans. Offering a template many would adopt, he wanted "to stop Afrocentric education in the schools."

For neutral observers like *Publishers Weekly,* it was an interesting but failed effort. Magnet, *PW* wrote, "offers many examples of societal ills but fails to make a convincing case that the legacy of the counterculture is the culprit." But for would-be thought leaders on the right, eager to hammer away at blaming the '60s, it was time to sing. "The book of the decade," burbled syndicated columnist Mona Charen, "the most insightful analysis of what has gone wrong in America during the past thirty years I've seen."

Cleta Mitchell moved to Washington in 1991, another ambitious far-right conservative looking to have an impact, taking a job with a pro–term limits group, and before long was close friends with Ginni Thomas. As Denver Riggleman, an expert on Ginni Thomas after all his time studying the texts and other sources, compared the two: "They both might be true believers, but Cleta seems to be much savvier, and she's also a little bit more practical," he said for this book. "Cleta, when it comes to election law and things like that, she does try to ground herself in law, even though I would say what she's pursuing is absolutely bonkers in some respects. So the best way you can say it is that Cleta is just much more practiced and sounds much more sane even when covering insane topics."

Ginni Thomas has never been one to be shy about flaunting her power, as one longtime Washington pollster illustrated with a story about Ginni asking him to do some polling for her in recent years.

"Can you do it for free?" she asked.

"Why would I do that?" the pollster asked.

"Because I'm Ginni Thomas," she said.

Told the story, Riggleman commented, "Yes, that's exactly what she would say. It's an arrogance of ignorance. It's so elitist, based on fantasy. I called her 'the high priestess of the GOP' and 'the high priestess of QAnon.' She holds both of those champion belts at the same time. What's really scary is she's able to merge fantastical belief with access. She's the exemplar of what QAnon has done to the GOP and what conspiracy theories and Christian nationalism have done to the GOP."

The Amigas, all three brassy personalities who came across as cocky even when they had nothing to be cocky about, reeked of Washington power. Their network of connections was absurdly powerful and had free access to the flood of money sweeping over Washington. If FDR had brought the world an alphabet soup of organizations looking to put dollars in the pockets of the poor during the Depression, through one means or another, from the Works Progress Administration to the Civilian Conservation Corps, Washington in the heyday of the Amigas was a place in which a new alphabet soup of organizations flourished to put dollars in the pockets of ambitious political extremists and their opportunist fellow travelers happy to hoover up whatever loot they could and pretend to believe in something. You needed a scorecard to keep up with all the groups fanning right-wing money into the capital—or you could just try to keep up with the Amigas. They were all three election deniers neck deep in the push to overturn the 2020 election, and moving forward, through the 2024 election cycle, we can count on more nefarious—and very dangerous—efforts to undermine the will of the people and our system of checks and balances, all in an ultraconservative push to grab power. The most important part of that was to pack the courts.

## CHAPTER 15

# JANUARY 2010: DARK MONEY UNLEASHED

Trying to plot the downward trajectory of the Supreme Court over Clarence Thomas's years as a justice, leading up to the *Dobbs* earthquake, the most momentous—and most bizarrely argued—ruling of all might be the January 2010 ruling on *Citizens United*—one in which Thomas shockingly failed to recuse himself, despite having been the clear beneficiary of Citizens United's mudslinging to back off Thomas critics during his confirmation hearings. That ruling, with its twisted argument asserting that political donations amount to free speech, has had such dramatic repercussions in unleashing dark money—crucially, Leonard Leo's dark money. If one were to take a step back, not having witnessed all that has unfolded to disfigure and destabilize American democracy, few facts are more disturbing than the reality that one individual, whose religious-extremist views and power make him a kind of American Ayatollah, now controls more than a billion dollars in dark money with which he can operate as an agent of special interests. It's ironic that a plot to take over America would have as its alleged legal foundation the half-baked notion of originalism, which amounts to stiff and self-congratulating arguments for denying the arrival of modernity, when the Founding Fathers would have reacted in horror to the prospect of a self-appointed king in the Leo mold gaining so much power and having so little accountability.

Citizens United, the same sleazy outfit Floyd Brown founded after making a splash with his Willie Horton attack ad, the same nonprofit that launched personal attacks on senators during the Clarence Thomas confirmation hearings, had moved on to a documentary-length attack on Hillary Clinton. *Hillary: The Movie* was crude and formulaic, quoting various half-famous people calling Hillary a liar and worse. McCain-Feingold, passed in 2002, prohibited corporate-funded ads and other "electioneering communication" from being aired within sixty days of a general election—or thirty days of a primary. Citizens United, represented by none other than Federalist Society leader Ted Olson, went all the way to the Supreme Court fighting for its right to run the smear on Hillary whenever it wanted. It was a convoluted case, full of backroom intrigue and twists and turns, but the upshot was clear enough: The Supreme Court ruled that corporations were free to donate unlimited funds to any candidate they wanted, whenever they wanted and that certain nonprofits could conceal the identity of their backers.

The ruling stands out as a particularly glaring instance of honest judicial reasoning flying out the window in the service of muscling through a verdict because of its political import. Justice Anthony Kennedy's rationale in his majority opinion came across then—and in retrospect comes across only more glaringly so—as hands-over-eyes wishful thinking masquerading as plausible argumentation. This was the tipping point, the historical moment at which the right wing claimed blatant judicial activism as its own, after years of dining out on complaints about the "activist" liberal Warren Court of a bygone era. Their argument in a nutshell: It's only judicial activism when the liberals do it! It's only abuse of power when the other side does it! We can do no wrong! Can't you *see* that?

"[I]t has long been a staple of conservative thought to criticize 'judicial activism'—the practice of unelected judges imposing their own policy judgments to overrule the will of the people's elected representatives," Jeffrey Toobin summed up in *The New Yorker* within days of the ruling.

> But it is hard to imagine a more activist decision than the Citizens United case. Congress passed the McCain-Feingold law, and President George W. Bush signed it, in the knowledge that the Supreme Court had repeatedly blessed restrictions on corporate political activity. But Justice Anthony Kennedy's opinion blithely overturned Court precedent, and rejected the work of the elected branches—all in service of the bizarre legal theories that (1) corporations have the same rights as human beings, and (2) spending money is the same thing as speaking. This was judicial activism of the most egregious kind. Indeed, it wasn't as much a judicial opinion as it was Republican talking points.

This was judicial opinion as a case of taking cues from the same Leonard Leo machine that was in turn dictating those Republican talking points and logrolling pliable thought leaders and media pundits. It was above all the work of a Federalist Society–funded–and–fostered network of activist-conservative attorneys with a post–Powell Memo mindset of inverting what they saw as the excesses—and threats—of the '60s counterculture experimentation and quest for alternative power. They were, without seeming to recognize it, far more radical than the radicals they claimed to be mimicking.

This was an essential step forward in the Leo program to

overwhelm democracy and in its place create a radical-religious-extremist alternate reality with which the rest of us were expected to live. The doctrine of originalism and the spirit of the larger Federalist Society takeover are both predicated on the notion that our collective ability to understand the meaning of our own experiment in democracy, and specifically the words of our country's founding documents, does not matter. Certain, select individuals, like priests in the Dark Ages, can see the true meaning, which—they tell us—has nothing to do with what these documents seem to us to mean.

As Justice John Paul Stevens took note in his dissent to *Citizens United,* in fact the Framers did put down markers on the need to keep corporations in check. Stevens cited this quote from Thomas Jefferson himself: "I hope we shall . . . crush in [its] birth the aristocracy of our monied corporations which dare already to challenge our government to a trial of strength and bid defiance to the laws of our country."

Stevens added: "The Framers thus took it as a given that corporations could be comprehensively regulated in the service of the public welfare. Unlike our colleagues, they had little trouble distinguishing corporations from human beings, and when they constitutionalized the right to free speech in the First Amendment, it was the free speech of individual Americans that they had in mind."

President Barack Obama famously spoke out in his 2010 State of the Union speech, just days after the *Citizens United* decision, saying, "Last week the Supreme Court reversed a century of law that I believe will open the floodgates for special interests, including foreign corporations, to spend without limits in our elections. I don't think American elections should be bankrolled by America's most powerful interests, or worse, by foreign entities."

Justice Samuel Alito, a man lacking in both self-awareness and manners, was caught on camera shaking his head during

Obama's speech and insisting, "Not true!" as the president spoke about foreign entities. Think about that. Was Alito so foolish not to see what would happen? Or so proud not to mind lying?

In another era of the court, Justice Potter Stewart had famously observed of obscenity, "I know it when I see it." *Citizens United* was obscene, on its face. We knew that when we saw it, as a nation. So much of the animus of the Federalist Society–led takeover of the court had to do with an arrogance bred of fear, a pomposity powered by insecurity, the wail of young Sam Alito at Princeton seeing his fellow students embracing a freedom he did not understand, a freedom that scared the bejesus out of him. He craved a set of rules he could understand. He sought power in rejection. He and others of his ilk did this without any real understanding of what they were rejecting, and compounded the arrogance of this elision with an imperious superiority that tried—a little too transparently—to turn weakness into strength. As but one example, having endured my share of pain over the years as a gay man living with intolerance on the right, I do not think there is anything ennobling or laudable about a doctrine built around pretending it's the nineteenth century.

*Citizens United* gave the lie to the effort to camouflage the radicals of the Thomas Court in the sober, respectable tradition of the Supreme Court at its best. There is nothing sober about this bunch. They create a world of hallucination and projection, a world of do whatever you want, because who is going to stop you? For a man from another era, like Justice John Paul Stevens, author of the powerful and blistering dissent in *Citizens United,* the horror of so much being squandered so callously and cheaply must have registered as a deep shock indeed.

Stevens, born in 1920, was a lifelong Republican and a conservative. He was pursuing a master's degree in English literature until, in December 1941, the month of the Pearl Harbor attack, he enlisted in the Navy. He then served as an intelligence officer in the Pacific theater, earning a Bronze Star for his brilliant work as a codebreaker. Republican president Gerald Ford appointed Stevens to the Supreme Court in 1975, calling him "the finest legal mind I could find"—and really meaning it. Ford later wrote: "I am prepared to allow history's judgment of my term in office to rest (if necessarily, exclusively) on my nomination thirty years ago of Justice John Paul Stevens to the U.S. Supreme Court." At the time of the *Citizens United* decision, Stevens was three months away from his ninetieth birthday; he'd seen a lot in his thirty-four years on the high court, but never anything quite so disturbing as this.

Stevens thought for himself. He actually wrote the first drafts of his opinions, which comes through. "In a democratic society, the longstanding consensus on the need to limit corporate campaign spending should outweigh the wooden application of judge-made rules," Stevens writes in culmination. Yes, that was a dis. "At bottom, the Court's opinion is thus a rejection of the common sense of the American people, who have recognized a need to prevent corporations from undermining self-government since the founding, and who have fought against the distinctive corrupting potential of corporate electioneering since the days of Theodore Roosevelt. It is a strange time to repudiate that common sense. While American democracy is imperfect, few outside the majority of this Court would have thought its flaws included a dearth of corporate money in politics."

What must Clarence Thomas have thought, heeding the power and clarity, the wisdom and humanity, of those words? Thomas was to largely join the majority opinion, but he broke with his fellow ultraconservative judges on Part IV of the decision, concerning "disclosure, disclaimer, and reporting requirements." His position? "I dissent from Part IV of the Court's opinion, however, because the Court's constitutional analysis does not go far enough." Specifically, Thomas favors total anonymity in campaign contributions—just imagine what THAT would mean for his friends from Leonard Leo to billionaire Harlan Crow.

As a May 2023 analysis from Americans for Tax Fairness would show, the Crow family, which had given lavish gifts to Thomas over the years to buy influence, "dramatically" increased "their average annual political spending to more than $1.5 million after *Citizens United,* versus $163,241 pre–*Citizens United*. Their total post–*Citizens United* political spending is $20.5 million, versus $5.3 million in all the reported years prior." David Kass, executive director of Americans for Tax Fairness, added: "The Crows used their fortune to buy access to and curry favor with one of the most powerful officials in Washington, then benefitted from his central role in loosening rules meant to limit the influence of money over politics and policy. It's a vicious cycle that can only be short-circuited by restoring meaningful campaign-finance rules."

It was a further illustration of the profound damage the majority ruling in *Citizens United* had inflicted on the country. As Stevens wrote in his opinion,

> In the context of election to public office, the distinction between corporate and human speakers is significant. Although they make enormous contributions to our society, corporations are not actually members of it. They cannot vote or run for office. Because they may be managed and controlled by nonresidents, their interests may conflict in fundamental respects with the interests of eligible voters. The financial resources, legal structure, and instrumental orientation of corporations raise legitimate concerns about their role in the electoral process. Our lawmakers have a compelling constitutional basis, if not also a democratic duty, to take measures designed to guard against the potentially deleterious effects of corporate spending in local and national races.

And hit home with: "Corporations have no consciences, no beliefs, no feelings, no thoughts, no desires. Corporations help structure and facilitate the activities of human beings, to be sure, and their 'personhood' often serves as a useful legal fiction. But they are not themselves members of 'We the People' by whom and for whom our Constitution was established."

Clarence Thomas, in contrast, citing the "advent of the Internet," worked himself into something almost resembling eloquence in his conclusion: "I cannot endorse a view of the First Amendment that subjects citizens of this Nation to death threats, ruined careers, damaged or defaced property, or pre-emptive and threatening warning letters as the price for engaging in 'core political speech,' the 'primary object of First Amendment protection,'" he writes in endorsing full donor anonymity.

These words might carry more moral weight if Thomas were not so closely aligned with Leonard Leo and the Federalist Society, a group that, through whatever indirect channels it sought in a Vladimir Putin–like attempt at deniability, attacked Brett Kavanaugh accuser Christine Blasey Ford in the press, leading to harassment and even death threats. We can infer that the Thomas argument is that he wants his side to do the harassing, and he wants to empower his side further and take down the other side. It's tribalism on the high court, not jurisprudence. Grievance and power, power and grievance, all Clarence Thomas has ever been about.

Does that sound a little harsh? Hard to back up? Actually, not at all. If Clarence Thomas possessed any honor—or even a sense that he ought to wonder what it would be like to possess honor—he would have recused himself from the *Citizens United* decision. He was aided in his nomination to the high court when Citizens United spent more than $100,000 in support of him to produce and air commercials attacking anyone opposed to him, as I covered in Chapter 8, which led to millions of dollars in free media coverage resulting from the ad buy.

Following the *Citizens United* ruling, Thomas faced mounting criticism, with a group called ProtectOurElections calling him out and demanding his disbarment. "Justice Thomas was obligated under the Supreme Court's June 2009 decision in *Caperton v. Massey,* to disqualify himself from Citizens United," Kevin Zeese, an attorney with ProtectOurElections, said in a statement.

> Indeed, the facts of the two cases are eerily similar, as we now know, with Citizens United Foundation actually supporting Thomas' nomination and creating what amounted to be millions of dollars in advertising and publicity to attack opposing Senators. Yet, Justice Thomas, just months after the ruling in *Caperton,* proceeded to sit in judgment of Citizens United without sua sponte recusing himself or disclosing the conflict. Justice Thomas owed his spot on the Court to Citizens United Foundation, and he repaid that debt with his favorable ruling in Citizens United. Clearly, his bias undermined the fairness of the judicial system.

Another group, Common Cause, cited Thomas's attendance at a Koch brothers funding conference as grounds for recusal in the case. The Kochs raise money at these conferences for their various causes, and the network stood to benefit from the loosening of campaign finance rules.

If power begets power, which we know it does, then dark money begets dark money. Thomas should have recused himself but instead was one of five justices who delivered to Leo the ability to turbocharge his powerful network of nonprofits while keeping donors anonymous. The power of Thomas and Leo was only just ramping up—and it would take years for anyone to survey the extent of the damage to the viability of the U.S. experiment in democracy.

# PART 3
# LEO'S TIME

## CHAPTER 16

# MARCH 2016: THE ART OF THE DEAL

I t's shocking to check the date and see how early in the calendar year it came: March 16, 2016. That was when President Barack Obama nominated Merrick Garland, chief judge of the U.S. Court of Appeals for the D.C. Circuit, to the Supreme Court—only to have the nomination swallowed up in a vortex of right-wing situational ethics, a straightforward usurping of democracy. Garland was a moderate with a law-and-order reputation chosen to attract Republican support, but Mitch McConnell, first elected to the U.S. Senate from Kentucky in 1985 as a pro-choice moderate, was not a man who saw life in public service as requiring great consistency: Stacking the courts with the help of Leonard Leo of the Federalist Society and his larger network was his one true calling, and all else fell by the wayside.

Antonin Scalia, right-wing bulwark of the court, announced in June 2015 that he would be retiring, but would wait one year, since he thought that would deny Obama the chance to name his successor and tip the balance of the court. This was Scalia's prerogative, and it was telling: Given all he knew of Washington, he assumed he would have to hold out a year, leaving only a few months of the Obama presidency, if he wanted to deny the president his pick.

Soon after Scalia's death, President Obama countered the argument of highly partisan Republicans that he should hold off on naming a successor, even though at that point Obama had eleven months left in his term. "These are responsibilities that I take seriously, as should everyone," he said. "They are bigger than any one party. They are about our democracy. They are about the institution to which Justice Scalia dedicated his professional life, to make sure it functions as the beacon of justice that our Founders envisioned."

What were the facts? It was rare to have an opening for the Supreme Court come up in the last year of a presidency, but not unprecedented. Seven times since 1900, a president had made a nomination to the high court in an election year—and no president had refrained from making a choice in such a circumstance, as Amy Howe wrote in an analysis at SCOTUSblog. The first such situation in the twentieth century, Howe related, came on March 13, 1912 (compared to March 16 for Garland), when Mahlon Pitney was nominated by President William Taft to succeed the first John Marshall Harlan, who died the previous October—and Pitney was confirmed. In 1916 President Woodrow Wilson actually made two nominations—Louis Brandeis on January 2, 1916, and John Clarke on July 14—both were confirmed. And so on. In none of those instances was it deemed unworkable to follow the dictates of the constitutionally mandated need for succession.

Even before Obama's nomination of Garland, McConnell declared any appointment by the sitting president to be null and void, and repeated that declaration after the nomination. There was no precedent for such action since the Civil War and Reconstruction. Moreover, the blockade was unconstitutional under Article II, which requires the Senate to give "advice and consent" on nominations, as McConnell well knew. He just didn't care. For him, the salient question was what he thought he could get away with, no matter how wrong he knew it was. "The American people should have a voice in the selection of their next Supreme Court justice," McConnell argued, disingenuously, in a statement. "Therefore, this vacancy should not be filled until we have a new President."

To provide a veneer of rationale for the nakedly political move, McConnell muddied the waters by invoking what he decided to call the "Biden Rule" on Supreme Court nominations. Spoiler alert: There was no such rule. It did not exist. Never had. So McConnell was writing fiction when he claimed "the Senate will continue to observe the Biden Rule so that the American people have a voice in this momentous decision." Continue? What was he talking about? The Senate had never observed any such thing.

As to the pretext for McConnell's formulation, any honest scrutiny makes McConnell look worse, far worse, not better. In his earlier days as chairman of the Senate Judiciary Committee, the year after the Clarence Thomas confirmation hearing, Joe Biden did give a speech on nominations to the Supreme Court and did urge some restraint on any president with a Supreme Court vacancy in the last year of his or her presidency. However, Biden's advice was directly the opposite of what McConnell claimed. Rather than inflaming a political fight, and turning that fight into a tool to move votes in an election, Biden wisely counseled action on filling a vacancy either should wait until after Election Day (a key point—*not* until the following year), or a president should choose a moderate, uncontroversial figure for the Supreme Court—someone like Merrick Garland. As Biden put it at the time, "If the president consults and cooperates with the Senate or moderates his selections, then his nominees may enjoy my support." Biden wrote the speech himself. It was a surprisingly statesmanlike oration, in fact, and also included Biden's vow that he would oppose any Supreme Court nominees who avoided answering direct questions on legal philosophy, as Clarence Thomas had done in his confirmation hearing the year before.

"In my view, politics has played far too large a role in the Reagan-Bush nominations to date," Biden observed, and went on to say, "it is my view that if a Supreme Court Justice resigns tomorrow, or within the next several weeks, or resigns at the end of the summer, President Bush should consider following the practice of a majority of his predecessors and not—and not— name a nominee until after the November election is completed."

So the so-called Biden Rule on Supreme Court appointments, upon which McConnell rested his entire argument for unscrupulous action, was—like "Borking"—a terminology that in fact meant the opposite of what ambitious right-wing extremists in Washington would have it mean. McConnell was defending the indefensible on fraudulent grounds, and he surely knew it.

"It's frankly ridiculous," Vice President Biden commented in March 2016, accurately enough pointing out, "There is no Biden Rule."

Immediate criticism of McConnell's outrageous power play was muted somewhat by the fact that Democrats, especially Obama and his advisors, held out hope that in the end Garland would receive a hearing—and be confirmed. Another complicating fact was the dawning political reality, the same month Garland was nominated, that the reality TV show Republican candidate with a history of running businesses into the ground might actually wind up with the Republican nomination for president—and reshuffle the deck of American politics in ways no one could predict. Democrats hoped Trump panic would help their cause in moving forward with the Garland nomination.

"You have the confluence of Donald Trump looking like the Republican nominee, and when the American people see they could have this mainstream guy [on the Supreme Court] or will have someone Donald Trump puts in there, what do you think they are going to say?" wondered New York senator Chuck Schumer.

Democratic senator Amy Klobuchar of Minnesota told *The New York Times* that during confirmation hearings for Obama nominees Elena Kagan and Sonia Sotomayor, "many" of her Republican Senate colleagues told her they would have supported Garland at the time, if he had been nominated earlier. "It's kind of hard to get away from the fact that he, in the past and now, has been viewed as a consensus person," she told the *Times*. "This is about how this burden of standing up for an independent judiciary—even if you may never get confirmed—is so important in this incredibly polarized time."

Republican senators were reduced to mumbling brief hollow talking points rather than defending the indefensible. Orrin Hatch of the Judiciary Committee was on record as having praised Garland about as lavishly as he praised any Democrat, declaring in 1995, during the Clinton administration, "I believe he is not only a fine nominee, but is as good as Republicans can expect from this administration. In fact, I would place him at the top of the list."

As constitutional law scholar Laurence Tribe, who taught Garland at Harvard, said on NBC News,

> One of the longest serving Republicans in the Senate, Orrin Hatch, publicly said right after Justice Scalia died that the President would do well to nominate Merrick Garland to fill the Scalia vacancy. He is a first-rate jurist, he is as good as anyone I know at building bridges, he is a dedicated public servant, he is a truly wonderful person, and he is someone that nobody has anything bad to say about—except that he has the misfortune of being nominated by a president whom some Republicans frankly seem to have regarded from the very first day as an illegitimate holder of that office. . . . Since

the Civil War, the Senate has never just refused to engage a nominee at all. It doesn't have to confirm, but it has always voted. When that court is rendered basically dysfunctional in lots of cases, because there are a lot of cases where it's going to come out 4–4 along ideological lines, when that happens not only do we have a dysfunctional Congress, but we end up having an impotent Supreme Court.

Even Republicans admitted their own polling showed the public strongly in favor of giving Obama's nominee a hearing, in fact running two-to-one in favor of doing the right thing. To put in perspective how egregiously offensive McConnell's political stance was, how rankly amoral, all one had to do was refer back to the law journal arguments of a young Republican aide in 1970, on his way to a job in the Nixon Justice Department. "Senators sought to hide their political objections beneath a veil of charges about fitness, ethics and other professional qualifications," that young Republican operative—one "A. Mitchell McConnell Jr."— had written at the time in a Kentucky journal.

I'm tempted to start a GoFundMe campaign to raise a million bucks and offer it to Senator Mitch McConnell to sit down and read and review—on camera, for posterity—the text of his article in Volume 59 of the *Kentucky Law Journal*. McConnell opened that article with a nod to French philosopher Paul Valéry, quoting him as follows: "All politicians have read history; but one might say that they read it only in order to learn from it how to repeat the same calamities all over again." Calamities like using one's power as Senate majority leader to aid and abet a would-be dictator whom one (not so secretly) despises, putting democracy itself in peril? Yes, wise words indeed.

McConnell goes on to declare, in that article more than half a century ago, "The Supreme Court of the United States is the most prestigious institution in our nation and possibly the world. For many years public opinion polls have revealed that the American people consider membership on the Court the most revered position in our society." The elder McConnell would see what he could do about changing *that*.

Young McConnell, not yet the cynical shell of a man he would become, lays out a chillingly prescient warning when he writes in the article, "Respect for law and the administration of justice has, at various times in our history, been the only buffer between chaos and order." Offering his "recommendations" about "the proper role of the Senate . . . in advising and consenting to Presidential nominations to the Supreme Court," young McConnell concludes: "It will always be difficult to obtain a fair and impartial judgement from such an inevitably political body as the United States Senate. However, it is suggested that the true measure of a statesman may well be the ability to rise above partisan political considerations to objectively pass upon another aspiring human being."

Well said, young McConnell. What a ringing indictment, seen in such vivid detail, the contours of McConnell's evolution from young up-and-comer, if not exactly idealistic then at least intellectually searching, to a handout-collecting entrenched operator whose nose somehow ignored the stench of blatant corruption but was ever attuned to the enticing smell of greenbacks on offer. McConnell knew there was money behind the monstrous effort to upend public trust in the high court by blocking the Obama nomination, and Leonard Leo and his network would go all in on the fight.

The Religious Right was an important element in that growing network. As *The New York Times* would later report, from the time of the Thomas confirmation fight onward, "Federalist Society lawyers forged new ties with the increasingly sophisticated network of grass-roots conservative Christian groups like Focus on the Family in Colorado Springs and the American Family Association in Tupelo, Miss."

The network of nonprofit groups funneling money to chum

the waters pushing for the Senate to defy all decency and precedent and block the Garland nomination included millions from
close Leo associates Neil and Ann Corkery, secretive extreme-
Catholic activists who spearheaded a group called the Wellspring
Committee, which as such groups do busily sought to push an
agenda so long as it could escape accountability, then shut down
in December 2018 when awkward public questions were raised
about its revenue sources. According to Lisa Graves's True
North Research, the group, heavily funded by Charles Koch and
his allies, funneled more than $50 million to use for the Garland,
Gorsuch, and Kavanaugh nominations. An estimated $7 mil-
lion of that total went to attack ads targeting senators favoring
decency and moving forward properly on holding hearings on
the nomination of the notably moderate and centrist Garland,
whom Obama moved forward precisely because, in line with the
actual "Biden Rule," he was a natural consensus-builder favored
and respected by many Republicans.

As *Politico* reported on March 24, 2016, eight days after
Obama announced the nomination, the Judicial Crisis Network,
originally founded by Ann Corkery in 2005, threw reality out the
window to spin a fantasy of Garland as some kind of dangerous
liberal. "The Judicial Crisis Network, the chief big-pocketed outside group giving air cover to Republicans in the Supreme Court
fight, is launching a $1 million ad campaign against Sen. Michael
Bennet (D-Colo.) warning Coloradans of the 'liberal' Merrick
Garland. The campaign . . . spans television, radio and digital
ads. The TV ad argues that Garland, as a Supreme Court justice,
would issue rulings that would roll back Second Amendment
rights and harm businesses." The ad, representing rank political
gamesmanship, predictably enough included a voiceover urging,
"Tell Senator Bennet and President Obama no, no more political
games with the Supreme Court."

This was part of Judicial Crisis Network's first wave of ads,
a $4 million campaign focused also on Iowa, New Hampshire,

North Dakota, Ohio, and West Virginia. *Politico,* after giving JCN fire-breathing spokesperson Carrie Severino a platform to froth about "liberal domination of the court," concluded: "The Senate Republican Conference has been largely in sync against moving forward on Garland's nomination this year. But that united front has begun to splinter."

The Judicial Crisis Network was founded during the George W. Bush administration under a different name, the Judicial Confirmation Network, and then with a Republican in the White House had as its goal an up-or-down vote on every nominee. Its key early supporters included Leonard Leo and real estate magnate Robin Arkley II of Northern California, up near the Oregon border, a major early funder. The new name was apt. For the right, the Garland nomination was a *crisis.* Garland replacing Scalia would tip the balance of the court back toward the center. Would the 5–4 right-wing majority hold?

As Media Matters for America reported back in 2009, JCN— under whichever full name—had a lengthy and sordid record of peddling disinformation.

"JCN was active in the opposition to Sonia Sotomayor's Supreme Court nomination, misrepresenting her judicial record to suggest she was an 'activist' judge," Media Matters reported in 2016.

> JCN ran a web ad making the false claim that Sotomayor had a "100 percent reversal rate as a court of appeals judge," which was subsequently taken offline. But Wendy Long, the JCN counsel at the time, continued to peddle similar claims in the media without challenge. Long was quoted in Congressional Quarterly alleging that "Sotomayor has an extremely high rate of her decisions being reversed, indicating that she is far more of a liberal activist than even the current liberal activist Supreme Court." Long also appeared on CNN days later with the misleading claim that Sotomayor "had plenty of cases . . .

overturned unanimously" by the Supreme Court. In reality, Sotomayor's reversal rates were deemed by legal experts and fellow judges to be "lower than the overall Supreme Court reversal rate for all lower court decisions from the 2004 term through the present" and "typical."

The bold and brazen move to stop Garland had behind it the religious zeal of Leonard Leo and his network. The Kochs themselves may not have been religious extremists, so far as anyone has been able to determine, but the machine they funded was stocked with a high proportion of extreme-Catholic holy warriors, intent on rolling back women's right to choose and focused on other social issues.

The Corkerys, for example, were Opus Dei. In 1990, Ann Corkery spoke to *The Palm Beach Post* about her membership in the militant Catholic group, much favored by Pope John Paul II, which at the time, the *Post* estimated, had about 3,000 members in the United States, about 50 in Florida, and a total of 76,000 worldwide.

Corkery hosted the meeting of Opus Dei that the *Post* reporter attended and was identified as a "supernumerary," the third category of Opus Dei member, allowed to marry and live at home. "Numeraries," the article explained, "live in communities and commit themselves to chastity," and "associates," the other category, "are also celibate but live independently." The article also explained that "celibate members engage in the practice of physical mortification, which some outside the society may consider unusual."

As an Opus Dei flyer explained at the time, "The central aspect of the spirituality of Opus Dei is the view that ordinary work can be transformed into a means of personal holiness and of helping others to reach holiness." Ann Corkery, who had previously worked as an attorney, echoed that idea, telling the *Post:* "Through your work, you're sanctified. You work so you can get closer to Christ. . . . If I was writing a brief, I tried to make it perfect. Not just for my company, or my clients, but for God."

That same year, Corkery spoke to a reporter from the *South Florida Sun Sentinel* about her Opus Dei membership and said, "People don't understand sacrifice, the whole idea of why anyone would inflict pain, because the modern notion is to avoid suffering. Why do it? Not to be . . . sadomasochistic. It's to share the great love Christ has for us. Selfishness is the enemy of love."

The article explained that Corkery, then thirty, stopped practicing law to focus on raising her two children.

> She was skeptical about Opus Dei before she became a member. "But everyone I met in Opus Dei, I loved," she said. Including her husband, Neil, who was an Opus Dei member when they met. "My husband really encouraged me, although he himself left Opus Dei," Ann Corkery said. "But he was never ostracized when he left." Neil Corkery found Opus Dei to be too structured. "I didn't think it was necessary to go through all of the requirements," he said. But he said the organization has added a positive dimension to his marriage.

Both Neil and Ann Corkery have largely avoided newspaper interviews—or social media presence—since then, but Ann Corkery did share this glimpse into her commitment to Opus Dei. "People think we're being ruled by Spanish priests who are sending orders to us," she said. "When I joined, I was waiting and waiting to find the big secret, but there was no big secret."

The big secret, over the years that followed, was how much Opus Dei and the strain of activist-right Catholicism it increasingly represented would gain so much influence over the inner workings of the American system. Following the demise of Wellspring, Leonard Leo—listed as the only trustee—would work with Neil Corkery to set up another funder for the Judicial Crisis Network, this one dubbed the Rule of Law Trust (ROLT). This new conduit reportedly would suck in more than $80 million in its first year, 2018, according to True North Research. It was all part of a larger power grab that went behind the court capture to embrace a program of revolutionary change set in motion by the Powell Memo, but which over the years had taken on an increasingly religious-war fervor.

McConnell flouted the Constitution, all the while arguing for fidelity to the text of our national charter when it suited him. But he got the campaign issue he wanted: That fall, again and again, Trump treated the Supreme Court as a touchstone. Exit polls showed the issue of the courts cemented Trump's lead in the Electoral College. *That is, McConnell's gambit elected Trump.* The results of the election left Democrats powerless to stop McConnell from eliminating the filibuster for Supreme Court nominees, paving the way ultimately for three Trump picks to win confirmation. For McConnell, the ends justified the means. In a 2016 speech, he declared, "One of my proudest moments was when I looked Barack Obama in the eye and said, 'Mr. President, you will not fill the Supreme Court vacancy.'" Two years later, as the Thomas Court was taking shape with two new Trump-appointed justices, McConnell said the decision not to act upon the Garland nomination was "the most consequential decision I made in my entire career."

———

Donald Trump was never slowed down as a candidate by the sorts of factors that tended to inhibit other politicians: personal history, past beliefs, reality itself. He saw no reason not to bring the same transactional approach he'd made his own in business to politics. No deal shaped his presidency more than the one he made with Leonard Leo and the Federalist Society.

In the spring of 2016, the month Garland was nominated, the Republican primary was in full swing, and Trump knew he had a problem with the evangelical right. Looming Supreme Court vacancies—perhaps three or four in the next four years—weighed heavily on the minds of conservatives. They saw generational damage to their movement if Hillary Clinton were to appoint liberals to the bench. This would tip the balance, and could create a liberal majority for many years to come. Trump saw that if he played his cards right, the court could be a unifying issue for him across various GOP constituencies. His internal polling showed that making commitments to the Religious Right could outweigh misgivings about his candidacy stemming from his famously loose personal morals, history of supporting abortion rights—and past financial support of major Democrats, including Hillary Clinton.

Then came a fateful meeting in March 2016, the first between Leo and Trump. As *Politico* later wrote, "Trump, with his extramarital dalliances, Big Mac appetite and apparent lack of religious faith, couldn't have stood in starker contrast to Leo, a devout Roman Catholic who attends daily Mass, has met three popes, and lives with his large family and wife of nearly thirty years in a brick home in the suburbs of Washington." The two men got down to business, and made a deal that would pay off for both: Trump would outsource—lock, stock, and barrel—his naming of Supreme Court justices and other judicial appointments to Leo, and Leo would vouch for him with the Religious Right and his army of rich donors and right-wing lawyers. The deal also represented a rapprochement between Trump and the Koch brothers network, which had earlier opposed Trump's candidacy but now was fully on board.

Trump released lists of potential high court nominees he pledged to appoint, later thanking the right-wing Heritage Foundation and the Federalist Society, including Leo specifically, for help compiling the lists. All three future justices—Neil Gorsuch, Brett Kavanaugh, and Amy Coney Barrett—would eventually appear on the Leo lists, easing social conservatives' doubts about

Trump's credentials and paving his way both to the nomination and to the presidency. The deal represented a complete overhaul of the court in just four years, cementing a 6–3 supermajority of donor-approved MAGA justices. They would, Trump promised, "automatically" reverse *Roe*.

Trump's election crystallized Leo's years of work building his conservative legal machine, building the Federalist Society to a membership of more than 40,000, and Leo wasted little time kicking the machinery he'd built into high gear. Leo had hundreds of millions of dollars in dark money at his disposal, undisclosed donations from wealthy right-wing conservative benefactors. By then, Leo had shepherded some 200 judges to confirmation on the federal bench, and more were on the way. Currently out of 179 active federal appellate judges (non-senior and senior status), 81 are members of the Federalist Society, 45 percent of all federal appellate judges. Out of these 81, 54 were appointed by Trump, meaning that 30 percent of the entire federal appellate judiciary were Federalist Society members handpicked by Leo.

In mid-November 2016, the Federalist Society's national lawyers' convention in Washington turned into a hot opportunity to snag appointments in the Trump administration, given Leo's outsized influence. Leo met with Trump in New York the day before the gathering began, and came away saying that Trump had not removed any names from the list of potential Supreme Court Justices that Leo and the Federalist Society had drawn up for him. The deal was intact. The Federalist Society was ascendant.

More than one thousand attended and the atmosphere was giddy and expectant; the list of guest speakers included Justices Clarence Thomas and Samuel Alito. "Anytime there's a major shift in the power of government," said Leo, "it's an enormous opportunity for what is probably the collection of the smartest, most talented and most publicly minded lawyers in the country to roll up their sleeves." In other words: An enormous opportunity for Leonard Leo. He wasn't wrong about that.

## CHAPTER 17

# APRIL 2017: GORSUCH GETS GARLAND'S SEAT

N eil Gorsuch, the man who would be installed on the Supreme Court in the seat that would have been Merrick Garland's if not for McConnell's illegitimate power grab, was an odd and conflicted figure who seems to have been deeply shaped by the teen trauma of having a flamboyant, formidable mother be publicly humiliated after a high-profile run in Ronald Reagan's cabinet. Anne Gorsuch, appointed by Reagan as the first woman to serve as administrator of the Environmental Protection Agency, had a highly controversial tenure that included diluting enforcement of the Clean Air Act—and was forced out of her job under an ethical cloud.

Neil Gorsuch's mother started out as a right-wing Republican firebrand who served in the Colorado House of Representatives in the 1970s—and was "a member of a conservative group called the 'House crazies,'" as the Associated Press reported. One fellow Colorado legislator found Gorsuch so "haughty," she dubbed her "Queen Anne," a sobriquet that morphed into "The

Ice Queen" during Gorsuch's time in Washington, D.C. Her surgeon father had instilled in her when she was quite young a belief that education was "the be-all and end-all," and when she was in grade school sent her to Mexico for summers to learn Spanish with nuns. A bright and ambitious student from an early age, she completed her undergraduate studies at the University of Colorado at Boulder at nineteen and her law degree at twenty-one. She worked as an attorney for Mountain Bell Telephone and, in an early sign of her propensity for ethical lapses, stated flat out in an interview that, elected to the Colorado House of Representatives, she saw no reason to abstain from votes potentially affecting the phone company's interests.

After Gorsuch was appointed by Reagan to her EPA role—chosen for being a brassy, take-no-prisoners type who could be counted on to horrify liberal proponents of safeguarding the environment by hobbling the agency's efforts—she and her family moved to Maryland and her oldest son, Neil, attended Georgetown Prep (the same Catholic school as Brett Kavanaugh). A look through his 1984 high school yearbook tells a dramatic story: In half a dozen pictures, young Gorsuch never smiles. He was no loner. The next year, he'd be elected senior class president. But in 1984 he looks sullen, depressed, almost on the edge of tears in one picture, of the International Relations Club; young Gorsuch, the only student among the twenty-one pictured in a double-breasted jacket, stands at one end, seemingly to lean against a wall for support, hands clasped tightly together, looking a little like the Timothy Hutton character in Robert Redford's 1980 family melodrama *Ordinary People.*

Neil Gorsuch looks deeply traumatized, and he was—a full year after his mother resigned from the EPA. As she wrote in her 1986 autobiography (written as Anne Burford), *Are You Tough Enough? An Insider's View of Washington Power Politics,* her stormy twenty-two-month run as EPA administrator was hard on her son, especially the ignominious circumstances of her 1983 ouster. Neil, she wrote, "got very upset." She repeats the word "upset" twice. "Halfway through Georgetown Prep, and smart as a whip, Neil knew from the beginning the seriousness of my problems," she writes. "He also had an unerring sense of fairness, as do so many people his age."

"You should never have resigned," her son told her "firmly," she relates. "You didn't do anything wrong. You only did what the President ordered. Why are you quitting? You raised me not to be a quitter. Why are you quitting?"

"Honey, relax," she told her son. "It isn't everything it appears to be. I can't explain it all to you now, but don't be upset."

She had a point about the circumstances of her ouster being complicated. As only the third EPA administrator since its founding in 1970, Gorsuch oversaw environmental cleanup at a pivotal time. A common move of post–Powell Memo–type conservatives, intent on letting big business run rampant with little restriction or regulation, was simply to slow-walk allocated funding, and Gorsuch ran into trouble for her agency's handling of the $1.6 billion Superfund for cleaning up toxic-waste sites. Gorsuch oversaw a reduction of EPA staff, and cuts in its budget—though, in fairness, she actually fought for fewer cuts than some in the Reagan administration wanted. Her use of the Superfund as a political tool—whether or not on orders of the White House— was an egregious violation of public trust.

As *The New York Times* reported in a bombshell revelation on March 7, 1983, "Last week, Richard Hauser, the deputy White House counsel, said one or more Reagan Administration officials had reported to the White House that they had heard the E.P.A. administrator say at an August 4 luncheon aboard the former Presidential yacht Sequoia that she was holding back more than $6 million in Federal funds to clean up the Stringfellow Acid Pits toxic waste site near Los Angeles to avoid helping the Senate campaign of former Gov. Edmund G. Brown Jr. of California, a Democrat. Mr. Brown subsequently lost the seat to the Republican candidate, Mayor Pete Wilson of San Diego."

Multiple congressional committees were investigating. The previous December, Gorsuch had also been cited for contempt of Congress for refusing a congressional subpoena to turn over documents to a subcommittee. Shortly afterward, she remarried and began going by the name Anne Gorsuch Burford. "Mrs. Burford has told aides that from the beginning she recommended that Congressional investigators be given full access to all documents," the *Times* reported, "but was overruled by the Justice Department and White House legal counsel's office."

Two days later, Burford resigned, clearly taking the fall to avoid further political harm to the White House—as her son correctly enough noted. As she wrote in her resignation letter to Reagan, "Without an end to these unfortunate difficulties, EPA is disabled from implementing its mandate and you are distracted from pursuing the critical domestic and international goals of your administration." Summed up *The Washington Post*, "Her resignation climaxed weeks of intensifying controversy over the EPA involving allegations of political manipulation, mismanagement and conflicts of interest that made her appear an unacceptable political liability to a growing number of senior White House aides and Republican politicians."

It's hardly a surprise that so public and mortifying a drama would leave Neil, as the oldest son, deeply shaken, and convinced of his mother's unjust treatment at the hands of callow Washington veterans. He internalized a deep-seated, almost religious conviction that the power and scope of government agencies needed to be reduced—his mother's mantra in her time at EPA. From his father, another Colorado attorney, his son inherited a love of the rugged nature of their home state, as an avid fly fisherman and skier; he also clearly had his mother's sharp mind and impatience with those he saw as less intelligent. From Georgetown

Prep he moved on to Columbia and Harvard Law, where soon after graduation he cowrote an essay for the libertarian Cato Institute—with Michael Guzman—on term limits that earned the approving attention of syndicated columnist George F. Will.

Like his mother, Neil Gorsuch cared little what anyone—especially anyone on the left—might make of his open partisanship. As a partner at the D.C. firm Kellogg, Huber, Hansen, Todd, Evans & Figel, he also wrote opinion articles for publications like *National Review Online,* including one in February 2005 that looks especially dubious in hindsight. In Gorsuch's telling, it was "American liberals" who had become "addicted to the courtroom, relying on judges and lawyers, rather than elected leaders and the ballot box, as the primary vehicle for effecting their social agenda." He adds, in words that ring true enough today, though clearly not in the way Gorsuch would have it, "This overweening addiction to the courtroom as the place to debate social policy is bad for the country and bad for the judiciary." A simple and concise damnation of what the Thomas Court has become.

In May 2006, Gorsuch was appointed to the Tenth Circuit Court of Appeals by President George W. Bush and confirmed by the Senate with no controversy. By 2014, Linda Greenhouse would be describing Gorsuch in the *Times* as "a rising star among Republican-appointed judges on the federal appellate bench." One year earlier, in 2013, Gorsuch had received his right-wing legal establishment coronation via an invitation to deliver a lecture at the Federalist Society annual dinner. "A culminating event at the society's yearly conference, the lecture was named for Barbara Olson [Ted Olson's wife], the conservative lawyer and TV commentator killed in the terrorist hijackings on September 11, 2001, when her flight from Dulles was plunged into the Pentagon," Joan Biskupic wrote in *Nine Black Robes*. Earlier Olson lecture speakers included Antonin Scalia, in 2004, and John Roberts, in 2007.

Very much his mother's son, Gorsuch opened his speech with

what for him was a feel-good round of venting on the subject of rampant federal regulation, a surefire warm-up for that crowd. "Today we have about 5,000 federal criminal statutes on the books, most of them added in the last few decades, and the spigot keeps pouring, with literally hundreds of new statutory crimes inked every single year," Gorsuch said early on. "Neither does that begin to count the thousands of additional regulatory crimes buried in the federal register. There are so many crimes cowled in the numbing fine print of those pages that scholars have given up counting and are now debating their number." This was no rabblerousing speech. Gorsuch felt no need to make headlines with a controversial address to raise his profile. He was content with a dry oration, leavened with the occasional attempted joke, that made serious points for what he saw as a serious audience.

Don McGahn, Trump's White House counsel, saw in Neil Gorsuch the mother's son: He was a committed opponent of federal regulation in all its various guises. Gorsuch made the long list of potential Supreme Court nominees candidate Donald Trump released during 2016, one of twenty-one, and when the list of possible choices was reduced to eight, after Trump's election, Gorsuch found himself still under consideration. McGahn would later joke that the White House had "insourced" rather than "outsourced" its process to the Federalist Society—so close in was the organization. In late January 2017, Gorsuch was formally nominated by Trump, the youngest Supreme Court nominee, at age forty-nine, since Clarence Thomas (forty-three) in 1991, to assume the seat on the court held by Scalia up until his February 2016 death—which should have been Merrick Garland's seat.

Gorsuch was hailed upon his nomination as in effect Scalia with better manners, an adherent to the Scalia pet theory of originalism, a nod to the Founding Fathers that in practice amounted to giving yourself license to rule however you want, based on political tides, and then claiming high-minded justification. Gorsuch dressed the doctrine up this way, with his own style of eloquence: The Constitution, he argued, "isn't some inkblot on which litigants may project their hopes and dreams for a new and perfected tort law, but a carefully drafted text judges are charged with applying according to its original public meaning." Scalia himself had put it this way, also eloquent, also backward: "The Constitution that I interpret and apply is not living but dead, or as I prefer to call it, enduring. It means today not what current society, much less the court, thinks it ought to mean, but what it meant when it was adopted."

Barring some science-fiction tools to go back in time, to gain some meaningfully complex understanding of the realities of the years in which the Constitution was hammered out and adopted, these pretty words are just that, smoke in the wind, lofty nothingness. "Originalism" was a slogan to push extreme interpretation, a tool, nothing more or less than that. Its power, if it had power, came not in eloquence or in fine reasoning, as the gushing encomia too often put it, but in how it was used as a lever. The rise of originalism charted the rise of Federalist Society power that brought the takeover of the courts. "What drove the increasing acceptance of originalism on the Supreme Court was Scalia's uncompromising commitment to his personal judicial philosophy and the growth of the conservative Federalist Society in academia, spawning, in turn, more and more advocates of the theory," NPR reported. From Reagan to Bush, Republican presidents had the good fortune to fill seven Supreme Court seats. "At each rotation, the new justice was more conservative than the person he or she replaced. That, too, reflected the increasing conservative drift of the Republican Party, with evangelicals and other social conservatives gaining more power and influence."

Neil Gorsuch apparently learned from his mother's ordeal the dangers of lying to Congress, and, though only fitfully, was actually at times direct and honest in handling questions from Congress after Trump nominated him to fill the long-vacant Scalia seat on the Supreme Court. How had Gorsuch come to President Trump's attention?

"I was contacted by Leonard Leo," he answered.

Leonard Leo, once again, said he was taking a short leave of absence from the Federalist Society to spearhead the Trump administration drive to confirm, though of course Leo would continue to coordinate his network of dark money to push millions of dollars wherever it might help influence media figures or lawmakers, an arrangement of questionable legality. In selecting Gorsuch for Scalia's spot, Trump had asked specifically why he thought past Republican nominees had shifted left—or lacked "backbone," as he put it. There would be no such doubts about Gorsuch, who had defended administration antiterror policies as a Bush Justice Department official, and who had been elevated to the Tenth Circuit Court of Appeals by Bush. Gorsuch had been recommended for the lower court appointment by Philip Anschutz, a right-wing Christian billionaire industrialist who supported antigay causes and groups, such as the Leo-aligned Alliance Defending Freedom and the Family Research Council. Anschutz, a major donor to the American Enterprise Institute, the Federalist Society, and the Heritage Foundation, also owns the right-wing *Washington Examiner,* part of the conservative movement's vast media ecosystem. It was all in the family for Gorsuch.

Gorsuch favored a broad definition of religious freedom inimical to advocates of church-state separation, raising grave doubts about where he would stand on *Roe v. Wade.* Despite his well-known positions and philosophy, under questioning in his Senate confirmation hearing, Gorsuch misleadingly told Dianne Feinstein that he would respect the precedent of *Roe.* Clearly coached to dissemble by emphasizing his belief in the "value" of precedent, he told her: "Part of the value of precedent, it has lots of value. It has value, in and of itself, because of our history, and our history has value intrinsically. But it also has an instrumental value in this sense. It adds to the determinacy of the law."

Dick Durbin of Illinois then quizzed Gorsuch about a passage in one of his books in which Gorsuch wrote, "The intentional taking of human life by private persons is always wrong." Durbin asked how that position squared with legal abortion. Gorsuch said, "Senator, as the book explains, the Supreme Court of the United States has held in Roe v. Wade that a fetus is not a person for purposes of the Fourteenth Amendment and the book explains that." Durbin continued: "Do you accept that?" Gorsuch replied, "That is the law of the land. I accept the law of the land Senator, yes."

Gorsuch, the tool of a highly partisan Federalist Society spending spree to install him and judges like him, was asked by Sheldon Whitehouse about the dark-money juggernaut arrayed behind him.

"Is it any cause of concern to you that your nomination is the focus of a $10 million spending effort, and we don't know who is behind it?" Whitehouse pointedly asked.

Gorsuch's deflection was breezy and supercilious.

"Senator," he replied, "there is a lot about the confirmation process today that I regret. A lot."

"Yes?" Senator Whitehouse asked.

"A lot," Gorsuch repeated. "When [Supreme Court Justice] Byron White sat here, it was ninety minutes. He was through this body in two weeks. And he smoked cigarettes while he gave his testimony. There is a great deal about this process I regret. I regret putting my family through this."

For the son of disgraced EPA administrator Anne Gorsuch, this last admission was personally revealing, but other than that, it was pure boilerplate, pure misdirection.

"But to my question?" Whitehouse persisted.

"Senator, the fact of the matter is, it is what it is, and it's this body that makes the laws," Gorsuch droned. "And if you wish to have more disclosure, pass a law, and a judge will enforce it, Senator."

Or the Thomas Court will strike it down, citing *Citizens United* as precedent—as Gorsuch well knew.

Whitehouse, in his landmark series of Senate speeches outlining the dangers of the Federalist Society power grab, spoke in March 2022 about how Gorsuch defined the approach of would-be Federalist Society–anointed judges auditioning for a starring role, an intriguing exposition that also applies to Kavanaugh and Barrett. "Ambitious right-wing lawyers aspiring to the Federal Bench aren't dumb," Whitehouse noted dryly. "They will follow the path that guides them to their goal. So the maximum adherence auditioning began."

Whitehouse had noted the example of a circuit judge who could not help but notice colleagues on the bench choosing certain cases, and writing certain rulings, that smacked of look-at-me posturing. They were, this judge observed, "auditioning"—as Whitehouse added, "auditioning for the Federalist Society gatekeepers."

How exactly does this auditioning take place? As with any audition, you have to know your audience. The big donors being wooed care about issues like guns and easing limits on campaign spending and corporate political power; right-wing social issues; and of course, the evergreen right-wing topic of reducing the size of the "administrative state." Again, as with any audition, you have to make sure to be heard. You have to *project* and have your voice carry. "Write opinions so extreme that they stand out and donors take notice," Whitehouse summed up. And finally, find ways to give legal wins to the big donors.

Gorsuch put on a clinic in pulling the right strings, above all harping away constantly at the "administrative state," a concept developed in the right-wing precincts of legal academia, such as the Antonin Scalia Law School at George Mason University. "To do that," Whitehouse said, "he deployed radical legal theories cooked up and propagated in the scheme's legal theory hothouse, where they developed schemes, kind of reverse-engineering them to give victories in cases." He also made sure to come across as passionate about the right's version of religious freedom, "which usually translates to dismantling the separation between church and State, which is another scheme favorite."

The result of the Gorsuch confirmation hearings was foreordained; Leonard Leo had made sure of it. "You know, the hearings matter so much less than they once did," Leo commented to *New Yorker* reporter Jeffrey Toobin, sitting in the back of the hearing room as the Gorsuch nomination was being considered. "We have the tools now to do all the research. We know everything they've written. We know what they've said. There are no surprises." Not, that is, as long as Leo could enforce his will. In addition to having misled the Senate in his confirmation hearings on stare decisis, Gorsuch was also unquestionably illegitimate due to the unprecedented and unconstitutional maneuverings of Mitch McConnell prior to his ascension. This was, straight up, a stolen seat.

———

Like Thomas and Alito, Gorsuch also had a secretive right-wing benefactor with interests before the court, the aforementioned Phil Anschutz. The connection became problematic in the 2024 term, when the court heard a case that established the Chevron deference, which holds that federal courts should defer to federal agencies' interpretation of congressional statutes. Chevron deference has long been in the crosshairs of the conservative legal movement and its war against the "administrative state." If federal agencies lost power to regulate business and that power fell into the hands of the Leo-packed courts, a decision overturning the Chevron deference would be a boon to big business, which is where Anschutz figures in.

Anschutz holdings are vast, including oil and gas, fossil fuel extraction, and real estate. His ties to Gorsuch date from the 1990s, when Gorsuch was his lawyer. According to *The New York Times*, Gorsuch is a "semi-regular" speaker at a policy conference sponsored by Anschutz at a ranch in Colorado. And Gorsuch had a real estate investment with two top Anschutz deputies, the sale of which Gorsuch failed to disclose as required by law.

Gorsuch has long campaigned against the Chevron deference, a fact that did not go unnoticed when he was picked for the high court. And Anschutz has close ties to organizations involved in the litigation. He has funded Americans for Prosperity, the Koch group representing the plaintiffs in the case. Groups filing amicus briefs against the Chevron defense have also been supported by Anschutz, including the Mountain States Legal Foundation, the Pacific Legal Foundation, and the National Right to Work Legal Defense Foundation. It probably goes without saying that Anschutz has also written checks to Leo's Federalist Society.

Gorsuch's vote in the case seems in the bag. Court reform groups like Accountable.Us have called on the justice to recuse himself, a request Gorsuch will never grant. Unfortunately, although there is a federal law on the books, for the Supreme Court recusal issues are left to the justices themselves to decide. And the Thomas Court members appear blind to the instances where their impartiality is in question.

## CHAPTER 18

# OCTOBER 2018: KAVANAUGH CHANNELS THOMAS

I f some Democrats had a soft spot for the intellectual caliber of judges like Antonin Scalia and Neal Gorsuch, they had no such illusions about Brett Kavanaugh—Ken Starr's angry hatchet man, Ted Olson's wing-man in *Bush v. Gore,* then staff secretary to George W. Bush, a sensitive political position responsible for coordinating all documents going to and from the president at a fraught time when the United States was engaged in a contro- versial "War on Terror." Kavanaugh had neither the experience nor temperament to qualify for a seat on the U.S. Circuit Court for the District of Columbia, the second-most-powerful court in America and often a stepping-stone to the Supreme Court.

In July 2003, Bush nominated his close aide to the circuit court. Democrats strenuously objected to Kavanaugh's partisan background and successfully stalled the confirmation for *three* solid years. When Bush put Kavanaugh forward again for the post in January 2006, it was a replay of a familiar tactic, nomi- nating a highly political, highly ideological figure not despite controversy but in part because of controversy, since the noisy political fight that would ensue had the desirable effect of getting religious-extremist voters energized. As *Newsday* explained the strategy in May 2006, "With just six months to go to the midterm elections, Republicans are pushing the judicial nomination of a White House insider to reignite the partisan battle over the courts and re-energize their conservative base.... The White House lately has been feeling the heat of conservative activists, who have sought to impress their sense of urgency on the issue of the federal courts, which they tie closely to social issues including abortion, gay marriage and property rights."

Democratic senator Dick Durbin of Illinois in 2006 memorably called Kavanaugh "the Forrest Gump of Republican politics." In the eventual hearing, Durbin and other senators accused Kavanaugh of lying to the Judiciary Committee when he denied his involvement in formulating the Bush administration's detention and interrogation policies while he was on the White House staff. Memos later surfaced proving that, yes indeed, Kavanaugh lied to get confirmed. It wouldn't be the last time.

Sheldon Whitehouse, in his speech on Federalist Society judges "auditioning" for spots on the Supreme Court, singled out Brett Kavanaugh as the most egregious practitioner of this crude art form. On March 30, 2015, for example, Kavanaugh delivered a speech at Catholic University, which has close ties to Leonard Leo, as part of the Pope John XXIII Lecture Series, later reprinted in the *Catholic University Law Review* as "The Judge as Umpire: Ten Principles." Kavanaugh had already checked a box or two right there, appealing to the Catholic mentality of so many in the influence group on whom he sought to make an impression, and he was not shy about laying it on thick.

"This school is rightly proud of its Catholic heritage," Kavanaugh said. "In line with the Gospel of Matthew, one of the stated missions of this law school is to care for the poor, the neglected, and the vulnerable. This university and this law school stand for those principles and do it very well. For my part, I am a product of Catholic boys schools in this area."

Moving into the body of his speech, Kavanaugh sought first to suck up to Chief Justice John Roberts, who had famously compared the role of Supreme Court justice to that of a baseball umpire, calling balls and strikes. "That notion, that a judge is just an umpire, has been criticized," he said. "Some say, 'Judges are just politicians in robes.' Or, 'Judges are advocates; they're partisans.' Or 'Judges are policymakers.' Or 'Judges are not mere robots.' The varying objections reflect, in my view, a misapprehension of what a judge does and should do—and also a bit of a misapprehension of what an umpire does and should do."

Kavanaugh, a former *Yale Daily News* sportswriter, clearly felt himself an expert on both baseball and the law. Next up was time to suck up to a conservative icon of the court, all in the service of what might be called a creative way of pretending to value precedent. "To be a good judge and a good umpire, you also have to follow the established rules and the established principles," Kavanaugh said. "A good umpire should not be making up the strike zone as he or she goes along. Judges likewise should not make up the rules as they go along. We see this in statutory interpretation, for example. A good judge sticks to the established text and canons of construction that help guide us in interpreting ambiguous text. Justice Antonin Scalia has had a profound influence on statutory interpretation. One of the things he has helped to do is to narrow the areas of disagreement about how to interpret statutes. Every judge now seems to start with the text of the statute."

It was, to the gathered crowd at Catholic University, a folksy, colorful comparison. One small problem. Talk to an actual expert on baseball, of which I am most certainly not one, and they will explain that every umpire working in baseball calls a slightly different zone; it is fantasy to imagine some theoretical perfect zone they call, at least until such time as robot umpires are employed. Similarly with the lie at the heart of originalism, that "statutory interpretation" can exist in a vacuum.

Ruth Marcus of *The Washington Post,* in her book *Supreme Ambition: Brett Kavanaugh and the Conservative Takeover,* writes that his colleagues on the appeals court noted that he was friendly enough, and would seem to listen to arguments, but they never made any difference in his thinking. Meanwhile, she writes, Kavanaugh "displayed a propensity for filing separate concurrences and dissents, actions that some colleagues took as judicial grandstanding and, more to the point, an effort to position himself for a Supreme Court seat."

That effort often extended to contorting his ideas and judicial philosophy for the benefit of his intended audience. "Kavanaugh pumped up the 'major questions' doctrine—one of the hothouse legal theories pushed by the far right," Whitehouse said in his speech on auditioning. "It says that courts should ignore an Agency's authority to solve a problem if the court thinks the problem is too big. Big regulated companies love having regulatory Agencies hobbled. So this was catnip for scheme donors."

In all, Leo produced three lists of potential Supreme Court nominees to Trump. Kavanaugh was not on the first list he handed Trump. He also wasn't on the second list. But all his campaigning eventually paid off with a spot on the third. "Like Barrett, Kavanaugh did his own publicity," Whitehouse said. "He spoke at fifty-two—count them, fifty-two—Federalist Society events over his career. You almost couldn't keep him out."

The unseemly aspects of Brett Kavanaugh's nomination to the Supreme Court actually date back to before an opening even occurred. After Trump's election, the Trump family reportedly set their sights on persuading Justice Kennedy to step down so the president could appoint a second justice to the bench. First

Daughter Ivanka Trump and her husband, Trump advisor Jared Kushner, had a relationship with Justin Kennedy, Anthony Kennedy's son, and brazenly set out to exploit it. In 2005, Justin Kennedy helped secure for the Trumps $700 million in loans from Deutsche Bank, where the younger Kennedy worked, to construct a skyscraper in Chicago, despite Trump's repeatedly defaulting on business loans. *The New York Times* reported that Trump was able to convince Justin Kennedy and other top executives that "the Chicago development was a guaranteed money-maker" and further signaled "the Trump family's commitment to the project" by informing the bank that Ivanka Trump would be "in charge of the operation." Justin Kennedy continued to help the Trump family with loans when he moved on from Deutsche Bank and established his own Florida firm, and would attend public events with the Trumps, like the U.S. Open tennis match.

After Trump's inauguration, the family launched a full charm offensive—for example, sitting Ivanka next to Justice Kennedy at an inaugural lunch. Ivanka also visited Justice Kennedy at the Supreme Court, bringing her daughter. President Trump himself sought to leverage the relationship with Justin Kennedy, talking to Justice Kennedy about how "special" his son was. "Trump's flattery," author David Enrich writes in his book *Dark Towers: Deutsche Bank, Donald Trump and an Epic Trail of Destruction,* "was part of a coordinated White House charm offensive designed to persuade the ageing justice—for years, the court's swing vote—that it was safe to retire, even with an unpredictable man in the Oval Office." Safer still if one of his own former clerks would be tapped to replace him.

A chance to fill Kennedy's seat, giving Trump his second Supreme Court appointment in his first eighteen months, represented a golden opportunity to fulfill one of his most important campaign promises to his followers—and dramatically change the complexion, and direction, of the Supreme Court. Replacing Kennedy, a true swing vote, with Kavanaugh would move the court appreciably to the right and be a big step toward overturning *Roe*.

Two law professors evaluated Kavanaugh's appellate court decisions for *The Washington Post,* rating his decisions in four areas: rights of criminal defendants; support for rules regarding stricter enforcement of environmental protection; upholding the rights of labor unions; and siding with those bringing suits alleging discrimination. They found that between 2003 and 2018 he had the most conservative voting record on the D.C. Circuit in three of those policy areas, and the second-most in the fourth. The Trump vetting team also had access to a 2017 speech Kavanaugh gave to the conservative American Enterprise Institute praising William Rehnquist's dissent in *Roe v. Wade.*

With the Senate narrowly divided, Kavanaugh circled Republican Susan Collins of Maine, a supporter of abortion rights, as perhaps the most critical vote to secure, and in fact she did cast the deciding vote in his favor. After their meeting, Collins issued an extraordinary statement saying Kavanaugh had promised to uphold *Roe* as inviolable precedent. "To my knowledge Judge Kavanaugh is the first Supreme Court nominee to express the view that precedent is not merely a practice and tradition, but rooted in Article III of our Constitution itself," her statement read. "In other words, precedent isn't a goal or an aspiration; it is a constitutional tenet that has to be followed except in the most extraordinary circumstances."

After the *Dobbs* decision in June 2022, with Kavanaugh in the majority, Collins made another extraordinary statement, telling *The New York Times,* "I feel misled." Kavanaugh had told her—according to her office's notes—"Roe is forty-five years old, it had been reaffirmed many times, lots of people care about it a great deal, and I've tried to demonstrate I understand real-world consequences. . . . I am a don't-rock-the-boat kind of judge. I believe in stability and in the Team of Nine." Under oath, falsely seeking to assure the Senate he would uphold *Roe,* Kavanaugh testified he respected *Planned Parenthood v. Casey,* the 1992 Pennsylvania abortion case upholding *Roe,* as "precedent on precedent." He intended no such thing.

———

By mid-September, with Collins's support, the Kavanaugh nomination seemed headed for approval by a razor-thin margin. Then news leaked in *The Intercept* that weeks earlier a woman named Christine Blasey Ford had come forward to the top Democrat on the committee, Dianne Feinstein, with an explosive allegation of sexual misconduct when she and Kavanaugh were both high school students in Maryland. Feinstein, honoring Ford's request for anonymity, had reported the allegation to the FBI but otherwise took no action and didn't even inform her committee colleagues of the charge. The delay, warranted or not, assured there would be no time to fully consider the charge.

With Republicans in control of the committee, hearings were set on Ford's allegation, but the hearings were to be held in only one day and there were to be no witnesses other than the accuser, Ford, and the accused, Kavanaugh. Incredibly, this had been the same rigged setup in the Thomas-Hill face-off.

Taking the stand under oath, Ford looked visibly uncomfortable, explaining, "I am here today not because I want to be. I am terrified." She testified that Kavanaugh and his friend Mark Judge, both "visibly drunk," had locked her in a bedroom, where Kavanaugh, then seventeen, groped her and tried to take her clothes off while Judge watched. She said she "believed he was going to rape me," and feared for her life as he held his hand over her mouth. Ford stated that she escaped when Judge jumped on the bed, knocking them to the floor.

When it was his turn to respond, Kavanaugh's histrionics were reminiscent of Clarence Thomas's twenty-seven years earlier. A visibly emotional Kavanaugh sought to turn the tables on the Democrats, claiming that Ford's accusations were somehow a "political hit job" by left-wing Democrats "on behalf of the Clintons," for his work on the Starr report. "A good old-fashioned Borking," Kavanaugh declared. There was no evidence that Ford, a psychology college professor in California, had a partisan agenda in coming forward. In citing the example of overtly political Robert Bork, an antiabortion political extremist, Kavanaugh in fact was highlighting his own lack of legitimacy, as a former political operative with extreme views, for a seat on the high court.

The furor over Ford's allegations against Kavanaugh forced the Trump White House to agree to a truncated FBI investigation of Kavanaugh's background—very truncated. Eighty-three complaints were logged against Kavanaugh with a judicial conduct panel—including one by Deborah Ramirez, a Yale classmate who told *The New Yorker* Kavanaugh exposed himself and thrust his penis in her face at a college party. Ramirez, like Angela Wright in the Anita Hill case, would not be allowed to testify, as Republican Judiciary Committee chairman Chuck Grassley controlled the hearings. The judicial conduct panel dismissed the case, saying they had no authority over Supreme Court justices.

Kavanaugh, in his rebuttal to Ford, had gone to great lengths to deny the portrait she had sketched of him as a teenager, a drunk and rowdy carouser. "I liked beer," Kavanaugh memorably told the senators and the nation. "I still like beer. But I did not drink beer to the point of blacking out." It was an assertion others would emerge to contradict.

Ford's live testimony came across to most neutral observers as far too detailed to be made up, as when she relayed to the senators and television audience, "Brett groped me and tried to take off my clothes. He had a hard time, because he was very inebriated, and because I was wearing a one-piece bathing suit underneath my clothing. I believed he was going to rape me. I tried to yell for help. When I did, Brett put his hand over my mouth to stop me from yelling. This is what terrified me the most, and has had the most lasting impact on my life. It was hard for me to breathe, and I thought that Brett was accidentally going to kill me."

Ford's description of how she escaped was compelling and believable. She described Kavanaugh friend Mark Judge as "ambivalent . . . at times urging Brett on and at times telling him to stop." She made eye contact with Judge and "thought he might try to help me, but he did not." Then, rather than try to figure out whether to stop or egg on his friend, Judge decided to horse around. Judge, Ford recalled, "jumped on the bed twice while Brett was on top of me. And the last time that he did this, we toppled over and Brett was no longer on top of me. I was able to get up and run out of the room."

The falling-off-the-bed detail leaped out immediately to Timothy Don, a friend of both Judge's and Kavanaugh's at Georgetown Prep in Maryland, where he was one year behind them. "You couldn't make that up," Don says now. "That's exactly how it would have gone down."

Speaking of Kavanaugh's performance in the hearings, and of other judicial nominees following a similar playbook, Don added: "I find it incredible that people at that level will just flat-out lie. You're there with your hand on the Bible taking the vow and you just straight-up lie? It's super sad. It's like, Dude, just don't take the job! You don't have to do it."

At the time, pressure mounted for Judge—who dismissed the Ford allegations in a brief interview with *The Weekly Standard*—to testify before the confirmation hearings. "How could we want to get the truth and not have Mr. Judge come to the hearing?" New York's Chuck Schumer pointedly asked, but in the end Judge escaped with a perfunctory FBI interview whose details were never revealed. Judge ducked the press—and has been basically hiding ever since.

"He's never really been interviewed, and it's kind of weird, isn't it?" Don observed recently. "That never came out, which suggests to me: I guess we know what you know. The silence was as damning as anything he could say. I don't know how much Judge remembers, since he was shitfaced through all of high school."

Don knew of what he spoke. Judge, later a conservative writer for such publications as *The Daily Caller,* in fact wrote a memoir about his heavy drinking in high school. Judge, one of Kavanaugh's closest friends in school, wrote in praise of male sexual aggressiveness, penning the sentiment that "if [a] man is any kind of man, he'll allow himself the awesome power, the wonderful beauty, of uncontrollable male passion."

Ford's testimony, whatever spin the right-wing machine wanted to put out there, unnerved many Kavanaugh supporters, as years earlier I had seen the accusations against Clarence Thomas during his confirmation hearings unnerve his inner circle, many of whom knew or suspected the accusations were on target. The right-wing sleaze machine took their best shot. Kavanaugh defender Ed Whelan, clearly terrified that the allegations had a basis in fact and would sink the nomination, tried a wild attack on Twitter, using a series of tweets to try to push the notion that Ford was accusing the wrong man. Whelan, president of the Ethics & Policy Center, a right-wing Washington think tank where Leo sits on the board, saw his desperate scenario quickly shot down by Ford herself, who forcefully rejected it, and soon Whelan was excoriated for his reckless charges. Jake Tapper of ABC called them "stunningly irresponsible." Whelan, clearly fearing Ford might sue, apologized on Twitter, accusing himself of "an appalling and inexcusable mistake of judgement."

Charles Ludington, the former basketball player and Kavanaugh friend, was part of a group of former Yale students who worked together after Ford's allegations emerged to compare recollections and rigorously fact-check incidents they could recall taking place. For Ludington, who had often seen Kavanaugh drunk and out of control, his Senate testimony crossed a line of basic decency. "I was just watching it going, 'OK, OK,'" Ludington says. "The more he spoke, the more he lied. About the meaning of all those words [slang among his classmates] that everybody knew he was lying about, 'the devil's triangle' and 'boof' and all those things. . . . He was lying about the meaning of words. He was lying about his behavior and I said: That's it. You shouldn't be able to lie."

Ludington called the FBI to say he had information about Kavanaugh to report. Soon he was national news. Ludington was mentioned in a *Washington Post* article on the confused state of the Kavanaugh investigation, reporting on his intention to go to the FBI field office in Raleigh, North Carolina, and give a statement "detailing violent drunken behavior by Kavanaugh in college."

In a statement shared with *The New York Times,* Ludington wrote, "When Brett got drunk, he was often belligerent and aggressive. . . . I do not believe that the heavy drinking or even loutish behavior of an eighteen- or even twenty-one-year-old should condemn a person for the rest of his life. However . . . if he lied about his past actions on national television, and more especially while speaking under oath in front of the United States Senate, I believe those lies should have consequences."

NBC News and other outlets picked up the story, with a headline blaring "Yale Classmate to Tell FBI of Brett Kavanaugh's 'Violent Drunken' Behavior." The NBC report, on the weekend after Ford's testimony, also quoted a statement from Susan Collins saying that she was "confident that the FBI will follow up on leads that result from the interviews."

But in the case of Ludington, the interview never happened. The FBI changed its mind. They didn't even want to talk to the former Yale friend of Kavanaugh's. "First they said come in," Ludington said in a recent interview. On his way to the FBI field office, he was told, "Don't bother coming in." Instead, he was told to submit his account online, and assured, "We will be in touch with you." No one ever called. Nothing Ludington turned in was ever followed up on.

None of the complaints filed to the FBI, including Debbie Ramirez's, were investigated by the bureau. They were simply forwarded to the Trump White House, which was directing a cover-up. Soon the White House announced that after reviewing the FBI file it had found no corroboration of the accusations. The investigation was a farce and a sham. The FBI leadership, in a clear spirit of self-preservation, chose political expediency and had its investigators doing the absolute minimum of work looking into Kavanaugh's background. This was a blatant cover-up that impugned the credibility of the FBI. The articles that were published about the White House letting the FBI loose to do its job were a fraud and smoke screen; nothing was behind them.

Outrage at this travesty reached a boiling point two years later in July 2021, when the FBI belatedly responded to a letter from Senators Sheldon Whitehouse and Chris Coons seeking more information on the so-called FBI investigation, and the 4,500 tips received, with a short note saying "all relevant tips" were forwarded to the White House counsel's office. As Ruth Marcus wrote in *The Washington Post,*

> What were these "relevant tips"? How many were there? How potentially serious? The letter doesn't say, and we don't know. What did then–White House Counsel Donald McGahn do with the "relevant tips"? That, we do know: not a damn thing. McGahn had no interest in discovering what his hand-picked nominee had done, or not done. He had every interest in ensuring that Kavanaugh be confirmed, facts be damned. If there was any follow-up within the FBI itself, there's no indication of that. And that is the outrage here. The FBI's investigation into sexual assault allegations against Kava-

naugh wasn't designed to uncover the truth. It was a shoddy enterprise whose mission was to satisfy enough disquieted senators—Republicans Jeff Flake of Arizona, Susan Collins of Maine—to get Kavanaugh across the finish line.

Ludington, a six-foot-eight bench player for Yale that year, remembers going to a September 25, 1985, UB40 concert at the Palace in New Haven with his six-foot-ten Yale basketball team-mate Chris Dudley, who would go on to play in the NBA—and Kavanaugh. At the time, Kavanaugh was actually writing arti-cles about basketball for the student paper, the *Yale Daily News,* including one in November 1985 in which he extolled Dudley's prowess and recalled how he "dominated games at the end of the year." Ludington explained, "Mostly I knew him because he was sort of a groupie, one of the few groupies for the basketball team." Ludington agreed with Dudley to invite Kavanaugh along to come to the concert, assuming he'd say no. "It didn't seem like his kind of music, from what I could gather, but sure enough, he wanted to go," he says.

Afterward, the three decided to stop off for a drink at a club called Demery's, on Broadway, that was known as one of the few places in New Haven where students and locals regularly mixed. At Demery's, the three Yale students spotted someone hanging out who reminded them of Ali Campbell, the UB40 lead singer. They really thought it might be him, and kept staring. Eventually, the man in the bar—who, it turned out, was most definitely not Ali Campbell—got tired of the staring.

"What the hell are you guys looking at?" he asked.

"I don't know, man, don't worry about it," Ludington remem-bers saying. "We just thought you were a lead singer of UB40."

"Well quit looking at me," the man said.

And that, Ludington says, was when Kavanaugh yelled "FUCK YOU!!!" at the stranger in the bar, and the guy yelled the same thing back, and then Kavanaugh threw the contents of his drink into the man's face. "The next thing you know, Chris, he and Brett started going at it," Ludington says. "As they started fighting, Chris then slammed his glass up against the guy's ear, and that's what got Chris landed in jail. My goal at that point was to pull our star center off this guy, knowing this was going to be bad."

It was understood at Demery's that town-gown tension was a given, something to be careful about, a third rail to avoid, but Kavanaugh seemed utterly oblivious. "There was just no awareness," Ludington says. "It was the height of immaturity on Brett's part to respond like that to a guy who was obviously insecure in this environment and he sees three Yalies and is feeling intimidated."

Kavanaugh, having started the fight with the man, later identified as Dom Cozzolino, was questioned by New Haven police afterward, as was Dudley. Both appeared in the resulting police report. "Upon our arrival we met Mr. Cozzolino," the New Haven police officers reported. "He stated that a very tall subject hit him in the ear with a glass. Mr. Cozzolino was bleeding from the right ear. He also stated that he was in a verbal altercation with an unknown man." In other words: Kavanaugh.

Any honest FBI investigation seeking to determine if Kavanaugh's past behavior supported Christine Blasey Ford's portrait of the young Kavanaugh as given to binge drinking and impulsive behavior, or supported Kavanaugh's bland insistence that he was the picture of rectitude, would have required a thorough consideration of Charles Ludington's account of that night. Instead, the cover-up machinery paved right over this and innumerable other accounts.

Kavanaugh, in his testimony, had moments where he brought into question his temperament for the job in his answers to senators—especially in the case of an outrageous exchange with Amy Klobuchar.

"So you're saying there's never been a case where you drank so much that you didn't remember what happened the night before or part of what happened?" Klobuchar followed up, asking Kavanaugh about his drinking.

"It's—you're asking about, yeah, blackout," Kavanaugh answered. "I don't know. Have you?"

"Could you answer the question, Judge?" Klobuchar tried again. "I just—so, you—that's not happened. Is that your answer?"

"Yeah, and I'm curious if you have," he said.

"I have no drinking problem, Judge."

Lisa Graves, a former Senate Judiciary Committee staffer, appeared on *Democracy Now!* with Amy Goodman, focused on that exchange. "I think you did see Brett Kavanaugh behaving belligerently to the Senate," she said. "It was actually extraordinary, the degree to which he was completely disrespectful and contemptuous of the senators who were asking genuine questions about how to reconcile his claim that this never happened, with the testimony of Dr. Ford that it did, and that he was drunk when it happened. . . . I think that when you look at his statements, what you see is a man, in some ways, in deep denial about who he was and who he may still be."

Ludington, who earned a PhD from Columbia in philosophy and history, went on to a career as a North Carolina State University professor, and has authored three books, including *Food Fights: How the Past Matters to Contemporary Food Debates*. Looking back on his time knowing Brett Kavanaugh at Yale, he sounds a sad, weary note. "I think the reason I grew apart is I got tired of his shtick," he says. "It was, drink a whole lot and start to yell about something, usually related to whatever it is that promoted his conception of masculinity, so therefore it's against what he deemed lesser men or women. It got really tiring really fast. It was one of those things that you could see it probably worked for him in high school, putting women down, putting men down who didn't live by his conception of masculinity. But obviously he was clearly trying to compensate for whatever insecurities he had, which is not atypical at all for college people in general."

Kavanaugh had cited Robert Bork in his emotional, self-serving performance before the Senate committee, and his fate would forever be yoked to that of the former Nixon accomplice. A Gallup poll conducted in mid-September 2018 found that Kavanaugh had the smallest amount of public support for confirmation of any nominee since Bork. Only 39 percent of those polled favored Kavanaugh being confirmed (with 42 percent opposed), whereas only 38 percent had supported confirmation for Bork (versus 35 percent opposed). As a point of comparison, Obama nominee Merrick Garland had the support of 52 percent of those polled against only 29 percent in opposition.

The picture Kavanaugh had presented to the nation during the hearings had alarmed a wide swath of the country. Millions thought his confirmation was tainted, for good reason. He also looked angry and petulant, his face contorted into a mask of self-pitying rage. Kavanaugh had the résumé, and the backers, but he clearly did not have the sort of judicial temperament, requiring equanimity, long associated with the honor and privilege of serving on the Supreme Court of the United States.

Retired justice John Paul Stevens, ninety-eight, went so far as to speak up in public on the Kavanaugh nomination. A few years earlier, Stevens had praised Kavanaugh. "At that time, I thought he had the qualifications for the Supreme Court should he be selected," Stevens said at a Florida event, reported in *The New York Times*. "I've changed my views for reasons that have no relationship to his intellectual ability," Stevens said. "But I think that his performance during the hearings caused me to change my mind."

In the end, the cover-up worked—that and lavish spending on Kavanaugh's behalf. This time, the Leonard Leo–led network outdid itself, with nearly $15 million coming from the Wellspring Committee alone, funneled to the Judicial Crisis Network, to muddy the waters on behalf of Kavanaugh, pushing saccharine blather about how he was "a person of impeccable character, extraordinary qualifications, independence and fairness."

When the Judiciary Committee began investing the FBI's role in the cover-up, one agent on the case told a Senate staffer, "Why are you asking questions about this? He was already confirmed." Such was the prevailing attitude inside the bureau.

Behind the scenes, Republicans were desperate to bury Debbie Ramirez's account of Kavanaugh's lewd behavior at Yale. It was critical corroboration for Ford and had the potential to sink Kavanaugh. In their twenty-eight-page report on the nomination, the Republicans sought to smear Ramirez with a story told by a friend of Leonard Leo's. The report floated the possibility that Ramirez had mistaken Kavanaugh for another classmate, the same charge the right had made against Ford. Yet the boy in question was in high school far from the Yale campus, not at Yale, at the time of the incident described by Ramirez.

Even though the information, provided to the committee by a Federalist Society lawyer based in Colorado, was discredited, the Republicans put it in anyway to cast aspersion on Ramirez. The committee report claimed there was "no verifiable evidence" to support Ramirez's claim. To do so, they had to ignore the story of another Yale graduate, Max Stier, describing a separate alleged incident in which he said he witnessed Kavanaugh expose himself at a different Yale party. According to a report in *The New York Times,* Stier had wanted to tell the FBI anonymously that he recalled having seen "Kavanaugh with his pants down" at a "drunken dorm party, where friends pushed his penis into the hands of a female student." Stier had agreed to let Senator Chris Coons of Delaware contact the FBI on his behalf and urged investigators to speak with him. Coons dashed off a letter to the FBI director. Stier was never contacted.

In the end, Susan Collins stuck by Kavanaugh, and he was confirmed 50–48 in a historically close vote. The following August a small item appeared in the *Portland Press-Herald*. Collins had appeared at Leonard Leo's 7,900-square-foot Maine residence, a Tudor-style mansion, for a fundraiser, attended by C. Boyden Gray, a Federalist Society chieftain. JCN announced that it was launching a six-figure ad campaign on Maine TV and digital media to "thank" Collins for backing the beleaguered nominee.

Kavanaugh held the distinction of not only having a past as a political operative deeply implicated in the dirty-tricks campaign against Bill Clinton, but also committing perjury three distinct times. Even before he was nominated to the Supreme Court, Kavanaugh had perjured himself in 2006 during his confirmation hearing for the U.S. Court of Appeals for the District of Columbia, claiming never to have seen documents that had been prepared by Senate Judiciary Committee Democratic staff members. This was a clear falsehood, under oath. The documents had essentially been hacked, and Kavanaugh was one of the beneficiaries. That was one undeniable case of perjury, and in his Supreme Court hearings, and in private meetings with senators, Kavanaugh again lied about his positions on stare decisis and *Roe*—and he lied again, repeatedly, when forced to confront his reckless, drunken sexual misconduct as a high school and college student, including the highly credible allegations leveled by Christine Blasey Ford. Among the extremist, illegitimate members of the Thomas Court majority, other than Thomas himself, Kavanaugh could claim the dubious distinction of being the most illegitimate.

# CHAPTER 19

# OCTOBER 2020: THE HANDMAID

Given Justice Ruth Bader Ginsburg's bouts of cancer, some urged her to step down during the Obama presidency so a like-minded replacement could be nominated. She decided to hold on, a risky move, and her cancer came back—and metastasized. Ginsburg died at home in her Watergate apartment on September 18, 2020, a major loss for the country. The election was less than two months away. It would follow from McConnell's own logic, in holding up the Garland nomination, that it was far too close to the upcoming election for the Republicans to try to rush through a Supreme Court nominee. That would be a mockery of McConnell's position on Garland, a surrendering of the last shred of honor the man might possess, and an abasement of the dignity of both the Senate and the court. Uncharacteristically, McConnell seemed unsure what to do. Peter Baker and Maggie Haberman reported in *The New York Times* that on the Friday night Ginsburg died, McConnell vowed "to hold a vote on a Trump nominee but would not say whether he would try to rush it through before the vote on Nov. 3 in what would surely be a titanic partisan battle. . . . A Trump administration official said there might not be enough time on the calendar to vote on a confirmation before the election."

Leonard Leo was also on record as holding off. In an October 2018 interview with PBS, he said, "If a vacancy occurs in 2020, the vacancy needs to remain open until a president is elected and inaugurated and can pick. That's my position, period." This of course was the same argument Republicans had used to deny a hearing and a vote on Merrick Garland.

Yet Leo soon began "amending his position," as his spokesman put it. His benefactors clearly wanted a 180. Even as Ginsburg's body lay in state, Leo and his network once again raced into action, lining up funds for ad buys and media influence campaigns, and religious right leaders spoke up to remind Trump: This is why we backed you. Trailing Biden in the polls Trump saw a "titanic partisan battle" over the Supreme Court as a chance to revive his flagging campaign, just as McConnell's Garland maneuvers helped Trump win the presidency in the first place. McConnell cast aside his doubt and decided to try to push through a nomination only thirty-eight days before Trump would face Biden on the ballot. It was a "cynical attack on the legitimacy of the court," as Democratic Senate leader Chuck Schumer put it, "the most illegitimate process I have witnessed in the Senate." The Republicans could have been right in 2016, or right in 2020, but not both times. (More likely, they were wrong twice.)

Trump quickly announced that his pick would be the religious conservative judge Amy Coney Barrett, a right-wing Catholic extremist and a favorite of the Religious Right, since she had clashed with Democrats over questions of her faith and impartiality in the confirmation hearings for her circuit court seat. She was the furthest right of the names Leo had handed Trump. Barrett had been a protégée and former clerk for both Laurence Silberman and Scalia, and in her first public appearance upon being announced, she rolled out the now shopworn Federalist Society two-step. At a hastily arranged Rose Garden ceremony, she sought to cast herself as an heir to the Scalia tradition, itself a carefully manufactured myth.

"His judicial philosophy is mine, too—a judge must apply the law as written," she said. "Judges are not policymakers, and they must be resolute in setting aside any policy views they might hold."

The ceremony itself was telling; in attendance stood a who's who of antiabortion conservatives: Gary Bauer, the longtime head of the Family Research Council, Matt Schlapp of the American Conservative Union, John Malcolm of the Heritage Foundation, Marjorie Dannenfelser of Susan B. Anthony List, Jeanne Mancini, president of March for Life, hard-right senators Josh Hawley and Marsha Blackburn, and Antonin Scalia's family— Maureen, Paul, and Eugene.

Here we were again. The Federalists expected the Senate and the public at large to accept the canard that they set aside their policy views when they donned their judicial robes when in fact the opposite was true: They were actually weaponizing the court to force their extreme social policy views on the country. Indeed, anyone who professed surprise at the perfectly predictable *Dobbs* decision just hadn't been paying attention. Recall that Alito had written to Ed Meese flatly stating he opposed abortion rights. Gorsuch had an expansive view of what the right calls "religious liberty," which he had used to deny contraception under the Affordable Care Act. Kavanaugh had given a speech praising Rehnquist's dissent in *Roe*. And now this: As a law professor at the University of Notre Dame, a premier Catholic institution, Barrett had signed political ads by antiabortion groups in Indiana. "Please continue to pray to end abortion," said one, sponsored by the St. Joseph County Right to Life, which called itself "one of the oldest continuously active pro-life organizations in the nation." The ad signed by Barrett identified its signatories as those who "oppose abortion on demand and defend the right to life from fertilization to natural death." Just as Thomas's appointment to replace Thurgood Marshall had been a perverse insult to civil rights, Trump's choice of Barrett to replace Ginsburg, a pioneer for women, was a perverse insult to women's rights.

"With ghoulish irony, Trump reportedly told his inner circle, 'I'm saving her for Ginsburg,'" Bridget Kelly of the Population Institute wrote in an essay for *Newsweek*. "It's a particular insult to women, as well as to Justice Ginsburg's memory, for Trump to propose such a candidate to replace her and claim he's doing it to advance women's equality. If he succeeds in appointing such a staunch opponent of reproductive rights to the Court, he'll advance his own agenda of turning women's rights back fifty years. Appointing Barrett could well result in the overturning of *Roe v. Wade,* and the assault on sexual and reproductive rights will not stop there."

As much as her friends talked of Barrett not being a woman of ambition, the appointment to the Supreme Court hardly came out of nowhere. Barrett, nominated by Trump in May 2017 to the U.S. Court of Appeals for the Seventh Circuit, turned her spot on the court into a platform for extensive auditioning. "In one case, Barrett's Seventh Circuit Court of Appeals declined to hear a challenge to an Indiana law on women's right to choose," Sheldon Whitehouse said in his speech on auditioning. "Barrett bucked the majority to stake out an eyebrow-raising position on the right, joining a dissent aimed directly at Supreme Court abortion precedent. On guns, Judge Barrett authored an opinion in a Second Amendment case called *Kanter v. Barr* that would have given a felon back his gun because this felony wasn't violent. Constitutional scholars' jaws hit the floor at that one."

UCLA law professor Adam Winkler, an expert on the Second Amendment, called that opinion by Barrett her "audition tape" for the Supreme Court, going out of her way to appeal to Mitch McConnell and the Federalist Society. Winkler told *The New*

*Yorker* that the "history and tradition" argument Barrett relied on in *Kanter*—to make it an audition tape—was both problematic and dangerous. "Barrett's logic could similarly overturn laws preventing people who were convicted of domestic violence from owning guns," reporter Margaret Talbot wrote. "Beating your wife wasn't a crime in Colonial America, Winkler pointed out."

Questions were also raised about Barrett's adherence to a religious sect that preached the subjugation of women. During her Supreme Court confirmation hearings, it emerged in press reports that Barrett was a lifelong member of People of Praise, a small Christian sect founded in the 1970s and based in South Bend, Indiana. People of Praise, where both Barrett parents were very active, is a secretive Christian faith group that considers women's obedience and subservience to men one of its central tenets. An offshoot of the charismatic movement within Catholicism, it embraced such intense practices as shared living, faith healing, and speaking in tongues.

Barrett's father, Mike Coney, offered this description of People of Praise in a long post on his church website in 2018 on his faith journey, which led him to become a deacon. "After ordination we felt a call to live life in a close knit Christian community, one like that described in the Acts of the Apostles, one that would help form our children into good Christians and strengthen our marriage and family," he wrote. "As a result, our family became members of an ecumenical lay covenant community called the People of Praise (POP). The glue which binds the members of the POP is a promise to share life together and to look out for each other in all things material and spiritual. Men and women separately meet weekly in small faith groups. In this ecumenical community my faith has been nourished and my commitment to my friend Christ has grown deeper and stronger and has borne good fruit."

Make no mistake, this is a fundamentalist form of Christianity. Barrett's father writes in the same essay of one night when he "began to speak in tongues" and "sensed a call from the Lord to serve." That's no knock on the value of religious affirmation, like his "continual" prayer, "Give me wisdom, knowledge, discernment and sound judgement," but the Barrett family's religious background was clearly one in which a strong adherence to the will of others was emphasized and women in general were seen as being in a subservient position to men.

A 2010 directory of People of Praise listed Barrett with the title of "handmaid," described as a leadership position for women in the community, according to *The Washington Post.* The title of handmaid was adopted for People of Praise in reference to the biblical description of Mary as "the handmaid of the Lord." A 1986 community handbook also obtained by the *Post* said each member is "personally accountable to God for his and her decisions" but also emphasized "obedience to authority and submission to head ship (men in the community)." As recently as 2017, Barrett sat on the board of a People of Praise–affiliated school.

Barrett's membership in what frankly amounts to a backward religious cult troubled Senator Dianne Feinstein in Barrett's circuit court nomination hearing. Knowing that the circuit courts are stepping-stones to the high court, and worried that was where Barrett was headed, Feinstein had a moment of striking clarity. Tackling the taboo issue head-on, Feinstein declared, "The dogma lives loudly within you, and that is a concern." The exchange with Feinstein made Barrett an instant favorite of religious conservatives and thus a front-runner for a future court vacancy.

For these religious conservatives membership in People of Praise was yet another signal of Barrett's bona fides. Yet at the time of the nomination several former People of Praise members came forward to criticize the group's practices. Most outspoken was Coral Theill, who identifies as a "handmaid survivor." She wrote a letter to the Senate Judiciary Committee asking to testify in the Barrett hearings. In the letter, Theill said she suffered "marital rape, illegal detention, illegal interrogation and kidnapping." She continued: "The entire time I was there, I was under the control of men and subjected to psychological abuse, including undue influence, threats, shaming and shunning my leaders and my husband. Coercive persuasion was used on my children to turn them against me. My husband and community leaders used coercive control, isolation and intimidation to strip me of my personhood, safety and freedoms guaranteed to me as a United States citizen."

Theill's letter went unanswered by Republicans—and Democrats.

In 2024, the plot took another turn when Barrett's father was named general counsel of the group and put in charge of investigating various complaints about how People of Praise treats its members. PoP survivors are concerned that Barrett is in a position to engineer a cover-up. "Elevating Amy Coney Barrett's father to a position where he can influence what goes public is a huge conflict of interest. It gives him the power to block information that might be embarrassing to her. Yet public scrutiny is exactly what's needed in order to protect children in the group," said a spokesperson for PoP Survivors, which has fifty-five members and is comprised of adults who grew up in the sect and are no longer affiliated with the group.

During Barrett's Supreme Court hearing, Democrats were reluctant to pursue People of Praise for fear that they would look like they were attacking Barrett's religious faith, but Feinstein was still clearly upset about her fealty to right-wing Catholicism. Yet rather than honestly stating her views, Barrett reverted to the Federalist Society language of textualism and originalism to mask the truth about her real views. She falsely told Feinstein she would "obey all the rules of stare decisis" with respect to *Roe,* and pledged respect for court precedents on abortion-related cases that might come before her. While Barrett did concede she did not consider *Roe* a "superprecedent," she quickly added, with a clear intent to mislead, "That does not mean *Roe* should be overruled." Meanwhile, right-wing dark-money groups run by Leo spent millions during the hearings putting out false messages that Barrett would set aside her personal views, follow settled law, and rule fairly.

Senator Josh Hawley gave up the game by making clear he already knew Barrett would vote to overturn *Roe.* "I think the judge's record as to her understanding of judicial role and *Roe* and how *Roe* fits into that is pretty clear," he said. "It certainly fits my threshold."

Hawaii's Mazie Hirono retorted, in her questioning of Barrett, that she was bothered by the nominee's "willingness to overturn *Roe v. Wade* . . . which Senator Hawley fully expects you to do because you have met his litmus test."

The stakes were high for the organized right—thus the brazen rush to confirm the judge in the few weeks they might have left in office. Before Barrett's appointment, John Roberts was the swing vote in a 5–4 majority, so he could set the pace for the reversal of legal precedents that right-wing lawyers had selected to target. With Barrett on the court, Justice Alito did not have to bend to Roberts's gradualism to get a fifth vote to destroy *Roe*'s precedents. Like Kavanaugh, Barrett was very narrowly confirmed, 52–48, with all Democrats and one Republican opposed. In June 2022, in signing Alito's opinion in *Dobbs,* Barrett provided the critical fifth vote to overturn it and cemented the Thomas five. Her very appearance put an exclamation point on the takeover of the high court: Barrett, the mother of seven, including an eight-year-old, was only forty-eight at the time; given an average life expectancy for women of 79.9 years, as of 2020, the very real possibility is that Barrett and her religious-extremist views could find a home on the Supreme Court for at least the next thirty years.

# PART 4

# A CROOKED COURT CANNOT ESCAPE TRUE REFORM

## CHAPTER 20

# JUNE 2022: THE *DOBBS* EARTHQUAKE AND BEYOND

For all the decades of scheming, manipulating, and paying off that went into it, the Supreme Court's June 2022 *Dobbs* decision to overturn *Roe v. Wade* and make abortion illegal in much of the country had an immediate effect that no one fully saw coming: It put a woman's right to choose on the ballot in a transformative way. Suddenly a large segment of the population was deeply energized. Every election for the foreseeable future would have added urgency—and increased participation. That was dramatically the case in November 2022 when women voters in different regions of the country turned out in overwhelming numbers to defend their rights. Voters in the pivotal state of Ohio not only approved a 2023 constitutional amendment enshrining a woman's right to abortion, they did so by a wide margin, 56.6 percent to 43.4 percent. It was hardly a surprise that California voters would also pass a ballot measure to support abortion rights, but so did voters in Michigan and Vermont. And in the deep red states of Kansas, Kentucky, and Montana, efforts to restrict abortion access in statewide votes were successfully turned back.

In November 2024 abortion is definitely on the ballot again, offering voters a stark choice between Biden and the Democrats—who endorsed passing legislation to codify *Roe*, which is really the only answer to this nightmare—and Republicans seeking a numerical edge in both houses of Congress in order to pass a national ban on abortion. Trump himself, ever the adaptable opportunist, staked out a position on the stump claiming he found a ban at six weeks too draconian, even as he continued to brag about his judges overturning *Roe* and would be pressured by the antichoice movement in office to issue antiabortion executive orders. But the larger GOP project was summed up in the figure of Speaker of the House Mike Johnson, a Holy Warrior for whom a national abortion ban is nothing short of a sacred mission, befitting a man who believes God speaks to him directly, as He once spoke to Moses, and gives him tips on leading the Republican House caucus.

The Leonard Leo machine had been building for years toward the overthrow of *Roe v. Wade*, and the October 2020 installation of Amy Coney Barrett as the youthful final piece of the Thomas Court puzzle made it a matter of months before the upheaval came. This was all about power and politics and chits coming due, not about legal niceties or decorum. The pressure to act was immense. "The conservative legal movement finds itself at its most precarious point since its inception in the early 1970s," former Alito clerk J. Joel Alicea, a law professor at Catholic University, wrote in a Winter 2022 essay in *City Journal*. "[I]t is precisely the movement's success that puts it in peril. . . . This, then, is the moment the conservative legal movement has fought to bring about. If the Court fails to overrule *Roe*, the ruling will likely shatter the movement."

The *Dobbs* case represented the culmination of an organized push by religious conservatives aligned with the Leo machine to find a test case they could advance upward to the Supreme Court as a lever either to weaken or overturn the *Roe v. Wade* precedent. It all started with the Religious Right organization Alliance Defending Freedom, originally founded in 1993 in Phoenix, Arizona, as the Alliance Defense Fund, specifically founded by "a group of religious broadcasters and Christian fundamentalists," the Associated Press reported at the time, as a "legal war chest" to fight a "civil war of values" on such issues as abortion and gay rights. The fund was overseen by Alan Sears, who would go on to coauthor a virulently anti-gay 2003 book, *The Homosexual Agenda: Exposing the Principal Threat to Religious Freedom Today,* characterized by the Southern Poverty Law Center as "an anti-LGBT call to arms that links homosexuality to pedophilia." A more or less typical passage of that Sears tract read: "The radical homosexual activist community has adopted many of the techniques used in Nazi Germany."

Over time the Alliance Defense Fund grew increasingly aligned with Leonard Leo. As *The New Republic* put it in a July 2022 article, "Leo's work builds on that of other great minds of the Christian right's legal juggernaut." From 2017 to 2022 ADF was led by close Leo ally Michael D. Farris, and the group's annual revenue of more than $100 million came from a web of mostly untraceable sources largely tied to Leo and his network. As *Politico* reported in December 2023, "ADF is funded by Leo-aligned DonorsTrust, among the biggest beneficiaries of Leo's network of nonprofits." *Ms.* magazine, attempting to follow the money in a June 23, 2023, article, put it this way: "Much of ADF's revenue has come from donor-advised funds (DAFs), pass-throughs that shield the true source of funds. Leo's network has increasingly relied on DAFs to pass money between groups in his network. Notably, Leo's Marble Freedom Trust gave Schwab Charitable Fund, which has given millions to ADF, almost $150 million in 2021, although there is no direct proof those funds or significant funds were directed by Leo to ADF because the DAF helps obscure who the true original donors are." Like a mafia boss's, Leo's wishes are sometimes as important as his specific instructions—and everyone playing this dark game with him well knows it.

In 2018 Mississippi passed a state law, the Gestational Age Act, banning most abortions after the fifteenth week of pregnancy, a law that ADF staff attorneys helped draft. ADF attorneys were also closely involved in planning the legal defense of the law when Jackson Women's Health Organization in Jackson, Mississippi, the state's only abortion clinic at the time, sued Dr. Thomas E. Dobbs III, a Mississippi state health officer, challenging the abortion ban's constitutionality. Lower courts ruled—following the Supreme Court's 1992 decision in *Planned Parenthood v. Casey*—that the Fourteenth Amendment's Due Process Clause protected a woman's right to choose an abortion beyond fifteen weeks, enjoining enforcement of the law.

The Supreme Court agreed to hear the case and held oral arguments on December 1, 2021. Mississippi solicitor general Scott Stewart, a former Clarence Thomas law clerk, argued for both *Roe* and *Casey* to be overturned, relying in his arguments on an emotional appeal. "They have no basis in the Constitution," he said. "They've damaged the democratic process. They've poisoned the law." Focusing on questions about the viability of a fetus at different stages in pregnancy, Stewart dubiously claimed that science supported his religious contention that fetuses are "fully human" starting "very early" in a pregnancy.

Those were the arguments made to give cover to a baldly political proceeding. Stewart knew full well that his mentor Thomas was on his side, along with Alito, Gorsuch, Kavanaugh, and Barrett and possibly Chief Justice Roberts. The fix was in. As Justice Sonia Sotomayor—joined in opposition by Stephen Breyer and Elena Kagan—noted that day during oral arguments, the ADF push to overturn *Roe* was moving forward—as the group itself admitted—"because we have new justices" on the Supreme Court. This was about having the votes, not about law—or science. Sotomayor, addressing Stewart, argued forcefully against tossing out precedent, which would seriously harm the court's reputation and open the door to unpredictable ripple effects.

"Will this institution survive the stench that this creates in the public perception that the Constitution and its reading are just political acts?" Sotomayor asked Stewart. "I don't see how it is possible."

Sotomayor's question would ring in the air, defining an era of Thomas Court runaway arrogance and abuse of power, but the Federalist Society justices were far beyond appeals to reason or conscience. When a draft of Samuel Alito's majority decision in *Dobbs* was leaked to *Politico* in May 2022—a leak that was in and of itself breathtaking—the tone and thrust of Alito's arguments, at least within the context of how Supreme Court justices have traditionally framed opinions, were disturbing and sinister in their utter lack of restraint or nuance. Was this an op-ed Alito was submitting to his friends at *The Wall Street Journal* hard-right editorial page or a legal opinion? A Fox News commentary or a decision from a justice sworn to uphold precedent or at least respect it?

"Roe was egregiously decided from the start," Alito asserted in the draft that was leaked, which sounded more like a taunt to critics than the words of a man attuned to the gravity of the events he and the rest of the Thomas Court were setting in motion. All five in the majority would sign on to this sweeping statement, which suggested they had come to the case with their minds already made up.

Just as Donald Trump had made clear that he considered himself the president only of those people who had supported him and continued to support him, Alito was signaling in effect that from his point of view, any critic of his arguments or his conclusions was, ipso facto, irrelevant to him. He couldn't care less. He had power and religious conviction on his side. This was not merely a matter of upending reproductive rights and interfering with women's freedom to make their own choices about their own bodies, this was a hard turn toward a radical new era of hard-right conservatives becoming increasingly assertive about enforcing their minority—and in many cases, fringe—views on the majority of the country. Radicalism was not just the outcome, it was the point. Tepid half measures were to be scorned.

Alito's opinion was intellectually shoddy to a shocking degree. In a startling indictment of the doctrine of originalism, which purports to take great interest in fidelity to an accurate view of history, Alito thumbed his nose at any kind of accurate historical awareness, focusing instead on the breezy—and wrong—generalizations of a polemicist. Alito in his *Dobbs* majority opinion leaned on the purported "fact" that the vast majority of American states outlawed all forms of abortion at the time the Fourteenth Amendment was ratified. Wrong: At least seven states actually permitted some form of abortion. This was no idle slip, but part of a systematic effort to rewrite history, typical of originalism, which all too often was "original" only in its willingness to twist and falsify history to get to a preferred result.

"The logic that Alito uses in the draft opinion leans heavily on history—history that he gets egregiously wrong," University of Illinois law professor Leslie J. Reagan, author of *When Abortion Was a Crime,* wrote in *Politico Magazine* in June 2022. "Alito explicitly dismisses the distinction between ending a pregnancy before or after quickening (around 16 to 20 weeks of pregnancy), a distinction that my research has found was critical to the way American women and American physicians traditionally thought about pregnancy. In early America as in early modern England, abortion before 'quickening' was legal under common law and widely accepted in practice. . . . Alito's draft opinion sidesteps this well-established history. Instead, he insults 21st-century Americans by citing the words of a 13th-century judge who endorsed human slavery and a 17th-century jurist who sentenced witches to execution and defended marital rape."

Many observers noted how radical a break with court tradition the decision represented. University of Virginia law professor Richard M. Re, who clerked for Kavanaugh on the U.S. Court of Appeals for the D.C. Circuit, excoriated not only the *Dobbs* decision itself but the method by which it was reached. The court "barreled over each of its normal procedural guardrails," Re was quoted as saying in *The New York Times.* "[T]he Court compromised its own deliberative process."

Expanding on the point for the University of Virginia Law School, Re wrote, "Gradualism should have won out in *Dobbs v. Jackson Women's Health,* exerting gravitational influence on the majority and dissenters alike. In general, the Supreme Court should not impose massive disruption without first providing notice of its contemplated course of action. . . . In essence, the majority claimed that only grand, decisive action could meet the challenge at hand. But by acting in haste, the Court compromised its own deliberative process and prevented the public from adequately preparing for an avulsive shift in the law."

The leak itself offered devastating proof, if more was needed, that the court was a highly political body, no better than any executive branch agency or committee of the Congress, or even political campaign, where inside players routinely leak to the press to gain advantage. The Supreme Court leaker, surely an opponent of *Roe* seeking advantage, was playing high-stakes political poker and had taken care to leave no fingerprints on the *Politico* story. But a prior leak, this one to *The Wall Street Journal* editorial board, whose members were close to a number of the right-wing justices and their clerks, was more revealing.

Shortly before *Politico* reported on the draft opinion, the *Journal* published an inside account of the court's internal deliberations, suggesting that Chief Justice Roberts, who wanted to uphold Mississippi's restrictive abortion law without overturning *Roe,* was working to persuade other justices, including Barrett and Kavanaugh, to join him in a narrower ruling. The *Journal* urged the two possibly wavering justices to stay strong on *Roe*. "Leaking the draft opinion—which Justices Barrett and Kavanaugh had voted to join, according to reporting at the time—would have trained immense pressure from conservative elites on both justices to stick with their original votes, thus preserving *Dobb*'s eventual five-member majority," Aaron Tang, a law professor at the University of California at Davis and a former clerk to Sonia Sotomayor, explained in *The New York Times*.

The obvious suspects in the leak were the justices themselves, who can and do operate with impunity. A case in point: Five months after *Dobbs* was handed down, a *New York Times* report on a stunning right-wing influence operation on an entire branch of government implicated Samuel Alito in a leak of another controversial Supreme Court decision he had authored back in 2014. The *Times* described a "Ministry of Emboldenment," run by a former antiabortion activist, the Reverend Rob Schenck, aimed at pushing certain justices through social pressure to "lay the groundwork for an eventual reversal of *Roe*."

According to the *Times,* Schenck encouraged allies and wealthy donors to his organization to "invite some of the justices to meals, to their vacation homes or to private clubs and to contribute an estimated 125K to the Supreme Court Historical Society" and then "mingle with the justices at its functions." Schenck "ingratiated" himself with court officials to gain access. "You can position yourself in a special category with regard to the justices," Schenck said. "You can have conversations, share prayer." It was in one of these conversations, Schenck said, that Alito or his wife had told conservative donors over dinner in advance that Alito had authored the decision in the Hobby Lobby case that allowed religious exemptions to the Affordable Care Act's contraception coverage requirements. Perhaps only *Roe* ranked as a higher priority for the religious right than the Hobby Lobby case.

Schenck offered a devastating critique of the dark bargain that had been made between evangelical leaders and Republican operatives, testifying in December 2022 to the House Judiciary Committee about a brass-tacks meeting he had attended on Capitol Hill. "The conversation went something like this," Schenck recalled. "You guys want *Roe v. Wade* overturned? We can do that for you. But you take the whole enchilada." In other words, religious leaders knowingly agreed to what Schenck called "a deal with the devil," an agreement to throw out their principles in the service of one objective—overturning *Roe.* As Schenck explained, "We would support everything on the conservative agenda whether or not we had conscientious conflict with it. The means were justified by the end of that."

---

The fiasco over the leaked Alito draft opinion only furthered the diminishment in power and legitimacy of Chief Justice Roberts, whose quixotic efforts to work with Justice Stephen Breyer to find a middle ground on *Roe* were effectively killed off by the leak, and whose bland, nothing-to-see-here handling of this crisis of legitimacy for the court made him seem out of touch to the point of feckless. (Breyer, in an interview for his book *Reading the Constitution,* essentially confirmed that his efforts with Roberts to preserve *Roe* were derailed by the leak.)

Roberts had directed the marshal of the Supreme Court, former Army colonel Gail Curley, to initiate a thorough investigation into who might have leaked the draft opinion. Curley, previously known, if she was known at all, as the one who banged her gavel and called out "Oyez! Oyez! Oyez!" when the Supreme Court justices arrived for another session of the court, was given little investigative power in taking on the assignment. Predictably, the investigation turned out to be a sham, coming up empty. Supreme Court law clerks and other employees, ninety-seven in all, were forced to cooperate with the investigation, not only being required to sign sworn affidavits but also supplying detailed call

and text message logs, but the Supreme Court justices themselves were apparently not subjected to thorough questioning—
they were, rather, *consulted*.

Curley, responding to a media furor after the report was
released, issued a follow-up statement that raised more questions than it answered: "During the course of the investigation,
I spoke with each of the Justices, several on multiple occasions,"
Curley wrote. "The Justices actively cooperated in this iterative
process, asking questions and answering mine. I followed up on
all credible leads, none of which implicated the Justices or their
spouses. On this basis, I did not believe that it was necessary to
ask the Justices to sign sworn affidavits."

It sounded like a whitewash, one more example of the lack of
true accountability for the justices—including, in all likelihood,
the one who leaked the opinion, or helped leak it, in effect rigging
the vote on this hugely important decision and further undermining the legitimacy of the court's ruling. "The marshal's leak
report does not even consider the possibility that the leak was
by a justice," former Supreme Court clerk Daniel Epps told *The
Washington Post*. "If that was simply declared out of bounds at
the outset, it's hard to take this investigation seriously."

*The Hill* was particularly excoriating. "If Curley has any experience or skill in conducting leaks investigations, her qualifications are less than obvious," James Zirin wrote in December
2022. "Roberts's appointment of Curley is understandable even if
it appears supremely obtuse. The judicial branch does not want
the executive branch of government looking over the shoulders
of its personnel. But if Roberts really wanted to get to the bottom
of it, his reliance on Curley was misplaced. There is the lurking
suspicion that Curley's investigation is, as Shakespeare put it,
but 'a dagger of the mind, a false creation.' "

Roberts had the court issue a statement assuring the public
that the leaked opinion "does not represent a decision by the

Court or the final position of any member on the issues in the case," and Roberts himself was quoted as saying, "To the extent this betrayal of the confidence of the Court was intended to undermine the integrity of our operations, it will not succeed. The work of the Court will not be affected in any way."

This was at best wishful thinking. Roberts could not have been more wrong, as he had to have known. The work of the court was dramatically shaped and the leak did in fact seal the votes where they stood. When the *Dobbs* decision was rendered in June, the Alito opinion was an almost verbatim repetition of the leaked opinion. The court had actually done it: There was no constitutional right to abortion, five justices had found, because the Constitution does not mention abortion and the right is not "deeply rooted" in the country's history. States, therefore, had authority to regulate access to abortion. Roberts had failed to attract a fifth vote that would have left *Roe* standing while upholding the restrictive abortion law in Mississippi.

Roberts had effectively lost control of the court when Barrett replaced Ruth Bader Ginsburg in 2020. As the five other right-wing justices could outvote the rest, Roberts could no longer preside over a conservative court that respected precedent. This was no longer the Roberts Court. In fact, it was more the Leonard Leo Court than it was anything else at this point, but really, it was the court of Leo's close friend Clarence Thomas.

The backstory of the case showed just how long a shadow Justice Thomas cast even when it was not at all obvious to the general public. Mississippi, in the long run-up to *Dobbs* moving forward, made a highly unusual move at one point and dramatically shifted their arguments in the case. A far more aggressive argument directly targeting overthrow of *Roe* was launched by the state's newly appointed solicitor, Stewart, who had clerked for Thomas from 2015 to 2016. Stewart remained very much involved in the network of former Thomas clerks overseen by

Ginni Thomas. "Roe and Casey are egregiously wrong," Stewart argued in Mississippi's main brief. Sound familiar? It should. Alito would echo the sentiment.

The month that Stewart brief was filed, he was at a West Virginia resort for an elite gathering, one of the more exclusive clubs offering entrée into the halls of conservative power in Washington. Ginni and Clarence Thomas were hosting former Thomas clerks, and of course Stewart would not miss such an important networking—and strategy—session. As *The New York Times* reported, "He had attended reunions in previous years, and now he was about to argue his first case—one of surpassing importance—before his former boss and the other justices."

To those paying close attention to the inner workings of the Supreme Court, the *Dobbs* decision was expected. There had been the award given to Clarence Thomas by an antiabortion group, not to mention his wife's fervent advocacy on the subject; the Alito memo against *Roe* to Ed Meese; Gorsuch's pandering to the Religious Right in his "religious liberty" opinions; Kavanaugh's speech casting aspersions on *Roe;* and Barrett's signing of antiabortion advertisements. Sometimes math was just math. Two plus two equals four. Add one more and you get to five.

But for the nation as a whole, the decision still registered as a shock because most of the country had not been paying close attention. The public had a reasonable expectation that the justices entrusted with the most prestigious job in the land were not liars; they tended to believe that they had testified truthfully when they said they had no predisposition against *Roe,* no personal biases on abortion, and a strong belief in stare decisis, meaning they would uphold the *Roe* precedent even if they disagreed with it.

Even after the *Politico* leak, polls showed women didn't believe their right to abortion would be taken away. It was not reasonable to think all five justices committed perjury. But that's exactly what happened. After the decision was released, Representative Ted Lieu said in a tweet, "Multiple SC Justices lied during their confirmation process about the view of #RoeVWade and stare decisis."

The result in the real world was a confusing patchwork of access to abortion services. At least twenty-one states with Republican leadership either passed or were in the process of passing antiabortion-related bills when the Supreme Court agreed to hear *Dobbs.* Thirteen states had so-called trigger laws that ban most abortions. They became enforceable when *Roe* was overturned. Another nine states had never repealed their pre-*Roe* abortion bans, which were now enforceable. Several states adopted, or began to enforce, laws that banned abortion without exceptions. States opposed to abortion were also considering bans on access to medication abortion. In many states, doctors faced criminal penalties for performing abortions—and in some cases, women themselves faced abortion-related charges. As of December 2023, fully twenty-one states restricted abortion, or imposed stricter limits than the standard under *Roe,* and more restrictions were expected.

The impact on women's health was immediate and grim. Horror stories abounded, for example of an Idaho woman who took to TikTok to share updates on her nineteen-day ordeal of going through a miscarriage, visiting the emergency room three times, and being denied access to surgery—six weeks into her pregnancy—because of the abortion ban in Idaho. Heartbreaking stories from Texas included that of Samantha Casiano, who found out the fetus she was carrying in her womb had anencephaly, an impairment of brain development that is always fatal, but Casiano could not afford to leave Texas to have an abortion. Casiano has now joined a lawsuit challenging Texas's abortion ban.

Amanda Zurawski of Austin, Texas, testified to Congress about her harrowing near-death ordeal. Her water broke when she was just eighteen weeks pregnant. The fetus was no longer viable, but Zurawski's doctors were afraid to terminate the pregnancy because of the vagueness of the Texas law, which theoretically allows for abortion to save the life of a mother but without clear guidelines. Doctors finally performed the abortion—but only when Zurawski developed an infection, and was near death because of sepsis. It was, Zurawski told Congress, a "horrific" ordeal, and she specifically called out her two U.S. senators in Texas, Ted Cruz and John Cornyn.

"I nearly died on their watch, and furthermore, as a result of what happened to me, I may have been robbed of the opportunity to have children in the future," she testified. "Because I wasn't permitted to have an abortion and the trauma and the PTSD and the depression that I have dealt with in the eight months since this happened to me is paralyzing."

The stories of the ordeals women were going through post-*Dobbs* struck a chord with voters nationally, both Democrats and Republicans. For example, the polling firm PerryUndem found that voters, asked to compare two similar ballot measures, favored the one offering women full reproductive freedom and the right to make "all decisions," including on abortion. "Tresa Undem, one of the firm's founders, was so surprised by the result that she asked her staff to quadruple-check the numbers, and then conducted another poll and follow-up interviews to ask voters why they responded the way they did," Kate Zernike wrote in *The New York Times* in December 2023. "Those polls found that respondents who had heard stories about women with pregnancy complications being forced to travel out of state for abortions were overwhelmingly likely to support a ballot measure—that included 57 percent of Republicans. Even 46 percent of voters who said abortion should be illegal in most cases were likely to support a ballot measure establishing a right to abortion, if they had heard these stories. And over and over, voters explained their preference by saying they did not want the government involved in deciding who gets an abortion."

The immediate verdict on the political importance of *Dobbs* was quickly registered: American politics had dramatically shifted. *Dobbs* made abortion a major issue in the November 2022 midterm elections. "In 2022, 27 percent of Democratic ads for the House, Senate, and governorships talked about abortion, thirteen times higher than the share of Democratic ads that mentioned it two years earlier," *Politico* reported. "Republicans, on the other hand, largely avoided the topic: Only 5 percent of GOP ads mentioned abortion. . . . In total, Democrats sunk nearly $358 million into abortion-related ads in House, Senate and gubernatorial races, according to AdImpact. . . . Republicans, in contrast, spent about $37 million on abortion-related ads."

The widely predicted "Red Wave" for the Republicans never materialized. Democrats held control of the Senate while the Republicans captured the House very narrowly. Exit polls attributed the Democratic surge to pro-choice sentiment among women voters. They showed voters highly motivated by *Dobbs*—in Michigan, where voters passed an amendment to the state constitution enshrining reproductive rights, 45 percent of voters said abortion was the most important issue in determining their vote.

The verdict on the court was equally powerful. A clear majority of all Americans disapproved of the court's decision to overturn abortion rights—62 percent, according to Pew Research, with close to half of all Americans (42 percent) strongly disapproving. Among Democrats and independents who leaned Democratic, Pew found, 82 percent disapproved of the decision. Among Democrats, approval ratings of the court hit a record low at 25 percent—and then slipped further to 17 percent in a subsequent poll.

Far more important than one midterm election, *Dobbs* activated women voters in a way that showed no signs of abating in the immediate aftermath of the ruling. State elections around the country, for example in Wisconsin, would demonstrate how deeply motivated a broad swath of female voters had become to push back hard against the broader social-conservative attempted takeover of America. "One year after the Supreme Court ended the constitutional right to abortion, the issue reverberates almost as strongly as it did in the days immediately following the decision," Dan Balz wrote in *The Washington Post* in June 2023. "Politically, the landscape has been altered significantly, with little reversal in sight."

It was incumbent on the Democrats, from President Biden on down, to put the courts on the ballot in 2024, as a galvanizing and unifying issue for Democrats, and to persuade independents. Young people—a voting cohort Biden was struggling with—disapprove of the Supreme Court by 73 percent according to a Quinnipiac University poll in March 2024. As president, Trump could appoint two young replacements for Justices Alito and Thomas, who are in their seventies and thought to be ready for retirement. Many of the great issues in the campaign from abortion to gun control, from environmental regulation to voting rights, are all implicit in the question, "Whose side is the Supreme Court on?" A president and his cabinet have wide authority to affect abortion-related policy through executive action, and Trump will be beholden to the ever more radical anti-abortion movement. At stake, too, are dozens of federal appellate judgeships. It's critical that the Federalist Society's hold on these appointments be broken.

Yet going into the 2024 national elections, the possibility remained that Republicans could regain control of both houses of Congress and seek to further curtail women's rights. "If you don't know already, if Republicans win control of the House and Senate in 2024, they are going to pass a national abortion ban," Senator Chris Murphy of Connecticut, a Democrat, said in July 2023. "It's 100 percent certain. Just so we're clear about the stakes." So much for the transparently disingenuous argument, flogged for years by antichoice activists, that their effort to roll back *Roe* was all about states' rights.

*Dobbs* was really the beginning of the damage the Thomas Court was intent on inflicting on the country. In the following term, the Supreme Court ruled that a wedding website designer could discriminate against a gay couple because a Colorado law that prohibited her from doing so allegedly violated her First Amendment rights. Just a few days before the decision came down, it was revealed that the web designer had never been asked to design a site by anyone. The case was a right-wing scam. Worse still, Gorsuch's majority opinion said that religious speech has historically occupied a preferred position in American society and is therefore untouchable. But religious speech in fact has been regulated alongside other forms of speech since the founding. The court also ruled that affirmative action policies in publicly funded universities are unconstitutional. In his concurring opinion, Thomas argued that the Equal Protection Clause, the basis for affirmative action programs, had always been intended to be race-blind. Thomas had his history backward: Racial discrimination was prohibited, but actions intended to benefit Black Americans, such as affirmative action, were always permitted.

As of this writing, the court is expected to issue major rulings in 2024 that could further the long-term right-wing agenda of undermining government regulatory authority, a major Federalist Society goal. A case involving the Securities and Exchange Commission could lead the Thomas Court justices to hamstring the SEC and other federal agencies by placing restrictions on their enforcement activities. Similarly, the court appeared to have the Consumer Financial Protection Bureau in its crosshairs. The agency, established after the 2008 financial crisis, has been an effective advocate for consumers, monitoring the activities of credit rating agencies, debt collectors, and lenders, and achieving billions of dollars of restitution and canceled debts. The right-wing-dominated Fifth Circuit Court of Appeals took action against the agency in 2022, citing its unusual funding mechanism, through the Federal Reserve System, and the Thomas Court majority looks likely to take action to further undermine the consumer watchdog agency, once again backing elite corporate interests.

The perversity of the doctrine of originalism will be on vivid display with Clarence Thomas's incendiary rationale on gun regulation leading to more activity on gun rights. Thomas, infamously, articulated his new standard writing for the conservative majority in the 2022 case *New York State Rifle & Pistol Association v. Bruen,* declaring, "The government must demonstrate that the regulation is consistent with the Nation's historical tradition." As *Politico* noted, highlighting the obtuseness of the Thomas formulation, "How do 18th century traditions apply to 21st century conundrums involving modern technology and sensibilities? What would James Madison's generation have thought about 'ghost guns,' a type of homemade, sometimes 3D-printed firearm?"

In 2024 the Supreme Court was expected to take up another ruling from the right-wing Fifth Circuit, on *U.S. v. Rahimi,* this one invalidating a federal law denying any individual with a restraining order for domestic violence from legally possessing a firearm. Improbably enough, the Fifth Circuit ruled that even individuals so dangerous as to have been hit with a restraining order for domestic violence should be legally entitled to guns. As the Brennan Center succinctly pointed out, "Domestic abusers are among the last people in the world who should be carrying guns: women are five times more likely to die in a domestic violence situation if a gun is present."

In pushing back the clock, originalism turns back progress. In *New York State Rifle & Pistol Association v. Bruen,* in 2022, the Thomas Court created out of thin air a new "standard" for evaluating the constitutionality of gun control laws. The court held that only laws "consistent with the Nation's historical tradition of firearm regulation" will be deemed constitutional. As Natalie Nanasi of Southern Methodist Law School wrote in *Wake Forest Law Review,* "The Fifth Circuit's decision in Rahimi highlights the unworkability of the *Bruen* test. Women's rights were virtually nonexistent when the Second Amendment was ratified. Domestic violence was tolerated, and it was not until nearly 200 years later that protective order statutes were enacted across the United States. Looking to the past to justify modern day gun safety laws gravely threatens women's rights and safety." Hard to find a more succinct demonstration of the danger of originalism.

The court will also return to the issue of abortion rights in a case involving the federal government's approval of mifepristone, widely and safely used for medication abortions. A new right-wing organization formed as an umbrella group of anti-abortion organizations, the Alliance for Hippocratic Medicine, seemed to be a pop-up just to challenge the drug's use. The group was secretly funded by Leonard Leo through a number of pass-through entities in his empire. The money trail began with the Catholic Association Foundation, which it says "engages on issues that are compelling based on the teachings of the church," and pursues antiabortion efforts as a top priority. Leo has sat on the CAF board and funded the organization. CAF in turn funded the American Association of Pro-Life Obstetricians and Gynecologists, which is a member of the Alliance for Hippocratic Oath. Once again, Leo's shell game defeated transparency.

In bringing the case in Amarillo, Texas, the alliance was judge shopping: They knew the judge on the case would be Matthew Kacsmaryk, a Trump appointee and a former counsel of the conservative First Liberty Institute, which also has financial ties to Leo. Kacsmaryk has been a stalwart of the Federalist Society since law school and founded a lawyers chapter in Fort Worth. He ruled that the FDA wrongly approved mifepristone and under his ruling its use was banned. The case is under Supreme

Court review at this writing. During oral arguments, at least two justices, Alito and Thomas, appeared to entertain the idea that an antiobscenity law from 1873 could be used to ban abortion. Antiabortion zealots were advocating behind the scenes that a second Trump administration could ban abortion without the approval of Congress by invoking the Comstock Act.

Polls show the public does not trust the court to rule impartially in cases involving former President Trump. In one Trump case, the Supreme Court ruled unanimously that Colorado cannot disqualify Trump from the ballot under the Fourteenth Amendment's insurrection ban, even though the plain text of the amendment seemed to require it. Critics pointed out that the originalists on the court had to do backflips to reach their desired result.

In February 2024, the court took up the Trump argument that the Constitution prohibits any prosecution of a former president for "official acts" he engaged in while in office. Lower courts had already nixed the outlandish "immunity" argument. Rather than deferring to the lower courts, the justices in effect delayed the prosecution for about five months, meaning that his trial could be delayed until after the November election. The court could have moved much faster if it wanted to.

Leonard Leo's victory on rolling back women's rights led him to begin plotting new conquests. In 2022, the Chicago financier and antiabortion activist Barre Seid granted Leo $1.6 billion— yes, you read that right—to fund a now sprawling network of nonprofits that, beyond transforming the judiciary, would extend into Republican efforts to suppress the votes of minority populations and unleash broadsides against big corporations for pushing environmentally and socially responsible policies. "The idea behind the network and the enterprise we built is to roll back liberal dominance in many important sectors of American life," Leo told *The New York Times* in an unusually candid October 2022 interview. "I had a couple of decades or more of experience rolling back liberal dominance in the legal culture, and I thought it was time to take the lessons learned from that and see whether there was a way to roll back liberal dominance in other areas of American culture, policy and political life."

Leo had been focused for years—decades—primarily on the goal of overturning *Roe,* but his focus had shifted over the years to include a mounting commitment to enact major changes in a variety of issues, both on business and social issues. As his level of personal compensation climbed dramatically, Leo seemed to grow more bold, some might argue more reckless, and served notice that he would do his best to keep pushing the Supreme Court justices he had installed to enact sweeping change, as dramatic as possible and as quickly as possible. As Cardozo Law School professor Kate Shaw told ABC News: "The five most conservative members of the court are interested in a maximalist strategy, basically to move the law as far and as fast as possible."

## CHAPTER 21

# REAL REFORM STARTS WITH EXPANDING THE SUPREME COURT

President Joe Biden's April 2021 announcement that he'd issued Executive Order 14023 establishing a Presidential Commission on the Supreme Court of the United States, "comprised of a bipartisan group of experts on the Court and Court reform debate," reverberated widely at the time as a major move expected to lead to decisive action. In a telling sign of fear on the right, the ultraconservative *Wall Street Journal* editorial page immediately branded the whole exercise as suspect, wildly speculating that the panel of experts being formed was "better understood as the commission on packing the Supreme Court." Continued the *Journal,* "The White House is trying to make this seem like routine political business, but don't be fooled."

Such were the expectations set in motion of major action. However, as soon became apparent, the commission included respected names across the political spectrum, like Laurence Tribe of Harvard, one of the most influential voices in the country and a sharp critic of the Thomas Court, but failed to include prominent voices calling for an expansion of the court, most notably former Kennedy clerk Daniel Epps, coauthor—with Vanderbilt law professor Ganesh Sitaraman—of a widely cited 2018 plan to expand the court to fifteen justices.

As Epps himself observed in a *Washington Post* column on July 15, 2021, "Expectations that Democrats will be able to substantially reform the Supreme Court—perhaps by adding new members—have nosedived recently." So much for the feverish warnings of the *Journal.* "Even before President Biden's blue-ribbon Supreme Court commission met for the first time," Epps continued, "progressives were lamenting that its generally moderate and bipartisan members were unlikely to endorse bold changes to the court's structure. And even if they did, major reforms appear politically impossible with Democrats' extraordinarily narrow advantage in the Senate. So court-packing is almost certainly off the table, as most likely are term limits for justices. But that doesn't mean Supreme Court reform is dead."

There is nothing sacrosanct about the current complement of nine justices on the Supreme Court. When the Supreme Court was first established, by the Judiciary Act of 1789, the number stood at six. Much wrangling ensued. President John Adams, at the end of his term, did what he could to undermine his successor, Thomas Jefferson, by pushing through another Judiciary Act that set the number of justices at five. Under Jefferson the number of justices went from five to six—and then to seven. By 1837, under Andrew Jackson, the number was up to nine—briefly up to ten under Abraham Lincoln—but since 1869 has stood steady at nine justices.

President Franklin Roosevelt pushed hard to change that number in 1937. Irate over the conservative Supreme Court's rulings pushing back against his sweeping New Deal programs, Roosevelt set out on a bold plan to add justices to the court. In a March 1937 Fireside Chat radio address to the nation, Roosevelt sought to build support for legislation to expand the court, insisting, "This plan of mine is not attacking of the Court. It seeks to restore the Court to its rightful and historic place in our system." Even many Democrats were cool to FDR's plan, which struck them as a power grab, but openings on the court soon shifted the dynamic. In short: The system worked. Roosevelt, who had no Supreme Court openings to fill in his first term, would have five openings in his second term, from January 1937 to January 1941—including Hugo Black, nominated and confirmed in August 1937, and Felix Frankfurter, nominated and confirmed in January 1939.

As Biden's Supreme Court Commission wrote in its final report,

> Many observers—at the time and since—charged Roosevelt with overreaching. . . . Other commentators contend, however, that the plan in fact achieved some of its objectives. The Supreme Court's constitutional doctrine did undergo changes in 1937, and certain of those changes proved enduring. That spring, the Court began upholding major pieces of New Deal legislation, despite challenges that the statutes exceeded Congress's Article I powers—in particular, the commerce power and the taxing and spending power. Roosevelt did not succeed in "packing" the Court, but neither did he have to abandon his New Deal agenda.

No such natural correction looms now. To address the stench of corruption and abuse of power now emanating from the high court by adding more justices now would require only a simple majority vote in both houses of Congress. However, in 2021, Democrats' hold on the Senate was indeed narrow—with in effect a 50-50 split, and Democrats only gaining control through Vice President Harris's tiebreaker vote. In the House, Democrats held 222 seats to 215 for the Republicans. With such narrow margins, major reform legislation was a nonstarter.

A few lawmakers did nevertheless move forward with legislation. Congressman Hank Johnson introduced House Resolution 2584, the Judiciary Act of 2021, in April 2021, which called for the Supreme Court to be expanded to thirteen justices. Ro Khanna of California, a creative thinker, introduced a House resolution in August 2021 calling for a fundamental shift in how justices are appointed, including eighteen-year term limits for Supreme Court justices and a stipulation that presidents are required "to appoint a Supreme Court Justice every two years." If the number of justices grew to more than nine, longer tenured justices would lose their votes.

Sheldon Whitehouse introduced a Senate bill in February 2023, focused on the sorry state of Supreme Court ethics. The Whitehouse bill sought to "adopt a code of conduct for Justices and establish procedures to receive and investigate complaints of judicial misconduct," and to "adopt rules governing the disclosure of gifts, travel, and income received by the Justices and law clerks that are at least as rigorous as the House and Senate disclosure rules." It also sought to "establish procedural rules requiring each party or amicus to disclose any gift, income, or reimbursement provided to Justices."

Senator Chris Murphy of Connecticut also introduced a Supreme Court reform bill in February 2023, the Supreme Court Ethics Act, which called for a code of conduct for Supreme Court justices and sought to establish a mechanism to investigate complaints and offer a yearly report on the result of those investigations.

In May 2023, Senator Ed Markey reintroduced the Judicial Act of 2023, joined by Senators Tina Smith and Elizabeth Warren, and Representatives Hank Johnson, Jerrold Nadler, Cori Bush, and Adam Schiff, which again called for expanding the Supreme Court to thirteen. "Congress can determine the size of the Supreme Court; it has already added and removed seats on the Court seven times throughout its history," the sponsors noted. "At a time when the American people's confidence in the nation's highest court has fallen to a record low and Congressional Republicans have already employed their far-right judicial playbook by disregarding norms and precedent in the confirmations process, Congress must take action by once again expanding the Court."

Biden's Commission on the Supreme Court failed to make the kind of splash many had hoped for when it was first announced, but its final report, issued in December 2021, contributed to the larger tide moving against the Thomas Court. Accountability could not be put off indefinitely, it was clear. As *The Washington Post* wrote at the time, "A bipartisan panel of legal scholars examining possible changes to the Supreme Court voted unanimously ... to submit to President Biden its final report, which describes public support for imposing term limits but 'profound disagreement' about adding justices."

The report itself veered toward generalizations, but in its own way offered devastating support for the need for change. "Calls for and by Democrats to expand the size of the Court first appeared in substantial numbers upon the announcement of his retirement by Justice Kennedy, who had long been seen as the median Justice on a divided Court, and during the subsequent controversial nomination process of Justice Kavanaugh," one section read.

These calls increased in late 2020 when Senate Republicans confirmed Justice Barrett, with Democrats arguing that Republicans had contradicted their own prior arguments that Justices should not be confirmed in close proximity to a presidential election. According to news accounts, "(a)s soon as it became clear that the Republican-controlled Senate would almost certainly confirm Judge Amy Coney Barrett, creating a 6–3 conservative majority on the court," a number of Democrats "argued that if Democrats won in November, they should seriously consider increasing the number of jus-

tices." Public discussion of Court expansion surged notice-
ably between 2019 and 2020. In 2020, more than 400 articles
appeared in the *New York Times, Wall Street Journal, Washington Post,* and *USA Today* invoking the term "Court packing"
in the context of the Supreme Court in contrast to approxi-
mately 100 articles in 2019.

Law professor Laurence Tribe and retired U.S. district judge
Nancy Gertner, who both sat on that Supreme Court Commission,
came around to the view that drastic measures were urgently
necessary to expunge the stench. "[T]he anti-democratic, anti-
egalitarian direction of this court's decisions about matters such
as voting rights, gerrymandering and the corrupting effects of
dark money . . . haven't been just wrong; they put the court—
and, more important, our entire system of government—on a
one-way trip from a defective but still hopeful democracy toward
a system in which the few corruptly govern the many, something
between autocracy and oligarchy," the two wrote in a December
2021 *Washington Post* opinion article. "Instead of serving as a
guardrail against going over that cliff, our Supreme Court has
become an all-too-willing accomplice in that disaster. Worse,
measures the court has enabled will fundamentally change the
court and the law for decades. They operate to entrench the
power of one political party: constricting the vote, denying fair
access to the ballot to people of color and other minorities, and
allowing legislative district lines to be drawn that exacerbate
demographic differences."

In November 2023, the Supreme Court made news by belatedly announcing a code of conduct governing the ethics of its
members, a clear attempt to respond to mounting public outrage, but any PR value the announcement might have garnered
was undermined by the glaring lack of any actual mechanism
for enforcement of the vaunted new code. The toothless code of
conduct was a step in the right direction, even fierce critics of

the Thomas Court could agree, but a small step that had to be followed by many others, not the kind of genuine shift that would turbocharge the need for more action.

The court issued a statement explaining, with deep condescension, that the code was being put forward by the court to "dispel" what the statement called any "misunderstanding" by the public about the allegedly high standards of conduct of the court. Actually, the problem was that the public understood, not that it misunderstood, what was going on.

For the record, the Supreme Court did, theoretically at least, agree to be bound by a requirement, for example under "Canon 2: A Justice Should Avoid Impropriety and the Appearance of Impropriety in All Activities," including that of B, "Outside Influence," which spelled out, "A Justice should not allow family, social, political, financial, or other relationships to influence official conduct or judgment. A Justice should neither knowingly lend the prestige of the judicial office to advance the private interests of the Justice or others nor knowingly convey or permit others to convey the impression that they are in a special position to influence the Justice."

This provision, if adhered to even partially, would have completely shut down the Thomas family business, a lucrative influence operation, in no time—but there were no immediate indications of any actual change in because the provision relies on self-enforcement.

Still, the code if nothing else amounted to a somewhat ambitious cataloguing of aspirational virtue, reading at times almost like the Boy Scout Handbook, for example in this provision in the "Responsibilities" section: "A Justice should be patient, dignified, respectful, and courteous to all individuals with whom the Justice deals in an official capacity."

Taken on a deeper level, the markers put down in the document did in fact lend ammunition to critics of the court seeking, for example, to push justices to recuse themselves in cases of egregious conflict of interest—as in Justice Clarence Thomas participating in any Supreme Court decision relating to the January 6 attempted insurrection in which his own wife was an acknowledged co-conspirator.

Here was the language the Supreme Court unveiled: "A Justice should disqualify himself or herself in a proceeding in which the Justice's impartiality might reasonably be questioned, that is, where an unbiased and reasonable person who is aware of all relevant circumstances would doubt that the Justice could fairly discharge his or her duties."

For example, if: "The Justice or the Justice's spouse, or a person related to either within the third degree of relationship, or the spouse of such person, is known by the Justice: (i) to be a party to the proceeding, or an officer, director, or trustee of a party; (ii) to be acting as a lawyer in the proceeding; (iii) to have an interest that could be substantially affected by the outcome of the proceeding; or (iv) likely to be a material witness in the proceeding."

Given such language, *Politico* made a point on many minds when it noted, in its news article announcing the code, "In a somewhat surprising development, no justice noted any opposition or dissent to the code, including Justices Clarence Thomas, who has faced the brunt of allegations over questionable ethics practices, and Samuel Alito, who has publicly argued against congressional proposals to impose an ethics code on the court."

Most of the reaction to the Supreme Court's code of conduct ran toward mockery of the limitations of the self-enforced code of conduct, but in a *New Republic* commentary, Simon Lazarus argued that seen in the broader context of the ongoing wars over the Supreme Court's lack of legitimacy and accountability, this small dose of self-surrender amounted to a valuable tool for critics.

"For these life-tenured justices, who for decades had spurned a code of conduct as unnecessary, useless, and unworkable, this

abrupt 180-degree about-face was grudging surrender to reformers' superior political momentum," Lazarus wrote.

> The justices' embrace of this code reflects—indeed, the Pre-
> amble explicitly acknowledges—their need to persuade the
> electorate that they are bound by explicit and meaningful eth-
> ical rules. Key provisions of their code measure up to those
> criteria. However, critics have focused on weasel words—in
> the code and the unsigned "Commentary" that follows it. . . .
> The overriding goal of reformers must be to maintain the
> political momentum that got them this win, in order to maxi-
> mize, preserve, and build on its terms. Gearing up for the bat-
> tles ahead means establishing a frame that highlights the best
> (not the worst) reasonable interpretation of the new code, to
> hold the justices to those robust standards, deter evasion and
> backsliding, and lay the groundwork for further advances.
> Because meaningful further advances *are* attainable.

———

The Supreme Court has long been far too drunk on its own power
ever to let plunging poll numbers or widespread condemnation
impel them to pursue genuine reform. "They don't give a damn,"
Larry Sabato, director of the Center for Politics at the University
of Virginia, said. "It doesn't make any difference. They could go
down to 5 percent, and they'd simply hire more guards. They'd
probably never be seen in Washington. They'd be in some Chalet
making the decisions. They don't care. They just don't care."

John Roberts demonstrated when he first became chief justice what an actual commitment to action looks like. He stated at
the time that there was a "crisis" around the court that required
urgent measures. In his January 1, 2007, year-end report he wrote
movingly of a problem that, Roberts felt, "has now reached the

level of a constitutional crisis that threatens to undermine the strength and independence of the federal judiciary." A constitutional crisis! Now that's urgency. What was the issue? "I am talking," Roberts continued, rattling the tin cup, "about the failure to raise judicial pay." And who could not feel sympathy for these deeply deprived men and women in black robes. Consider that as chief justice, Roberts in 2007 pulled in only a paltry $212,100 in salary.

Roberts, alas, has failed to tackle ethics reform with anything like that sense of urgency.

In fact, Roberts, who chairs the Judicial Conference of the United States, the body that sets ethics policy for every court below the Supreme Court, has been an obstacle for that body of judges to take up the question of an ethics code for the Supreme Court, observers say. Judges in the conference are concerned especially about what impact Thomas's misbehavior will have on public perceptions of the court and have grappled with whether to say or do anything about it. Roberts is likely shielding Thomas from further scrutiny but he also may have personal motivation for that stand. His wife, Jane Sullivan Roberts, made a career change two years after her husband joined the court rather than risking ethical questions, agreeing that it would be "awkward to be practicing law in the firm." Instead, she has worked since then as a top-level legal recruiter—and done very well, according to information revealed in a whistleblower complaint. Jane Sullivan Roberts reportedly earned more than $10 million in compensation from 2007 to 2014, including from firms with cases before the Supreme Court, though she keeps most of her work confidential.

"When I found out that the spouse of the Chief Justice was soliciting business from law firms, I knew immediately that it was wrong," Kendal Price, the whistleblower, who worked at the same recruiting firm as Roberts, told *Business Insider.* "During the time I was there, I was discouraged from ever raising the issue. And I realized that even the law firms who were Jane's clients had nowhere to go. They were being asked by the spouse of the Chief Justice for business worth hundreds of thousands of dollars, and there was no one to complain to. Most of these firms were likely appearing or seeking to appear before the Supreme Court. It's natural that they'd do anything they felt was necessary to be competitive."

The chief justice tossed a match onto gasoline when he spurned a request from Senate Judiciary Committee chairman Dick Durbin to appear before the committee in May 2023 to discuss Supreme Court ethics. "Testimony before the Senate Judiciary Committee by the Chief Justice of the United States is exceedingly rare as one might expect," Roberts wrote Durbin in declining the request. Yes, a fair point. Not as rare, however, as the full-fledged crisis of legitimacy raging for the Supreme Court in the 2020s. Roberts, apparently not realizing how ridiculous his duck-and-cover move looked, included with his letter to Durbin a "Statement on Ethics Principles and Practices," and added that all the current justices "subscribe"—by which he meant not that they are bound to comply, but "subscribe" in a lofty, theoretical sense.

Roberts would eventually buy himself a little time with the code of conduct announced later in 2023, but too much would be at stake in 2024 for public pressure for reform to abate or recede. Roberts can and will be pushed to do much, much better, and sooner or later it will dawn on him that history is poised to judge his tenure on the court very, very harshly. He looks like a pawn, a prop, a powerless puppet of the Federalist Society machine who has little real influence over the Thomas Court. He looks like a once proud figure whose announced intention at least to shepherd through some greater accountability for Supreme Court justices appeared, as of early 2024, to amount to a joke—a joke on Roberts, and a joke on the American people.

As weird and confusing as so much of the drama surrounding the corrupt Thomas Court was to many Americans, the conditions were ripe in 2024 for a profound and vigorous public accounting of the crimes of this court and of the urgent need to turn this existential crisis into an opportunity. Yes, the court can be saved, the essential third pillar of the U.S. system of government can, possibly, be renovated thoroughly enough to retain its structural integrity, halting the rapid erosion of viability recent years have brought. But that effort will require an end to numb sleepwalking and passivity, as if the train wreck that is the American judicial system were merely a roadside accident for rubberneckers to glimpse with wide eyes on their way past and nothing more.

Bold action is required, starting with expanding the court. Let's face it, the Supreme Court's legitimacy cannot be saved by baby steps, the members of the Thomas Court have debased themselves and the institution far too much for that. The stench of absolute power corrupting absolutely permeates. The inexorable downward slide of public perceptions of the court can only be halted by taking firm steps to counteract the packing of the courts with illegitimate justices.

I advocate a plan to add three new justices to bring the court from its current complement of nine to an even dozen, and I submit that having an even number on the court would be a clear improvement. Rather than having many key decisions rendered by a narrow, one-vote margin, consensus would have to be sought until the justices could cobble together seven votes in favor, versus five opposed. There might be more deliberating. There might be more arguments. All of that would do wonders in helping alter the perceptions of a general public that sees the court now as a political mechanism willing to force major change on the country on 5–4 votes.

Altering the makeup of the court would be a major step, and it's not one I advocate lightly. I watched with horror and fascination as the machine that built up Clarence Thomas and tried to knock down Bill Clinton—a machine of which I was a part—

mutated and grew massively into some freakish caricature of how it started, a movement founded on malice, a wrecking ball seeking to bring down what it claimed to see as the dastardly detritus of liberal overreach. Hostility and power lust fueled the drive to pack the court, and along the way collegiality and mutual respect bit the dust. It means nothing that Clarence Thomas is said to be friendly with liberal colleagues. He can afford to be friendly. He's vanquished all foes and achieved untold power and influence and done it while helping to steer the court in the direction of wreaking havoc with democratic ideals and imperiling the future of the country.

It took decades of single-minded organizing and dirty deals for a small group of right-wing religious conservatives to pack the court. It may take decades to restore the dignity of the high court and begin to rehabilitate its terrible image with the public as an openly political body enforcing its will on a population that broadly disagrees with its radical worldview. I have long been ambivalent about calls to expand the court; it's an admittedly dramatic step. But events have forced the idea toward the mainstream as an increasingly unavoidable step to respond to what amounts to a national emergency.

As constitutional law professor Kermit Roosevelt III, who sat on President Biden's Supreme Court Commission, was already framing the issue in a December 2021 *Time* magazine article, "I have always viewed expansion with great skepticism, as a last resort, the fire axe in the glass case on the wall. But we may well be at the point of breaking that glass now. Our constitutional system has produced a playing field that tilts toward the minority. This is not because wise Framers wanted it that way—they didn't foresee political parties at all. . . . Absent some decisive action, we could be looking at generations of minority control." Those words were written before the *Dobbs* decision—and Justice Thomas's clear warning that the Thomas Court would roll back freedoms across the board, including for gays and even couples using contraception.

The Supreme Court as it is now constituted represents the triumph of backroom schemers and power brokers over the open and sometimes chaotic work of actual democracy getting regular voters involved and having a say. How democratic does this sound? In seven of the last eight presidential elections, more people voted for Democrats than Republicans, and in the Senate, Democrats represent 40 million more people than Republicans, but, astonishingly enough, sixteen of the last twenty-one Supreme Court justices have been appointed by Republicans. Five of twenty-one have been appointed by Democrats. That's a travesty and it's unhealthy for democracy.

"When a bully steals your lunch money in the schoolyard, you have to do something about it, or else the bully will come back over and over again," says Senator Ed Markey, cosponsor of a bill to expand the court. "So we're in this fight, and we're going to reclaim these seats. We're not going to allow the bully to win."

It's time for Democrats to move beyond merely calling out the corruption of the Thomas Court to actively making a public case for court expansion and other serious measures. If the situation is as bad as we keep saying, or even half as bad, then action to halt or reverse the insidious degradation of the court is not only desirable, it's essential. It's not enough to be right, it's important to show you're fighting for what's right. Restoring some long-term viability to the court won't be easy, but it's the right thing to do.

———

Term limits for Supreme Court justices are also urgently needed—a move that would have the support of about two-thirds of the population, according to repeated public polling.

For example, a 2023 poll by the University of Massachusetts Amherst found that 65 percent of those polled favored Supreme Court term limits. A 2022 Associated Press–NORC Center for Public Affairs Research poll found 67 percent support for limiting Supreme Court terms, including a clear majority of Republicans (57 percent) and an overwhelming 82 percent of Democrats.

Lifetime appointments to the Supreme Court are an unsustainable anachronism. Consider that in October 1991, when Clarence Thomas joined the Supreme Court, the Soviet Union still existed. The United States was still engaged in a world-defining Cold War with the "Evil Empire." Soon after Thomas was sworn in, the Soviet Union collapsed. No one in 1991 had ever heard of the World Wide Web, because it only came into existence that year. Electric cars and space travel by anyone other than governments were science fiction. Isaac Asimov, Anthony Perkins, and Marlene Dietrich were all still alive. It was, in short, an unimaginably long time ago, culturally speaking, and yet all these years later, Clarence Thomas is still there, on the high court, wielding unchecked power over the rest of us.

No man or woman should have that much power. Advances in medicine and biotechnology have helped push the human lifespan far past what anyone could have imagined when lifetime posts on the Supreme Court were originally conceived. The average American life expectancy had reached 79.11 years by 2023, compared to 78.8 a decade earlier, 77.4 twenty years earlier—and 75.5 the year Thomas was approved. In the 1780s, when the Judiciary Act established the United States Supreme Court, average life expectancy in the United States was all of thirty-six. Let me repeat that: People could expect, on average, to live to the ripe old age of thirty-six. Not only has the time come for term limits to be imposed on Supreme Court justices, providing in effect an expiration date for their time on the bench, a strong case can be made that they need to be retroactive.

What would it take to add more justices or impose term limits? Given the current alignment of the Thomas Court with the Republican Party, voters would have to reject the monomaniacal power grab of Leonard Leo and his machine, reject the Christian Nationalism that has taken over the Republican Party, and elect Democrats in large numbers. To pass major judicial reform legislation, Democrats would need the White House and both houses of Congress and the Supreme Court itself on the 2024 ballot. "Having a margin of a seat or two isn't going to do it," Larry Sabato noted. "You'd have to have a landslide margin." That might never come again, Sabato warns. Then again, given the way power-mad Republicans have played with fire in recent years, growing ever more corrupt and unresponsive to the priorities of the majority of voters, a backlash could be inevitable.

# CHAPTER 22

# THE CONTINUING DANGER OF GINNI THOMAS

Like millions of others, I found the March 2022 banner headline stunning—but not *that* stunning. I was in my office in Washington when a friend texted me the bombshell news that *Washington Post* reporter Bob Woodward, the man who helped bring down Nixon, had another stop-the-presses exclusive: Ginni Thomas, wife of Supreme Court Justice Clarence Thomas, had been caught red-handed by January 6 investigators repeatedly texting Trump White House chief of staff Mark Meadows in late 2020 to foment insurrection. The texts were soaked through and through in hundred-proof QAnon madness, citing feverish Q conspiracy theories, but they were also shockingly direct, even mentioning her "best friend" (her husband, she later revealed) in a reference not lost on Meadows. These were not suggestions. They were a blunt reminder of how Washington power worked. The wife and thought partner of a Supreme Court justice, a well-connected activist in her own right, was pushing to illegally void the results of the November 2020 presidential election and throw the country into full-fledged constitutional crisis.

"Help This Great President stand firm, Mark!!!" Thomas had texted Meadows. "You are the leader, with him, who is standing for America's constitutional governance at the precipice. The majority knows Biden and the Left is attempting the greatest Heist of our History."

This was the Ginni Thomas I'd known for years, unhinged and proud.

To start with the first of the twenty-nine Ginni Thomas texts to Meadows, on November 5, 2020, she forwarded a YouTube link that was full nutty conspiracy theory, titled, "TRUMP STING w CIA Director Steve Pieczenik, The Biggest Election Story in History, QFS-BLOCKCHAIN." Pieczenik (spoiler alert: not actually "CIA Director") was best known up to then for pushing the conspiracy theory that the Sandy Hook Elementary School massacre, gruesomely documented, was actually a "false flag" operation to build support for gun control. Ginni Thomas was burbling to Meadows in the same text about how "watermarked ballots" in twelve states "have been part of a huge Trump & military white hat sting operation in 12 key battleground states where 20,000+ natl guard were deployed; Biden crime family & ballot fraud co-conspirators (elected officials, bureaucrats, social media censorship mongers, fake stream media reporters, etc) are being arrested & detained for ballot fraud right now & over coming days, & will be living in barges off GITMO to face military tribunals for sedition." Whether she was typing out this torrent of Q-infused verbiage, or had copied-and-pasted, the opening of the text is unmistakably Ginni Thomas: "I hope this is true," wrote the wife of a Supreme Court justice.

Scrolling through the article on my phone, I felt a deep and familiar dread. The bell was tolling for Ginni Thomas, the time had finally come for her to be forced to meet the consequences of her reckless and dangerous behavior, but I knew even then that if she somehow slipped away from accountability, she would ultimately become an even more dangerous figure.

Ginni Thomas openly supported insurrection, even if her language was a little less direct and a lot more colorful. On November 6, at 10:49 in the morning, she wrote Meadows a straightforward directive, "Do not concede." Followed by the hallucinatory "It takes time for the army who is gathering for his back," presumably some kind of reference to Isaiah's prophecy of armies gathering to overthrow Babylon, not far from gushing about the coming Rapture when the world will end and all good evangelical Christians will have their moment and everyone else can basically go to hell.

On November 10, having apparently exercised some rare self-discipline in waiting a few days to reach out and lobby the chief of staff some more, she wrote Meadows: "Mark, I wanted to text you and tell you for days you are in my prayers!! I hear fr Nancy Schulze you are working though??" (That would be Thomas friend and associate Nancy Schulze, cochair of the Congressional Prayer Caucus Wives Council and a member of the Thomas-aligned Council for National Policy.)

The text continued: "Listen to Rush, Mark Steyn, [Dan] Bongino, Cleta [Mitchell] and know the grassroots wants Truth to prevail over Lies!!!?????? Help This Great President stand firm, Mark!!! The Left tastes their power!!! ???? You are the leader, with him, who is standing for America's constitutional governance at the precipice. The majority knows Biden and the Left is attempting the greatest Heist of our History."

Given that Trump lost the popular vote to Biden in 2020 by more than seven million votes, nearly 5 percent of the total, it's a little hard to know what "majority" Ginni Thomas imagined she was talking about, and probably the less said about her choices in punctuation and capitalization, rendered verbatim, the better.

Here was Meadows's reply: "I will stand firm. We will fight

until there is no fight left. Our country is too precious to give up on. Thanks for all you do."

And here, verbatim, was Thomas's response: "Tearing up and praying for you guys!!!!!???????????????? So proud to know you!!??????"

And after 10 p.m. the night of November 10, she fulminated to Meadows about how "House and Senate guys are pathetic too . . . only 4 GOP House members seen out in street rallies with grass-roots." This from the wife of a Supreme Court justice who herself would attend the January 6 "Stop the Steal" rally, though she claimed, without proof, to have "got cold and left." Cold, perhaps, but cold feet never. Not Ginni Thomas.

In particular, a text from Connie Hair that Ginni Thomas forwarded to Mark Meadows on November 14 at 5:26 a.m. jumped out: "The most important thing you can realize right now is that there are no rules in war," read the inflammatory text. "You destroy your enemy's ability to fight. This is what is happening right now—the war is psychological. PSYOP. It's what I did in the military."

Going back to the Powell Memo, the fevered right generated much of its energy from fantasies about the power of the left, fantasies that were laughably at odds with the reality of a splintered, factionalized, easily distracted, often self-defeating leftist movement seemingly headed in a hundred different directions all at once. Donald Trump had lost by millions of votes, even Fox News had called Arizona for Biden early, and some revivalist tent undercurrent in his following wanted to turn this into Judgment Day.

Winning the election because more people supported you amounted somehow to a "psychological operation"? Trying too hard to understand the random ricocheting of such minds was enough to give anyone a headache, but then the startling facts hit home: These were words approved of and endorsed by Ginni Thomas, wife of a Supreme Court justice, close friends with Connie Hair, who was then chief of staff to House Freedom Caucus stalwart Louie Gohmert, and the email came from Hair herself. Thomas forwarded it to Meadows on November 14 at 5:26 a.m.

Keep in mind, when Hair references her background in "PSYOPS," she's going back to the same general period of time she was doing nude shower scenes with Pia Zadora, while complaining about how liberal Hollywood was harming U.S. culture. As Hair's Louisiana Freedom Caucus State Chair bio reads, "Connie served in the United States Army Reserve in psychological warfare (PSYOP) for eight years, doing double duty while she worked at Paramount Pictures in network television at the Hollywood studios. Seeing firsthand the destructive force the entertainment industry has become to America's culture, she abruptly left Hollywood to become fully involved in what was a hobby at the time—politics—to see what could be done about ending socialist Marxism's degrading influence on the nation's ability to self-govern."

Refreshing of Hair to admit that politics was "a hobby" to her. Her text in November 2020, forwarded by Ginni Thomas to Mark Meadows as a call to action, continued in the same tone of high dudgeon, nursing imagined grievance to justify extreme action: "They try to break our will to fight through demoralization, discouragement, division, chaos and gaslighting."

The words can't be dismissed given the fact they were shaping Mark Meadows's thinking at that crucial hour for democracy. "It is fake, fraud and if people would take a deep breath and look at things through that filter we will see this through and win," Hair wrote and Ginni Thomas forwarded. "The Constitution is on our side and it is worth fighting for. I believe in it. Our Founders and even those facing Omaha Beach have done MUCH more than we have since Election Day. I would suggest we all think in those terms because if we don't, and we allow this massive fraud to stand, we've lost our country anyway."

Lest anyone dismiss such inflammatory rhetoric as harmless,

consider that on January 1, 2021, Hair's boss Gohmert would echo the very same language, telling Newsmax that honoring the results of the election would represent "the end of our republic, the end of the experiment in self-government," and add: "The ruling would be that you got to go to the streets and be as violent as Antifa."

Those were his words, days before January 6, and he was part of a web connecting Ginni Thomas and Clarence Thomas to the White House. If that collusion doesn't strike you as a four-alarm fire for democracy, what does?

As Congresswoman Sheila Jackson Lee later said during a December 2022 House Judiciary Committee hearing on the politicization of the Supreme Court, "we do have a factual basis . . . that the wife of a justice was actively engaged in January 6th, [in] terms of its advocacy and other aspects of her participation." For Jackson Lee, who as a University of Virginia law student proudly earned an Earl Warren Scholarship, Ginni Thomas's role in January 6—and its implication of her husband, Justice Thomas—"strikes at the core of creating a more perfect union and the upholding of the Constitution that is a responsibility of the United States Supreme Court."

Denver Riggleman, the head of the data team working for the January 6th Committee, saw the linking of all three branches of government through Ginni Thomas's aggressive advocacy as a DEFCON 1 emergency. "I thought it would be the biggest thing we could have found was that we have a Supreme Court Justice's wife saying that she's talking directly to the Executive Branch, coordinating with the Legislative Branch and directly hooked to the Judicial Branch who's pushing this type of stuff out," Riggleman says. "We didn't just have the text messages, we had her emails, all those ridiculous things that we saw. I thought that it would be maybe the biggest portion of our investigative tool kit, but instead it became something that was very difficult for me to run with based on pushback from the entire committee."

Shocking but true: The discovery of the Ginni Thomas texts by January 6th Committee investigators led not to the immediate follow-up incumbent on any serious investigative effort, but instead to a cover-up. Clarence and Ginni Thomas were too big to fall. Their power was their protection. They had friends willing to pull strings to help them, even if it meant robbing the January 6th Committee's investigation of momentum and, ultimately, draining away some of its firepower.

Riggleman says it was the "entire committee" that forestalled further follow-up—and overall Washington-bred institutional caution surely played a role—but interviews with two Capitol Hill sources with personal knowledge speaking on background reveal a more dramatic truth, which might shock even some jaded Washington veterans not easily surprised by callow examples of power protecting power: Liz Cheney herself, the star of the hearings, doing her turn as independent-minded maverick Republican, did all she could behind the scenes to protect Ginni and Clarence Thomas and thwart the move to investigate further the implications of the Ginni Thomas texts to Meadows. There would be no subpoena for Ginni Thomas, much less her husband, no public testimony, only an informational interview in which she was not under oath.

At the time, it was already clear that Cheney was toying with a presidential bid in 2024, not merely a stop-Trump ploy but also a move in line with her own ambitions. Liz Cheney remained very close to her father, the former vice president widely seen as the ultimate power center in the George W. Bush White House. Also at work was the topography of overlapping Washington families, the Cheneys and the Thomases. Consider a snapshot from October 2007, during the disastrous U.S. war against Iraq stage-managed by then–Vice President Dick Cheney, whose intellectual dominance of affable but overmatched President George W. Bush was well established. Former Clarence Thomas aide Armstrong Williams hosted a book party for Thomas. Among the attendees were the vice president and his wife, Lynne. This fact alone is far from scandalous. In Washington people attend parties. But this appearance reflected deeper ties. As Williams wrote at the time in *The Hill,* "many people found it remarkable that Vice President and Mrs. Cheney stopped by for the occasion." A marker was being put down: Power courts power. Liz Cheney's parents were "standing and mingling like everyone else with admiration for Justice Thomas," Williams gushed. "They had come to see their mutual friend Clarence Thomas."

The naked power move by Liz Cheney and her team leading the January 6 investigation had to do with raw political math as she contemplated running for president in 2024—no Republican candidate could survive coming out against the right-wing court-packing project. When the January 6th Committee finally released its report in December 2022, the grace note was sounded: Not only did the 845-page report avoid connecting the dots on the vital role the Thomases played in pushing and, by extension, justifying the attempted coup d'état, the report—take a moment to process this—actually refrained from mentioning Ginni Thomas even once. Not one mention. In 845 pages. No wonder Ginni Thomas goes through life with the smug smile of a fanatic who knows she can take the law into her own hands with impunity.

---

The more information that came out about the layers of plotting behind the January 6 attempted coup, the more clear it became how many close associates of Ginni Thomas were involved. Ginni's network was wide and she was resourceful in using it to bolster her own moves. Congressman Mike Lee, a close ally of Ginni Thomas's, made a point of lobbying Meadows and Trump to lean on Sidney Powell, the attorney who would ultimately emerge as too crazy even for Trump World. Powell had legal chops as a former federal prosecutor, but already by that point had ventured far down the rabbit hole—even Trump called her schemes "crazy."

"We had steering committee at CPI tonight, with Sidney Powell as our guest speaker," Lee wrote Meadows at 10:23 p.m. on the Monday after the election, November 9. "My purpose in having the meeting was to socialize with Republican senators the fact that POTUS needs to pursue his legal remedies. You have in us a group of ready and loyal advocates who will go to bat for him, but I fear this could prove short-lived unless you hire the right legal team and set them loose immediately."

Who should they set loose? Figures like Sidney Powell. "Sidney told us that the campaign lawyers, who I do not know, are not focused on this and are obstructing progress," Lee continued. Translation: They were not going along with unhinged, halfbaked schemes. "I have no way of verifying or refuting that on my own, but I've found her to be a straight shooter. In any event, these actions need to be filed and announced in the next 48 hours or the public relations momentum we need to have behind it will start to dissipate."

On November 13, Ginni Thomas herself would push Sidney Powell on Meadows. "Just forwarded to yr gmail an email I sent Jared this am," she wrote. "Sidney Powell & improved coordination now will help the cavalry come and Fraud exposed and America saved. ?? Don't let her and your assets be marginalized instead . . . help her be the lead and the face?!?"

On November 10, at 6:23 p.m., Meadows received a text from extremist legal activist Michael Farris—one of many Meadows texts I obtained through sources and am making public here for the first time—reading in full, "Mark, I hope you're recovering. I was contacted by Jenna re election disputes. Wanting my help. Can you let me know if this is realistic?"

Jenna Ellis brought Michael Farris into the picture, and Farris would play an important—and widely overlooked—role in the conspiracy. Not only would Farris draft the legal brief Texas attorney general Ken Paxton would file to the Supreme Court in a failed bid to overturn election results in Georgia, Pennsylvania, Michigan, and Wisconsin, seeking to steal the election for Trump, Farris would also recruit close Clarence Thomas associate John Eastman into the plot.

Farris, a member of the Council for National Policy and also a donor to it, remained a largely obscure figure beyond the world of ultraconservative religious zealots pushing an extreme agenda through the courts. Farris grew up a Baptist in Washington State and then became a fundamentalist Christian. A political science major at Western Washington University, he earned a law degree at Gonzaga in 1976. Soon after, he harangued the Spokane City Council to stop allowing the sale of alcohol at the city's Opera House—"an impassioned, but unsuccessful plea," reported the local paper. In 1983 he moved from a Washington State leadership post with the Moral Majority to a position in Washington, D.C., with the evangelical Christian lobbying group Concerned Women for America, which claimed half a million dues-paying members. Farris left the Moral Majority, he clarified at the time, because founder Jerry Falwell was not extremist enough for him. "We represent a radical change," Farris told the Associated Press. Republicans and Democrats were all the same to him—"one wears Hush Puppies and the other wingtips." As to his beliefs, he was succinct: "There are those who believe the government is God and those who believe God is God, and that is how the battle lines for me are drawn."

A homeschooling advocate—and father of ten—Farris founded the Home School Legal Defense Association in 1983, a role in which he would eventually argue cases before the Supreme Court, and started dabbling in do-it-yourself meddling with the Constitution. In 2013 he cofounded a group called the Convention of States Project, seeking a national constitutional convention, a campaign summed up in a *Richmond Times-Dispatch* headline as "Effort Seeks to Reset Course for America." A photo with the article pictured a sparsely attended meeting—a telling reminder of what a fringe campaign this was.

Starting in 2017, Farris served as CEO of Alliance Defending Freedom, the anti-LGBTQ rights, antiabortion extremist group, funded by Leonard Leo, behind the Mississippi abortion case that led to the challenge to *Roe v. Wade.*

On December 5, 2020—in another of the Meadows texts made public here for the first time—Farris texted the chief of staff, "Mark, I was able to get John Eastman over the line. He's ready to file an original action in SCOTUS for the President. He needs to talk to you about two things. Can you call me so I can briefly give you the details? Mike."

Two days later, on December 7, Meadows wrote to Farris, apparently with Cleta Mitchell at his side: "From Cleta Mark," the text began, "Need to get you on a call with our new lawyer and Alex Kaufman. They think John Eastman's suit being filed today needs to ask SCOTUS to delay meeting of Electors until the election contests are completed. They make a good argument for that. We have talked with John. Not sure he's going to include it. Can you do call with us? ASAP?"

The Eastman legal appeal to the high court on behalf of Trump, submitted on December 9, formally requested that Trump be allowed to join a state of Texas lawsuit seeking to have election results thrown out in four other states, Pennsylvania, Michigan, Georgia, and Wisconsin. The Eastman document included florid language calling on the Supreme Court, in a "Prayer for Relief" section at the end, to "Enjoin Defendant States and their respective officials from using the constitutionally-infirm 2020 election results for the office of President to appoint Electors to the Electoral College," unless a specified—and convoluted—review of the 2020 election results were to occur. The Eastman document, quixotic at best, despite its high pretensions, went nowhere. On Friday, December 11, 2020, the Supreme Court ruled against Texas. As Reuters reported, the Supreme Court "brought an abrupt end to a long-shot lawsuit filed by Texas and backed by President Donald Trump seeking to throw out voting results in four states, dealing him a crushing setback in its quest to undo his election loss."

Far more important than this long-shot appeal to the high court was a series of memos Eastman wrote—often called "The Coup Memos"—purportedly attempting to make a legal case for Vice President Mike Pence to intervene and swing the election to Trump, or at least providing some gossamer-thin fig leaf of pretend legal cover. Based on Eastman's personal opinion that the Electoral Count Act of 1887 is "likely unconstitutional," he breezily proposed that Pence, presiding over a joint session of Congress to certify results, simply ignore the electoral tallies of seven selected states whose results Trump didn't like. In a tell of how weak an argument Eastman knew he had, he added, "The main thing here is that Pence should do this without asking for permission—either from a vote of the joint session or from the Court. Let the other side challenge his actions in court."

The clear hope here was that Pence, a deeply religious man, would supersede his loyalty to the Constitution in fealty to his boss and to a larger community of extreme-religious conservatives. The wonder, startling even now looking back, was that Pence did not go along with the plot.

———

The January 6th Committee's cover-up of Ginni Thomas's activities blocked the accounting that might have brought to wide public attention a true and thorough understanding of her role in helping orchestrate the events leading up to the January 6 insurrection—as well as a fuller picture of the danger she continues to represent.

At the time, the data investigative team found its moves suddenly questioned. "I think you had people in political positions who—I would say they have regrets that they didn't allow me to further the investigation into Ginni Thomas, especially after her interview and what's been found after the fact," Riggleman said.

That point is hard to argue. Ginni Thomas was brought in for a perfunctory interview with the January 6th Committee, a move that had about as much resemblance to real law enforcement work as Captain Renault in *Casablanca* announcing, "Round up the usual suspects!"

Even so, intriguing glimpses emerged. Why, for example, would Ginni Thomas confirm to the committee that, in one of the texts to Mark Meadows, she was talking about her husband the Supreme Court justice when she referenced a conversation with her "best friend"? Was she rubbing in the extent to which her power protected her? Was she in effect gloating? It sure seemed that way.

Let's go back to the texts. Shortly before 10 p.m. on November 24, Ginni Thomas sent Meadows a link to a Glenn Beck video, a video that clearly had her worked up in a state of high agitation, then followed up with a separate text to Meadows in which she scolded him: "If you all cave to the elites, you have to know that many of your 73 million feel like what Glenn is expressing. Me included. I think I am done with politics, and I don't think I am alone, Mark."

Meadows wrote right back: "I don't know what you mean by caving to elites."

"Sorry," Ginni replied. "I can't see Americans swallowing the obvious fraud. Just going with one more thing with no frickin' consequences. . . . the whole coup and now this . . . we just cave to people wanting Biden to be anointed? Many of us can't continue the GOP charade."

Meadows is wary.

"I didn't view the clip," he writes. "What is it about."

Just Glenn Beck ranting about being "fed up" that there are

never "consequences to all the hard work of showing progressive or d lies," she clarifies.

"You're preaching to the choir," Meadow tells her. "Very demoralizing."

That's all the encouragement she needs to rant some more, carrying on about "the stabbing in the back of anyone daring to still say there seemed to be fraud. All the Rs congratulating Biden. Your/his loyalists can't take this. It's so evil. Thank you for being in my choir then too!! If this doesn't turn, I am literally done with politics, and that's all I have done since my 20s. People hate the GOP!!! Or it's growing."

Meadows truly is in Ginni Thomas's choir, he's singing her tune. "This is a fight of good verses [*sic*] evil," he writes her. "Evil always looks like the victor until the King of Kings triumphs. Do not grow weary in well doing." (Galatians 6:9) "The fight continues."

To which Thomas replies, about half an hour after her previous text, "Thank you!! Needed that! That plus a conversation with my best friend just now. . . . I will try to keep holding on."

Let that sink in a little bit. Ginni Thomas was deep into a back-and-forth with the chief of staff to the president of the United States, citing Scripture to bolster their (apparently) joint conviction that extraordinary steps must be taken to fight the results of an election that ousted their candidate. She was distraught—until she talked to Clarence Thomas, with whom she clearly discussed what she was texting to Meadows.

What must Clarence Thomas have told her to calm her down? The investigators apparently didn't ask. We do know that Clarence Thomas himself emphasized in a February 2011 speech to the Federalist Society that he and "his bride" are "equally yoked." They "believe in the same things." In his eyes, her political activities, nakedly partisan, count as working "24-7 in defense of liberty." To anyone who would suggest Clarence Thomas in any way seeks to distance himself from her radicalism and extremism, the justice himself told the Federalist Society her feverish advocacy, in all its facets, "keeps me going."

Ginni Thomas's answers to the January 6th Committee were unsatisfying to say the least. Asked about her recollection of the Glenn Beck video, and of the thinking behind her words to Meadows, she repeatedly claims to have no memory, dodging every question, except when in a momentary flash of honesty and clarity she says, "I'm sorry these texts exist." On that point we believe her.

The "best friend" remark? "It looks like it was my husband."

And what did he say, exactly, that made her feel better? To the point where she could hold on?

"I wish I could remember," she says, claiming to "have no memory of the specifics," but adding, "My husband often administers spousal support to the wife that's upset."

Given the close partnership the two have had for decades, given the close entanglement of their political lives, her gambit of essentially making herself out as a hysterical wife strains credulity.

Here was how she continued in the "best friend" text to Meadows: "This rotten GOP . . . just like Fox and the NFL, they are whistling past the graveyard if they think proceeding without DJT [Trump] will work out. America has been educated and people want real leaders, not fake ones!! If globalists win and there is no truth either . . . I don't get the next play."

Even in the time I've worked on this book, I've watched the ground shift on the politics of the Supreme Court, and the growing awareness in particular of Clarence Thomas's corruption and illegitimacy—and the growing infamy of his insurrection-seeking wife—leaves Justice Thomas's jurisprudence severely compromised. By the end of 2023, with various court cases involving Donald Trump moving toward the Supreme Court, the pressure continued to climb with mounting calls for Thomas to recuse himself.

The point was not only that Ginni Thomas could literally be a material witness in the Justice Department's criminal case against Trump for his role in the January 6 attempted coup, based on her inflammatory texts to Mark Meadows alone. The issues went deeper than that. As former federal prosecutor Ankush Khardori argued in a December 2023 *Politico* article, "Justice Thomas should recuse himself because Ginni Thomas—an apparent true believer in Trump's election-fraud claims—is a victim of Trump's alleged crimes. That means that both Ginni Thomas and Justice Thomas have a direct reputational stake in the outcome of the proceedings—one that further calls into serious question the justice's ability to render an independent decision strictly on the merits of either case."

The political pressure only escalated in January 2024 when the Supreme Court agreed to hear a case taking up the Colorado top court's ruling that Donald Trump was ineligible for the November 2024 ballot, under the Constitution's anti-insurrection clause, given Trump's culpability for the January 6 insurrection. Considering Ginni Thomas's role in helping push for radical action in advance of January 6, it seemed increasingly outrageous for Clarence Thomas to refuse to recuse himself from the case, and yet all indications were that Thomas had no intention of even considering recusal.

Former Clinton administration official Robert Reich captured the absurdity of Thomas's position in a January 2024 post on Twitter/X. "Ginni Thomas was directly involved in efforts to overturn the 2020 election," wrote Reich. "She even texted Mark Meadows, Trump's chief of staff, lobbying him to help her cause. If the new SCOTUS code of ethics were worth anything, Clarence Thomas would be forced to recuse himself."

New York congressman Dan Goldman, an attorney for House

Democrats during the impeachment of Donald Trump, issued a letter calling firmly on Thomas to recuse himself. "Your wife was one of nine board members for a conservative political group that helped lead the 'Stop the Steal' movement, a movement which culminated in the January 6 attack that the Colorado Supreme Court deemed an insurrection," Goldman wrote. "It is unthinkable that you could be impartial in deciding whether an event your wife personally organized qualifies as an 'insurrection' that would prevent someone from holding the office of President. Furthermore, your wife of thirty-six years, Ms. Thomas, has shown a fervent bias in favor of Mr. Trump, and it is hard to believe that her bias has no impact on you, which is why reasonable people aware of the relevant facts and circumstances doubt that you can fairly discharge your duty to be impartial in hearing this case."

With the decision to recuse belonging to the justice himself, nobody expected Clarence Thomas to break with precedent and do the right thing.

# CHAPTER 23

# TIME TO IMPEACH
# CLARENCE THOMAS

Every day that Clarence Thomas remains on the Supreme Court is an affront. He should long since have been shamed into retiring and skulking off to a life of avoiding the public, and would have been if held to any fair and honest standards of accountability. That hasn't happened. The protectors of Clarence and Ginni Thomas are powerful and well funded. They're also complacent and arrogant. They don't believe anyone will take them on. Which is just why the fight has to be joined, and Clarence Thomas must be impeached, brought before a trial to air the abundant evidence of corruption and criminal conflict of interest. Even if he's not convicted in the Senate, the point will be made, and at least future justices might be warned away from such blatant and serial abuse of power and the public trust.

Like presidents, justices and judges can be impeached on a majority vote of the House of Representatives and convicted by a two-thirds majority in the Senate. I've been advocating for the impeachment of Thomas since October 2010, when I wrote a memo to then–Secretary of State Hillary Clinton detailing the case. The backstory of the memo was as follows: Years after I'd carried water for Thomas, helped by his friends and allies, the same people who had assisted me in lying to myself and the American people about the truth of Anita Hill's allegations confessed to me, now their trusted ally, that they'd been feeding me lies. Having the full force of that first round of lies exposed gave me in effect a decoder ring.

My four-page memo to Hillary, which surfaced publicly in 2015 after the Russians hacked her email, was pegged to a new interview in *The New York Times,* twenty years after the Thomas-Hill hearings, with Lillian McEwen, a former prosecutor, law professor, and judge who said that for Thomas pornography was "just a part of his personality structure," that he frequented a Washington video store that "catered to his needs," and that his interest in porn bled over into his personal relationships. McEwen, like other potential witnesses for Hill, had not been called to testify and her assertions stood in stark contrast with Thomas's sworn testimony in 1991 in which he denied having any sexual discussions with Hill. The memo also detailed differences between McEwen's 2010 accounts and Thomas's testimony in terms of his workplace behavior, including incidents in which Thomas remarked on the size of women's breasts or bra sizes, as well as provided evidence that Thomas supporters covered up evidence and intimidated witnesses. Yet under questioning from Democratic senator Patrick Leahy during the hearing, Thomas categorically denied any sexual discussion within the workplace, including with Anita Hill. Anita Hill herself, Angela Wright, and now Lillian McEwan have shown that Thomas's testimony was a bald-faced lie, and this could serve as Count 1 in an impeachment inquiry.

In August 2022, I published an op-ed in *The Huffington Post* (much of which I am repurposing here) arguing again that House Democrats should impeach Thomas while they still had the power to do so. This time, I had a new hook. Texts and emails showed that Ginni Thomas was in communication with the White House chief of staff and Arizona lawmakers, falsely arguing that the election was stolen and beseeching them to take wrongful actions to reverse it. Ginni Thomas also corresponded with lawyer John Eastman, the architect of the plot to reverse the election. In one communication, she mentioned having spoken with her "friend" about the election, a reference to her husband that she later admitted. She wrote, "Make a plan . . . and save us from the left taking down America." At the time, Ginni Thomas was serving on the board of CNP Action, the political advocacy arm of the Council for National Policy, which was urging Republicans to keep Trump in power.

In January 2022, after Ginni Thomas had sent those zealous pro-coup emails, Clarence Thomas was the sole dissenter in an 8-1 decision by the court requiring that the National Archives release Trump's records to the House committee investigating the January 6, 2021, insurrection. Given Ginni Thomas's active involvement in the events leading up to January 6—and especially since the twenty-nine text exchanges she had with White House chief of staff Mark Meadows in the weeks before appear to have been covered by the House document request—Thomas should clearly have recused himself from the case to avoid the appearance of impropriety. In other words, it looked like he was covering for his wife.

Federal law says judges and justices must recuse themselves cases where a spouse has "an interest that could be substantially affected by the outcome" and "where their impartiality might be reasonably questioned." In the National Archives case, Harvard Law professor Laurence Tribe concluded Thomas broke that law. That's Count 2.

The issue of Thomas and his failure to recuse himself with respect to his wife's political advocacy has been raised before. In 2011, seventy-four House Democrats said Thomas was required by federal law to recuse himself from any appeals involving the Affordable Care Act, since Ginni Thomas was a highly paid lobbyist working for clients seeking to overturn the law. Thomas also failed to recuse himself from the court's Muslim travel ban decision in 2018, even though, according to *The New Yorker,* Ginni Thomas was paid $200,000 in 2017 and 2018 by the Center for Security Policy, which submitted an amicus brief supporting the ban. These failures to recuse would be Counts 3 and 4.

Thomas also ran afoul of the law when he failed to disclose $686,000 his wife made at the Heritage Foundation between 2003 and 2007. Instead he checked boxes indicating Ginni Thomas had no investment income in those years. The Ethics in Government Act requires all high-ranking federal officials to file yearly financial disclosure statements for themselves and their spouses, signed under penalty of perjury, to guard against conflicts of interest. It's hard to believe that Thomas's multiple disclosure failures were simply unintentional accounting errors. University of Colorado law professor Paul Campos has called the Heritage Foundation omissions "criminal." These omissions would be Count 5.

Public scrutiny of Thomas's evident corruption ratcheted up dramatically in 2023 in the wake of the *ProPublica* reporting on his luxury vacations paid for by Texas billionaire Harlan Crow. As strained and flimsy as Thomas's self-justification was in the statement he issued after the bombshell reporting, the mere fact of Thomas issuing a rare self-defense functioned as confirmation of the story—and of the gravity of the situation. The disclosures were so dramatic, and so clearly part of a larger pattern, they were like bread crumbs to other investigative journalists looking to keep the story going with fresh disclosures of other examples of Thomas accepting expensive largesse he would, very conveniently, categorize as "personal hospitality" he failed to report. Accountability finally seemed to be coming for Clarence Thomas and his dangerous wife. Members of Congress have called for impeachment or resignation. Senators have written to the Department of Justice demanding investigation, though given the Thomases' track record of flaunting both their power and their impunity, all bets were off.

All federal judges except the Supreme Court justices are subject to a judicial code of conduct. It seems clear that if any other federal judge had committed the ethical violations Thomas did, he or she would be removed from office. Yet the absence of such a code does not mean Thomas walks away from his misconduct. In the case of the Harlan Crow flights around the globe, the tuition payments, and real estate transactions, the Ethics in Government Act requires all federal officials, including Supreme Court justices, to disclose such gifts and deals. There are both civil and criminal penalties that the Justice Department could pursue for violations of the act. In any event, even if the DOJ took no action, the failure to disclose the Crow gifts would be Count 6 in any impeachment.

The exposure of the scheme through which Leonard Leo used his network of nonprofits to personally enrich Clarence and Ginni Thomas goes well beyond ethics to the implication of illegality. The Leo payoffs to the Thomases would be Count 7.

Thomas's failure to recuse in the January 6th cases would bring my total count to 8.

I close this book with the admonition that Democrats must win back the House in the November 2024 elections and must use the opportunity that victory gives them to impeach Clarence Thomas because I am absolutely convinced that this course of action is essential to preserving our democracy. The stench of the Thomas Court has emanated from Washington for so long, some have grown inured to the stink and the rot it evokes. A big wake-up call like an impeachment inquiry can set the table for a necessary discussion on structural court reforms.

Many will say impeachment is a fool's errand. I strongly disagree. Even if the Senate would never convict Thomas, the impeachment in the House would send a message that this corruption would no longer slip under the radar. As a former right-winger turned Democrat, I often ask myself what my former colleagues would do strategically given a political opportunity. turned Democrat, I often ask myself what my former colleagues would do strategically given a political opportunity. If the shoe were on the other foot, Republicans would not hesitate to impeach a disgraced, vulnerable, and widely unpopular figure like Thomas; not only to punish him for past sins, but also to discredit and delegitimize with the public a host of spurious decisions undoubtedly coming down the line in the future from the Thomas Court with its radical MAGA 5–4 majority.

If we allow the country to be turned into a Christian Nationalist abomination in which a small minority dictates to the majority how it should live, if we don't fight for decency and the rights of the many, who will?

# ACKNOWLEDGMENTS

At Knopf, I'd like to recognize my terrific editor, Peter Gethers, and the supportive senior Knopf team: Reagan Arthur, Erinn Hartman, Jessica Purcell, and Claire Leonard, as well as Morgan Hamilton in Peter's office. Fred Chase did a careful copyedit.

My agent and friend Will Lippincott of Aevitas Creative Management was on board early with my concept and stayed on it every step of the way to publication.

During the course of my research, blockbuster reporting on Clarence Thomas's ethics problems was done by *ProPublica* (Joshua Kaplan, Justin Elliott, Alex Mierjerski, and Brett Murphy) and by *The New York Times* (Jo Becker and Julie Tate). Heidi Przybyla and Michael Kruse at *Politico* broke several stories on the Federalist Society and Leonard Leo, as did Ken Vogel of *The New York Times*.

I was informed by Jane Mayer in *The New Yorker* on Ginni Thomas; Margaret Talbot of the same publication on Samuel Alito; Michael Tarm of the AP, and Beth Reinhard and Alice Crites of *The Washington Post* on Amy Coney Barrett; Stephanie Kirchgaessner of *The Guardian* on Brett Kavanaugh; and Katherine Stewart's reporting on Christian nationalism.

278 Acknowledgments

Books I consulted include *The Rise of the Conservative Legal Movement: The Battle for Control of the Law,* by Steven Teles; *Ideas with Consequences: The Federalist Society and the Conservative Counterrevolution,* by Amanda Hollis Brusky; *The Education of Brett Kavanaugh,* by Kate Kelly and Robin Pogrebin; *Supreme Discomfort: The Divided Soul of Clarence Thomas,* by Kevin Merida and Michael Fletcher; *Supreme Ambition: Brett Kavanaugh and the Conservative Takeover,* by Ruth Marcus; and *Nine Black Robes: Inside the Supreme Court's Drive to the Right and Its Historic Consequences,* by Joan Biskupic.

Special recognition goes to Senator Sheldon Whitehouse and his book *The Scheme: How the Right Wing Used Dark Money to Capture the Supreme Court.* A series of Senate floor speeches on the Federalist Society scheme were also influential.

Over the years I've learned from the reporting and analysis of Linda Greenhouse and Adam Liptak of *The New York Times;* Ruth Marcus of *The Washington Post;* Nina Totenberg of NPR; and Dahlia Lithwick of *Slate*: Elie Mystal of *The Nation;* and Ian Millhiser at Vox.

I relied on research and other tips from Lisa Graves of True North Research and Alex Aronson of Court Accountability. I'd also like to thank the court watchers, legal experts, activists, and former clerks who shared their perspectives.

Friends and family are always a bedrock, thanks to all.

Finally, thanks to Steve Kettmann for his contributions to the manuscript. And a special thanks goes to my intrepid researcher, Frank Kline, for all his hard work. (Any errors in the book are mine.)

*David Brock,*
*April 2024*

# APPENDIX

Date: 11/5/20 23:55
from: Virginia Thomas
To: Mark Meadows

I hope this is true; never heard anything like this before; or even a hint of it. Possible??? TRUMP STING w CIA Director Steve Pieczenik The Biggest Election Story in History, QFS-BLOCKCHAIN 7 min video Dr Steve Pieczenik's info (who has very good intel contacts: Thu 5 Nov interview https://www.youtube.com/watch?v=qK3yQHHoHEA&feature=youtu.be) the QFS blockchain watermarked ballots in over 12 states have been part of a huge Trump & military white hat sting operation in 12 key battleground states where 20,000+ natl guard were deployed; Biden crime family & ballot fraud co-conspirators (elected officials, bureaucrats, social media censorship mongers, fake stream media reporters, etc) are being arrested & detained for ballot fraud right now & over coming days, & will be living in barges off GITMO to face military tribunals for sedition

Date: 11/6/20 10:49
From: Virginia Thomas
To: Mark Meadows

Do not concede. It takes time for the army who is gathering for his back. ??????

Date: 11/10/20 12:23
From: Virginia Thomas
To: Mark Meadows

Mark, I wanted to text you and tell you for days you are in my prayers!! I hear fr Nancy Schulze you are working though?? Listen to Rush, Mark Steyn, Bongino, Cleta and know the grassroots wants Truth to prevail over Lies!!!?????? Help This Great President stand firm, Mark!!! The Left tastes their power!!! ???? You are the leader, with him, who is standing for America's constitutional governance at the precipice. The majority knows Biden and the Left is attempting the greatest Heist of our History. ??????????????

Date: 11/10/20 12:34
From: Mark Meadows
To: Virginia Thomas

I will stand firm. We will fight until there is no fight left. Our country is too precious to give up on. Thanks for all you do

Date: 11/10/20 12:43
From: Virginia Thomas
To: Mark Meadows

Tearing up and praying for you guys!!!!!????????????????? So proud to know you!!??????

Date: 11/10/20 22:07
From: Virginia Thomas
To: Mark Meadows

Van Jones spins interestingly, but shows us the balls being juggled too. House and Senate guys are pathetic too . . . only 4 GOP House members seen out in street rallies with grassroots . . . Gohmert, Jordan, Gosar and Roy . . . where the heck are all those who benefited by Presidents coat-tails?!!!??. Watch this though. . . . if you haven't already. https://www .toptradeguru.com/news/cnns-van-jones-fear-trump-wins-as-long-as-he -doesnt-concede/ It is such a messaging war game/ information warfare being played to keep the truth from coming out. A Heist!

Date: 11/13/20 6:39
From: Virginia Thomas
To: Mark Meadows

Just forwarded to yr gmail an email I sent Jared this am. Sidney Powell &
improved coordination now will help the cavalry come and Fraud exposed
and America saved. ?? Don't let her and your assets be marginalized
instead . . . help her be the lead and the face?!?

Date: 11/14/20 5:06
From: Virginia Thomas
To: Mark Meadows

? The most important thing you can realize right now is that there are no
rules in war. You destroy your enemy's ability to fight. This is what is happening right now—this war is psychological. PSYOP. It's what I did in the
military. They are using every weapon they have to try to make us quit, to
give up on our system of government and processes. They try to break our
will to fight through demoralization, discouragement, division, chaos and
gaslighting. It is fake, fraud and if people would take a deep breath and look
at things through that filter we will see this through and win. The Constitution is on our side and it is worth fighting for. I believe in it. Our Founders
and even those facing Omaha Beach have done MUCH more than we have
since Election Day. I would suggest we all think in those terms because if
we don't, and we allow this massive fraud to stand, we've lost our country
anyway.—Connie Hair, Nov 13??????

Date: 11/19/20 3:31
From: Virginia Thomas
To: Mark Meadows

Mark, (don't want to wake you!) The intense pressures you and our President are now experiencing are more intense than Anything Experienced
(but I only felt a fraction of it in 1991). At stake: truth, evidence, facts and
America. Or will lies win?! I know you all are feeling an unbelievable negative intensity if you drink in media or weak people/messages. Look at a
calendar and set out the plan for getting truth, evidence out by dates certain. Sounds like Sidney and her team are getting inundated with evidence

of fraud. Make a plan. Release the Kraken and save us from the left taking America down?? Suggestion: You need to buck up your team on the inside, Mark. The lower level insiders are scared, fearful or sending out signals of hopelessness, vs an awareness of the existential threat to America right now. You can buck them up, strengthen their spirits. Monica Crowley may have a sense of this fr her Nixon days. ?? Northern VA Deplorables and others seem to be planning pop up spontaneous sign wavings this am for Stop The Steal! ???? Help the communicators share these kinds of messages (video below) as you guys garner truth and evidence. https://www .youtube.com/watch?v=yq3CKJtFQG4&feature=youtu.be Americans are praying for you all! Feel that and be the leaders God have made you into for this time!?????????? Ginni—You guys fold, the evil just moves fast down underneath you all. Lots of intensifying threats coming to ACB and others. So honor and respect you for helping this amazing President stand for all of us!!!!? This is Spiritual Warfare, as you must feel, Mark! It is about America continuing and this lonely leader and man!????????

Date: 11/19/20 7:09
From: Mark Meadows
To: Virginia Thomas

Thanks so much

Date: 11/19/20 8:02
From: Virginia Thomas
To: Mark Meadows

Loved Thanks so much.

Date: 11/19/20 12:34
From: Virginia Thomas
To: Mark Meadows

Tears are flowing at what Rudy is doing right now!!!!????????

Date: 11/19/20 12:36
From: Virginia Thomas
To: Mark Meadows

Emphasized Glad to help??

Date: 11/19/20 12:36
From: Virginia Thomas
To: Mark Meadows

Whoa!! Heroes!!!!

Date: 11/19/20 12:36
From: Mark Meadows
To: Virginia Thomas

Glad to help??

Date: 11/22/20 20:35
From: Virginia Thomas
To: Mark Meadows

Trying to understand the Sidney Powell distancing. . . .

Date: 11/22/20 20:36
From: Virginia Thomas
To: Mark Meadows

Wow!

Date: 11/22/20 20:36
From: Mark Meadows
To: Virginia Thomas

She doesn't have anything or at least she won't share it if she does

Date: 11/24/20 21:42
From: Virginia Thomas
To: Mark Meadows

https://video.parler.com/eG/xu/eGxuHsCsPirD.mp4

Date: 11/24/20 21:42
From: Virginia Thomas
To: Mark Meadows

If you all cave to the elites, you have to know that many of your 73 million feel like what Glenn is expressing. Me included. I think I am done with politics, and I don't think I am alone, Mark.

Date: 11/24/20 21:45
From: Mark Meadows
To: Virginia Thomas

I don't know what you mean by caving to elites

Date: 11/24/20 21:47
From: Virginia Thomas
To: Mark Meadows

Sorry. My phone was across a few rooms. I can't see Americans swallowing the obvious fraud. Just going with one more thing with no frickin consequences . . . the whole coup and now this . . . we just cave to people wanting Biden to be anointed? Many of us can't continue the GOP charade. ??

Date: 11/24/20 21:48
From: Mark Meadows
To: Virginia Thomas

I didn't view the clip. What is it about

Date: 11/24/20 21:49
From: Virginia Thomas
To: Mark Meadows

It's just him being fed up at there never bring consequences to all the hard work of showing progressive or d lies.

Date: 11/24/20 21:51
From: Mark Meadows
To: Virginia Thomas

You're preaching to the choir. Very demoralizing

Date: 11/24/20 21:53
From: Virginia Thomas
To: Mark Meadows

The fracturing now. The stabbing in the back of anyone daring to still say there seemed to be fraud. All the Rs congratulating Biden. Your/his loyalists can't take this. It is so evil. Thank you for being in my choir then too!! If this doesn't turn, I am literally done with politics, and that's all I have done since my 20s. People hate the GOP!!! Or it's growing. ??

Date: 11/24/20 21:58
From: Mark Meadows
To: Virginia Thomas

This is a fight of good verses evil. Evil always looks like the victor until the King of Kings triumphs. Do not grow weary in well doing. The fight continues. I have staked my career on it. Well at least my time in DC on it

Date: 11/24/20 22:22
From: Virginia Thomas
To: Mark Meadows

Thank you!! Needed that! This plus a conversation with my best friend just now . . . I will try to keep holding on. America is worth it! But this rotten GOP . . . just like Fox and the NFL, they are whistling past the graveyard if they think proceeding independent of DJT will work out. America has been educated and people want real leaders, not fake ones!! If globalists win and there is no truth either . . . I don't get the next play.

Date: 1/10/21 5:06
From: Virginia Thomas
To: Mark Meadows

I still adamantly ?? the President and you, friend!! We are living through what feels like the end of America. Most of us are disgusted with the VP and are in a listening mode to see where to fight with our teams. Those who attacked the Capitol are not representative of our great teams of patriots for DJT!!???????????? Amazing times. The end of Liberty???

# NOTES

## PROLOGUE: APRIL 1993: The Clarence Thomas Inner Circle and Me

viii Christopher Lehmann-Haupt, a respected daily reviewer—"Books of *The Times:* Peering Behind the Anita Hill-Clarence Thomas Matter," *New York Times,* April 26, 1993.

viii A reviewer in the Sunday *Times*—"The Case Against Anita Hill," *New York Times,* May 23, 1993.

viii the *Washington Post* reviewer—"A Revisionist's Nightmare," *Washington Post,* June 10, 1993.

viii on the *Wall Street Journal* editorial page—"A Revisionist's Nightmare," *Washington Post,* June 10, 1993.

viii George Will column—"Anita Hill's Tangled Web, *Newsweek,* April 18, 1993.

viii According to Gallup—"Gallup Vault: Anita Hill's Charges Against Clarence Thomas," *Gallup News,* September 21, 2018; "More People Believe Hill than Thomas, Poll Says," *Los Angeles Times,* reprinted in *Daily Oklahoman,* October 11, 1992.

viii a bombshell report—"The Surreal Anita Hill," *The New Yorker,* May 24, 1993.

ix dubbed "sleaze" by one *New York Times* columnist—"Opinion: Abroad at Home; Sleaze with Footnotes," *New York Times,* May 21, 1993.

ix "He spoke about"—"Nomination of Judge Clarence Thomas to Be Associate Justice of the Supreme Court of the United States," United States Senate Judiciary Committee, Part 4, October 11, 12, 13, 1991.

ix "his own sexual prowess"—Ibid.

x "Who put pubic hair on my Coke?"—Ibid.

x Though he denies it—"Book Author Says He Lied in His Attacks on Anita Hill in Bid to Aid Justice Thomas," *New York Times,* June 27, 2001.

xi "high-tech lynching for uppity blacks"—Ibid.

xi   "an alien pubic hair"—Ibid.

xi   "And now, I really am getting stuff"—Ibid.

xi   private compromise deal—"Senators' Private Deal Kept '2nd Woman' Off TV: Thomas: Democrats Feared Republican Attacks on Angela Wright's Public Testimony. Biden's Handling of the Hearing Is Criticized," *Los Angeles Times,* October 17, 1991.

xii   "You look good"—"Nomination of Judge Clarence Thomas to Be Associate Justice of the Supreme Court of the United States," United States Senate Judiciary Committee, Part 4, October 11, 12, 13, 1991.

xiv   Hendrik Hertzberg put it in—"Can You Forgive Him?," *The New Yorker,* March 3, 2002.

xvi   *ProPublica* revealed in 2023—"Clarence Thomas Had a Child in Private School. Harlan Crow Paid the Tuition," *ProPublica,* May 4, 2023.

xvi   Paoletta, predictably, indulged—@ MarkPaoletta, X, May 4, 2023.

xvi   Paoletta is depicted—"Clarence Thomas and the Billionaire," *ProPublica,* April 6, 2023.

xvi   *ProPublica* put it in an August 2023 report—"Clarence Thomas' 38 Vacations: The Other Billionaires Who Have Treated the Supreme Court Justice to Luxury Travel," *ProPublica,* August 10, 2023.

xvii   A July 2023 *Washington Post* report revealed—"Influential Activist Leonard Leo Helped Fund Media Campaign Lionizing Clarence Thomas," *Washington Post,* July 20, 2023.

xvii   "Justice Thomas: The most open"—Ibid.

xvii   in a letter to HBO's president—Ibid.

xviii   shows a relaxed, relatable version—"Clarence Thomas and the Billionaire," *ProPublica.*

xix   Here was the August 2023 headline—"Clarence Thomas's $267,230 R.V. and the Friend Who Financed It," *New York Times,* August 5, 2023.

xix   The Prevost Le Mirage XL Marathon—Ibid.

xx   Thomas gave a speech to a Goldwater Institute dinner—Goldwater Awards Dinner, November 19, 1999.

xxiii   By September 2022, Gallup was showing—"Views of Supreme Court Remain Near Record Lows," Gallup, September 29, 2023.

xxiv   according to a March 2023 Marquette University poll—"New Marquette Law School Poll National Survey Finds Continued General Trend of Lower Public Approval of Work of U.S. Supreme Court," Marquette University Press Release, March 24, 2023. "In the current survey, 33 percent favor the June 2022 decision in *Dobbs v. Jackson Women's Health Organization,* overturning *Roe v. Wade,* while 67 percent oppose that ruling."

xxiv   Women of childbearing age—"How Christian Nationalism Perverted the Judicial System and Gutted Our Rights," *The New Republic,* May 10, 2022.

xxiv   The vagaries of elections—Ibid.

xxiv   Yet moving forward—"How the Supreme Court Conservative 'Supermajority' Is Changing the Country," CNN, June 5, 2023.

xxiv "Clarence Thomas is an outlaw and a liar"—"David Brock Believed in Clarence Thomas. Now He Wants Him Impeached," *Huffington Post,* September 16, 2022.

xxvi Speaking in Arizona in 1999—Goldwater Awards Dinner, November 19, 1999.

## CHAPTER 1: October 1973: Nixon's Revenge

3 *New York Times* reporter Nan Robertson—New York Times News Service, "Pat Nixon Entertains 4,702 Republican Women: Girdle-to-Girdle in the East Room," *Louisville Courier-Journal,* April 16, 1969.

4 inspiring this prediction in a newspaper—"Blair Grad Is Top Clerk-Typist," *Omaha World-Herald,* June 21, 1974.

4 "Warrior woman: Ginni Lamp."—Westside High School Yearbook, Omaha, Nebraska, 1975, page 47. Via Ancestry.com database.

5 Thompson made his name—"Presenting: The Richard Nixon Doll (Overhauled 1968 Model)," July 1968, *Pageant.* Reprinted in Hunter S. Thompson, *The Great Shark Hunt: Strange Tales from a Strange Time* (Summit Books), 185.

7 memo, marked "CONFIDENTIAL"—"The Memo, by Lewis Powell," Washington and Lee Archives.

7 as explained in a *Fortune* magazine article—"Nader: An Assessment," *Fortune,* May 1971.

9 As the senator explained—Senator Sheldon Whitehouse, "The Scheme 1: The Powell Memo," May 27, 2021.

11 Jack Anderson, remarking—"Powell's Lesson to Business Aired," *Washington Post,* September 28, 1972.

11 As Sheldon Whitehouse connected the dots—Senator Sheldon Whitehouse, "The Scheme 2: Powell on the Court," June 8, 2021.

12 "I don't feel defiant"—Archibold Cox, "Saturday Night Massacre" Press Conference, October 20, 1973.

13 "Your Commander-in-Chief"—"The End Begins," *New York Times,* October 22, 1973.

13 article headlined—"Free Enterprise Radicals Score Federal Control," *New York Times,* May 29, 1970.

13 "I was thinking of resigning"—"Bork Irked by Emphasis on His Role in Watergate," *New York Times,* July 2, 1987.

13 Nixon praised Bork—"President Welcomes Saxbe to the Cabinet," *New York Times,* December 19, 1973.

14 McConnell gushed in his memoir—Mitch McConnell, *The Long Game: A Memoir* (Sentinel, 2016).

14 "kind of America *we want*"—"McConnell, Grimes Face Off," *Politico,* August 3, 2013.

## CHAPTER 2: October 1960: Radical Catholics

17 "In many ways, Archbishop Lefebvre is a man"—"Man in the News: Marcel Lefebvre; A Devotion to the Past," *New York Times,* July 1, 1988.

17  "He was born on Nov. 29, 1905"—Ibid.

18  "Vatican II was a sound defeat"—Massimo Faggioli, *Vatican II: The Battle for Meaning* (Paulist Press, 2012).

18  "The parallel I have drawn"—Marcel Lefebvre, *Open Letter to Confused Catholics* (Angelus Press, 1986).

19  "defiance of Pope John Paul II"—"Archbishop Lefebvre, 85, Dies; Traditionalist Defied the Vatican," *New York Times,* March 26, 1991.

19  issued a pastoral letter—United Press International, "Bishops in Puerto Rico Forbid Support of Marín," *Buffalo News,* October 21, 1960. Accessed via newspapers.com.

19  At San Juan Cathedral—United Press International, "Church Order Not to Vote for Marín's Party Splits Puerto Rico: Archbishop Booed," *Evansville Press,* October 24, 1960. Accessed via newspapers.com.

19  In the city of Arecibo—Ibid.

20  Archbishop Davis—"Gave No Thought to U.S.—Archbishop," *Press and Sun-Bulletin,* Binghamton (New York), October 29, 1960. Accessed via newspapers.com.

20  "Catholic life in Puerto Rico"—Ibid.

21  *The New York Times* reported from Madrid—"Franco-Pretender Rift Feared by Monarchists," *New York Times,* reprinted in *Des Moines Register,* January 4, 1960. Accessed via newspapers.com.

21  "My decisions on every public policy"—"Acceptance of Democratic Nomination for President," John F. Kennedy Presidential Library and Museum.

21  Protestant leaders—"Religion Unknown Element in Election," *Catholic Times,* November 11, 1960. Accessed via newspapers.com.

21  It took a strong performance in Houston—John F. Kennedy Address to the Greater Houston Ministerial Association, September 12, 1960.

21  Drew Pearson explained in his syndicated column—"Puerto Rico Bishops Hurt Kennedy Drive," reprinted in Muncie (Indiana) *Star Press,* November 6, 1960. Accessed via newspapers.com.

22  Theodore White, in *The Making of the President 1960*—Theodore White, *The Making of the President 1960* (Atheneum, 1961).

23  A *New Yorker* "Letter from Madrid"—"A Letter from Madrid," *The New Yorker,* November 12, 1960.

23  Deal W. Hudson, a former chair—Deal W. Hudson, *Onward, Christian Soldiers: The Growing Political Power of Catholics and Evangelicals in the United States* (Threshold Editions, 2010).

24  As Robert Hutchison wrote—Robert Hutchison, *Their Kingdom Come: Inside the Secret World of Opus Dei* (Thomas Dunne Books, 2006).

24  Opus Dei member John McCloskey—"An Opus Dei Priest with a Magnetic Touch," *New York Times,* June 12, 2015.

24  where, according to published reports—" 'Quite a Shock': The Priest Was a D.C. Luminary. Then He Had a Disturbing Fall from Grace," *Washington Post,* January 14, 2019.

25  which has included Leonard Leo—"Leonard Leo Has Reshaped the Supreme Court. Is He Reshaping Catholic University Too?," *National Catholic Reporter,* December 15, 2022.

25  He referred to *Roe v. Wade*—"Abuse of Discretion: The Inside Story of *Roe v. Wade,*" *National Catholic Register,* January 2014.

25  Pro-choice views are the result of—Ibid.

25  Homosexuality, in McCloskey's view—John McCloskey, "Homosexuality and the American Public Life," book review at https://www.catholicity.com /mccloskey/homosexuality.html.

25  McCloskey eventually had to leave Washington—"Opus Dei Paid $977,000 to Settle Sexual Misconduct Claim Against Prominent Catholic Priest," *Washington Post,* January 7, 2019.

25  One exception that seemed to pierce the code—"Washington's Quiet Club," *Newsweek,* March 8, 2001.

25  "Scalia is regarded as the embodiment"—Ibid.

26  In many ways, Leo was the heir—"How the Christian Right Took Over the Judiciary and Changed America," *The Guardian,* June 25, 2022.

27  both of whom have received awards—"The Benedict Leadership Award," Benedictine Leadership Institute.

27  "A majority of the Supreme Court"—"2022 John Paul II New Evangelization Award Leonard Leo Remarks," Catholic Information Center, November 22, 2022.

## CHAPTER 3: April 1982: The Federalist Society's Revolution

30  gave a speech at Yale Law School—"Review Essay: Brock's Word Against Hers," *Yale Journal of Law and Feminism* 5 (1993).

31  "I sense that we are at one"—"The Weekend at Yale That Changed American Politics," *Politico Magazine,* September/October 2018.

31  first conjured by Bork in a 1971 treatise—"Neutral Principles and Some First Amendment Problems," *Indiana Law Journal* 47, no. 1 (Fall 1971).

32  Bork, the AP reported—"Bork Nominated for High Court; Senate Fight Looms: Favorite of Hard-Line Right Wing," *Los Angeles Times,* July 1, 1987.

32  Bork went on to argue—"Yale Is a Host to 2 Meetings About Politics," *New York Times,* May 2, 1982.

33  "While there now exist"—Steven M. Teles, *The Rise of the Conservative Legal Movement: The Battle for Control of the Law* (Princeton University Press, 2010).

33  "Conservatives have long bemoaned"—Ibid.

34  Steven M. Teles, author of—Ibid.

34  "Do you share a judicial philosophy"—"Confirmation Hearings on Federal Appointments," United States Senate Judiciary Committee, July 11, August 22, August 27, September 13, October 4, 2001.

34  Leo himself is on record—"Ep 80: Leonard Leo Knows How to Win and How to Save Our Country," *American Optimist Podcast,* March 7, 2024.

35  wrote this account—United Features, "Reagan's 'Trickle-Down' Justice," Memphis *Commercial Appeal,* September 19, 1988. Accessed via newspapers.com.

35  "My grandfather was a very hard worker"—"Inside the Mind of Leonard Leo, Trump's Supreme Court Right-Hand Man," *Washington Examiner,* January 28, 2018.

36  "When you're that age"—"We Don't Talk About Leonard: Episode 1, Part 2, 'Most Likely to Succeed,' " *On the Media,* WNYC, September 29, 2023.

36  1983 edition of the Monroe Township High yearbook—"We Don't Talk About Leonard: The Man Behind the Right's Supreme Court Supermajority," *Pro-Publica,* October 11, 2023.

36  a gifted educator—"The Case of Jeremy Rabkin," *Cornell Daily Sun,* March 26, 2007.

36  "Ten years after Watergate"—As quoted in R. Emmett Tyrrell, "A Decision to Treat Freedom Frivolously," *Indianapolis Star,* June 1, 1983. Accessed via newspapers.com.

37  "Few legal scholars these days"—"The Charismatic Constitution," *The Public Interest,* Fall 1983.

37  Rabkin, inverting reality—"High Court Nonsense," *The American Spectator,* December 1984.

37  Working with Rabkin as his advisor—"Inside the Mind of Leonard Leo, Trump's Supreme Court Right-Hand Man," *Washington Examiner.*

37  interned for the Senate Judiciary Subcommittee—Ibid.

37  "In recent decades many have come to view"—"The Great Debate: Attorney General Ed Meese III—November 15, 1985," Speech by Attorney General Edwin Meese III Before the Federalist Society Lawyers Division, November 15, 1985.

38  "That speech had an enormous impact"—"Inside the Mind of Leonard Leo, Trump's Supreme Court Right-Hand Man," *Washington Examiner.*

38  he founded one himself in 1989—Ibid.

39  "every single federal judge"—Michael Avery, *The Federalist Society: How Conservatives Took the Law Back from Liberals* (Vanderbilt University Press, 2013).

39  One email from inside the Bush White House—Senator Sheldon Whitehouse, "The Scheme 5: The Federalist Society," July 27, 2021.

40  "focusing on key recent decisions"—Amanda Hollis-Brusky, *Ideas with Consequences: The Federalist Society and the Conservative Counterrevolution* (Oxford University Press, 2015).

41  whom Thomas has called—"Judicial Activist Directed Fees to Clarence Thomas's Wife, Urged 'No Mention of Ginni,' " *Washington Post,* May 4, 2023.

41  According to Sheldon Whitehouse—Whitehouse, "The Scheme 5: The Federalist Society."

42  "its choice of federal judges"—"How the CNP, a Republican Powerhouse, Helped Spawn Trumpism, Disrupted the Transfer of Power, and Stoked the Assault on the Capitol," *Washington Spectator,* February 22, 2021.

42   The group was a key player—"Conservatives Call on State Legislators to Appoint New Electors, in Accordance with the Constitution," *Conservative Action Project,* December 10, 2020.

42   In 2005 and 2006, JCN took in—"The JCN Story: How to Build a Secretive, Right-Wing Judicial Machine," *Daily Beast,* April 14, 2017.

42   the special interest funds available—"Leonard Leo's Court Capture Web Raised Nearly $600 Million Before Biden Won," True North Research, March 22, 2022; Senator Sheldon Whitehouse, "Scheme 18: Leonard Leo's $1.6 Billion Payday," September 13, 2022.

43   and also funneled cash to antigay groups—"How Abortion Pills Became the Target of Leonard Leo's Post-*Roe* Agenda," Accountable.us, August 25, 2023.

43   Leo's groups also pushed voter suppression laws—"The Honest Elections Project's Attack on Voting Rights," *Documented,* May 8, 2023.

43   According to *Politico,* $43 million—"Dark Money and Special Deals: How Leonard Leo and His Friends Benefited from His Judicial Activism," *Politico,* March 1, 2023.

43   He has also come under investigation—"D.C. Attorney General Is Probing Leonard Leo's Network," *Politico,* August 22, 2023.

43   "Since 2016," *Politico* reported—"Dark Money and Special Deals," *Politico.*

43   Federalist Society president Eugene Meyer—"Federalist Society for Law & Public Policy Studies," Form 990 for fiscal year ending September 2022. Accessed via ProPublica.

43   Just days prior to the publishing of—"What Ginni Thomas and Leonard Leo Wrought: How a Justice's Wife and a Key Activist Started a Movement," *Politico,* September 10, 2023.

44   Harlan Crow, the billionaire who gave—Ibid.

44   Leo joined the board—"Judicial Activist Directed Fees to Clarence Thomas's Wife," *Washington Post,* May 4, 2023.

44   Ginni quit Liberty Central—Ibid.

44   In an email sent to the offices—Author in possession of email.

44   reported here exclusively—Author in possession of email.

45   Liberty Consulting was propped up—"What Ginni Thomas and Leonard Leo Wrought," *Politico,* September 10, 2023.

45   The money flowed to Ginni—Ibid.

45   With Ginni on the payroll—Ibid.

45   JEP also filed a brief contending—Ibid.

45   In another shady transaction—"Judicial Activist Directed Fees to Clarence Thomas's Wife," *Washington Post,* May 4, 2023.

45   Ultimately more than 100K—Ibid.

45   In 2021, she signed a CAP letter—"Conservative Leaders: Remove Cheney and Kinzinger from House Republican Conference," *Conservative Action Project,* December 15, 2021.

## CHAPTER 4: April 1986: When Clarence Met Ginni

47   They met at an affirmative action conference—"Excerpt: Affirmative Action Conference: Toward a Color-Blind Society, Convened by the Anti-Defamation League of B'nai B'rith, 1986. Remarks of Clarence Thomas, chairman of the Equal Employment Opportunity Commission," *Kansas City Times,* June 13, 1986. Accessed via newspapers.com.

47   publisher Richard Viguerie lauded Thomas—"Taking a Close (and Critical) Look at Reagan's Cabinet Choices: His New Right Supporters Are Disappointed," *Los Angeles Times,* December 21, 1980. Accessed via news papers.com.

48   At a "black alternatives" conference—"Blacks Boost Conservatism," *Washington Post,* reprinted in *Hartford Courant,* January 1, 1981. Accessed via newspapers.com.

48   Thomas's appointment to the top civil rights job—"U.S. Weakening on Rights Charged," *St. Louis Post-Dispatch,* May 17, 1981. Accessed via newspapers.com.

48   Midge Decter, a leading neo-conservative—"Q & A: Clarence Thomas," C-SPAN, October 3, 2007.

48   Thomas at one point—Clarence Thomas, *My Grandfather's Son: A Memoir* (Harper, 2007).

49   As the Associated Press reported—Associated Press, "Commission Stirs New 'Comparable Worth' Argument," *Odessa* (Texas) *American,* June 18, 1985. Accessed via newspapers.com.

50   Much of the humor in the movie comes from—*Short Circuit,* script.

50   Thomas loved the movie—Thomas, *My Grandfather's Son.*

51   "The damn vacation is over!"—Ibid.

51   Soon after the Reverend Martin Luther King Jr. was murdered—"Judge Portrayed as a Product of Ideals Clashing with Life," *New York Times,* July 3, 1991.

51   As current Holy Cross president Vincent D. Rougeau wrote—"Clarence Thomas Was a Beneficiary of Race-Based Admissions at My School," *Boston Globe,* May 29, 2023.

52   Thomas is quoted as saying in Diane Brady's book—Diane Brady, *Fraternity: In 1968, a Visionary Priest Recruited 20 Black Men to the College of the Holy Cross and Changed Their Lives and the Course of History* (Spiegel & Grau, 2012).

52   Thomas attempted to claim—"Justice Thomas Scorns Media, Affirmative Action in Interview," *Los Angeles Times,* March 3, 2007.

52   At Holy Cross, Thomas "often dressed"—"Roots of a Conservative," *Atlanta Constitution,* February 23, 1990. Accessed via newspapers.com.

53   In a 1983 speech—"Thomas Once Praised Farrakhan in Speech: Judiciary: Court Nominee Says He Repudiates Anti-Semitic Views Later Attributed to Nation of Islam Leader," *Los Angeles Times,* July 13, 1991.

53   Among the points—"Clarence Thomas' Radical Vision of Race," *The New Yorker,* September 10, 2019.

53   Thomas was a hard-liner on the issue—Ibid.

53 "Looking out of a window"—Kevin Merida and Michael Fletcher, *Supreme Discomfort: The Divided Soul of Clarence Thomas* (Crown, 2008).

53 Later, Thomas would look back and say—*Created Equal: Clarence Thomas in His Own Words,* video documentary, January 31, 2020.

54 As the *New York Times* rather bluntly spelled out—"On Thomas's Climb, Ambivalence About Issue of Affirmative Action," *New York Times,* July 14, 1991.

54 As civil rights giant Rosa Parks herself said—"Thomas' Rulings Show a Man of Integrity," *Baltimore Sun,* November 17, 1996.

54 Longtime Washington columnist Carl Rowan went further—Carl Rowan, *Dream Makers, Dream Breakers: The World of Justice Thurgood Marshall* (Welcome Rain Publishers, 2002).

54 at one point William Bradford Reynolds—Merida and Fletcher, *Supreme Discomfort.*

55 In 1967, Marjorie Lamp was so headstrong—"3 Nebraska Clubs Quit GOP Women's Group," *Omaha World Record,* May 26, 1987. Accessed via newspapers.com.

55 "Her parents were the roots"—"Is Ginni Thomas a Threat to the Supreme Court?," *The New Yorker,* January 21, 2022.

55 Then in February 1972—"Mrs. Virginia Lamp Files for Legislature," *Omaha World-Herald,* February 15, 1972. Accessed via newspapers.com.

56 A *Fremont Tribune* article on her race—"Year of Women Sets Pace for New Valley Politician," *Fremont Tribune,* September 13, 1972. Accessed via newspapers.com.

56 She warned that if Georgia governor Jimmy Carter—"Valley Delegate: President Nice, but Not Qualified," *Fremont Tribune,* July 10, 1976. Accessed via newspapers.com.

56 In 1980, as a twenty-three-year-old law student—"District 2, Vote for 8, All from Omaha Unless Otherwise Stated, Reagan," *Lincoln Journal Star,* May 11, 1980. Accessed via newspapers.com.

56 Ginni finished second—"Leonard Peterson One of GOP Leading Convention Delegates," *Alliance* (Nebraska) *Times-Herald,* May 14, 1980. Accessed via newspapers.com.

56 "She was exuberant, enthusiastic"—"The Nominee's Soul Mate," *Washington Post,* September 10, 1991.

57 In February 1985 a poll was published—"Poll Backs Comparable Worth," *Billings Gazette,* February 13, 1985. Accessed via newspapers.com.

57 Ginni was honored in the July 1986 issue—*Good Housekeeping,* July 1986.

## CHAPTER 5: October 1987: The Deeper Meaning of "Borking"

60 On July 6, 1981—"Monday, July 6, 1981," Ronald Reagan Presidential Foundation and Institute.

60 O'Connor had cast a vote in the Arizona legislature—Linda Greenhouse, *Becoming Justice Blackmun: Harry Blackmun's Supreme Court Journey* (Times Books, 2005).

61    Scalia slipped through, too—"Antonin Scalia, of Virginia, to Be an Associate Justice of the Supreme Court of the United States, vice William H. Rehnquist," Congress.gov.

61    firing Archibald Cox—"Nixon Forces Firing of Cox; Richardson, Ruckelshaus Quit," *Washington Post,* October 21, 1973.

62    as Federalist Society founder Steven Calabresi later admitted—Steven Michael Teles, *The Rise of the Conservative Legal Movement: The Battle for Control of the Law* (Princeton University Press, 2008).

62    Bork was on record as believing—"Federal Offense," *The New Republic,* April 8, 2001.

62    supported poll taxes—"Bork Hearings Showed How Democracy Works; A Very Small Poll Tax," *New York Times,* October 23, 1987.

62    literacy tests for voting—Ibid.

62    mandated school prayer—"'Borking,' Explained: Why a Failed Supreme Court Nomination in 1987 Matters," *Vox,* September 27, 2018.

62    opposed the right to privacy that barred states—Ibid.

62    the use of contraceptives by married couples—"The Bork Hearings; Bork Is Assailed over Remarks on Contraceptive Ruling," *New York Times,* September 19, 1987.

62    and rights protecting homosexual conduct—"U.S. Court Upholds Navy's Discharge of a Homosexual," *New York Times,* August 18, 1984.

62    He had ruled for a company against workers—"'Borking,' Explained," *Vox.*

62    And in 1981, Bork had told Congress—"In Bork's Words: Abortion, Death Penalty, Gay Rights," *New York Times,* June 2, 1987.

62    Edward Kennedy of Massachusetts—"Robert Bork's America," C-SPAN, July 1, 1987.

63    was launched by People for the American Way—"1987 Gregory Peck Ad Against Robert Bork on SCOTUS," C-SPAN, March 20, 2016.

63    When asked a softball question—"The Bork Hearings; An Intellectual Appetite," *New York Times,* September 20, 1987.

63    In the words of *The Washington Post*—"In The End, Bork Himself Was His Own Worst Enemy," *Washington Post,* October 24, 1987.

64    Adam Serwer lucidly summarized—"The Care and Feeding of Supreme Court Justices," *The Atlantic,* October 3, 2023.

64    Texas author Bryan Burrough told NPR—"'Forget the Alamo' Author Says We Have the Texas Origin Story All Wrong," National Public Radio, June 16, 2021.

65    The legacy of Bork—"Robert Bork's Proud Legacy and the Senate's Shameful One," *Wall Street Journal,* August 31, 2018.

65    But the aggrieved right wing found it useful—"The Care and Feeding of Supreme Court Justices," *The Atlantic.*

66    and he was confirmed—"Anthony M. Kennedy, of California, to Be an Associate Justice of the Supreme Court of the United States, vice Lewis F. Powell, Jr., Retired," Congress.gov.

66  including, from 1993 to 1994—"Basketball, Popeyes, 2 Live Crew: The Year Neil Gorsuch and Brett Kavanaugh Clerked for Anthony Kennedy," *USA Today,* August 30, 2018.

66  David Margolick would write—"The Path to Florida," *Vanity Fair,* October 2004.

## CHAPTER 6: July 1991: Clarence Thomas, Revealed

70  Rudman, in his memoir, crowed—Warren Rudman, *Combat: Twelve Years in the U.S. Senate* (Random House, 1996).

71  he was celebrated on the front page—"Thurgood Marshall, Civil Rights Hero, Dies at 84," *New York Times,* January 25, 1993.

71  wrote *Louisville Courier-Journal* columnist—"Thoroughly Good," *Louisville Courier-Journal,* January 28, 1993. Accessed via newspapers.com.

72  Thomas had his intellectual pretensions—"7 Pols Who Praised Ayn Rand," *Politico,* April 26, 2012.

72  In a 1984 interview, Thomas asserted—"EEOC Chairman Blasts Black Leaders," *Washington Post,* October 25, 1984.

73  The *Washington Post* article announcing his nomination—"Bush Picks Thomas for Supreme Court," *Washington Post,* July 2, 1991.

73  she spearheaded a noisy group—"Confirmation Bias," *Slate,* April 7, 2016.

74  Thomas aced this assignment—"The President's News Conference in Kennebunkport, Maine," The American Presidency Project, presidency .ucsb.edu.

74  he immediately tried calling Ginni—"Bush Picks Thomas for Supreme Court," *Washington Post.*

74  "wonderful sense of humor"—"Supreme Court Nomination Announcement," C-SPAN, July 1, 1991.

74  "Only in America could this be possible"—Ibid.

76  the pair invited *People* magazine—" 'How We Survived,' " *People,* November 11, 1991.

76  *Washington Post* columnist Richard Cohen was excoriating—"What's Thomas Doing in People Magazine?," *Washington Post,* November 12, 1991.

77  Documents unearthed by *The New York Times*—"The Long Crusade of Clarence and Ginni Thomas," *New York Times Magazine,* February 22, 2022.

77  according to documents obtained by *Mother Jones*—"Inside Groundswell: Read the Memos of the New Right-Wing Strategy Group Planning a '30 Front War,' " *Mother Jones,* July 25, 2013.

77  The Eagle Forum, which opposes abortion rights—"The Long Crusade of Clarence and Ginni Thomas," *New York Times Magazine.*

77  Clarence Thomas has twice headlined—Ibid.

78  In September 2022, an analysis—"Revealed: Ginni Thomas's Links to Anti-Abortion Groups Who Lobbied to Overturn Roe," *The Guardian,* September 9, 2022.

78    in approaching the abortion issue—"Nomination of Judge Clarence Thomas to Be Associate Justice of the Supreme Court of the United States," United States Senate Judiciary Committee, Part 1, September 10, 11, 12, 13, 16, 1991.

78    Thomas had signed on to a White House working group—"Law and Natural Law: Questions for Judge Thomas," *Washington Post,* September 8, 1991.

### CHAPTER 7: January 1993: The Right Sets Out to Get Bill Clinton

81    reporting on Starr's nomination as solicitor general—"Appeals Judge Chosen by Bush to Be Solicitor," *New York Times,* February 2, 1989.

81    as author Jan Crawford Greenburg described it—Jan Crawford Greenburg, *Supreme Conflict: The Inside Story of the Struggle for Control of the United States Supreme Court* (Penguin, 2008).

82    and the next day the attorney general—"How Bill Barr Kept Ken Starr Off the Supreme Court (Resulting in David Souter)," *Reason,* August 17, 2021.

83    The Arkansas Project—"Almost $2 Million Spent in Magazine's Anti-Clinton Project, but on What?," *New York Times,* April 15, 1998.

83    Scaife had run afoul of the law—"Scaife: Funding Father of the Right," *Washington Post,* May 2, 1999.

83    An early funder—"Decades of Contributions to Conservatism," *Washington Post,* May 2, 1999.

83    Olson secretly helped prepare—"The President's Trial: The Lawsuit; Quietly, a Team of Lawyers Kept Paula Jones's Case Alive," *New York Times,* January 24, 1999.

83    I learned later that the troopers—Ibid.

84    including a rough-hewn former cop—David Brock, *Blinded by the Right: The Conscience of an Ex-Conservative* (Crown, 2002).

84    and an Arkansas bait-shop owner—"Justice Department Eyes the 'Arkansas Project,'" *The Observer,* April 6, 1998.

84    caused the sale of the magazine—"The Life and Death of *The American Spectator,*" *The Atlantic,* November 2001.

84    which he founded on the campus—Ibid.

84    In 1997, he published—R. Emmett Tyrell Jr. & Anonymous, *The Impeachment of William Jefferson Clinton* (Regnery, 1997).

85    "If Nixon deserved impeachment"—R. Emmett Tyrell Jr. and "Anonymous," *The Impeachment of William Jefferson Clinton: A Political Docu-Drama,* Review, "Is Impeachment Practical? Judge Robert Bork's Answer is YES."

85    He was the son—"The Roots of Ken Starr's Morality Plays," *Washington Post,* March 2, 1998.

85    was a Democrat in college—Ibid.

85    because he had psoriasis—"Kenneth Starr, Lawyer Who Led the Drive to Impeach President Clinton over the 'Zippergate' Affair—Obituary," *The Telegraph,* September 14, 2022.

85    Profiled as a high school senior—"Future Politician," *San Antonio Express-News,* October 26, 1963. Accessed via newspapers.com.

86  as Timothy Clifford wrote—"He's Used to Complex Cases," New York *Daily News,* January 21, 1994. Accessed via newspapers.com.

86  Even Republican senator Bob Dole—"GOP Lawyer Picked to Probe Whitewater: Presidency: Ex-N.Y. Prosecutor Fiske Is Chosen as Special Counsel by Reno," *Los Angeles Times,* January 21, 1994.

87  On June 17, 1993—"Who Is Vincent Foster?," *Wall Street Journal,* June 17, 1993.

87  one in a series—"The Journal and Vincent Foster," *Washington Post,* July 29, 1993.

87  Bartley and the *Journal* harrumphed—"Who Is Vincent Foster?," *Wall Street Journal.*

87  His note mentioned—"Wall Street Journal Editorial Writers 'Lie Without . . . ,'" *Baltimore Sun,* August 12, 1993.

87  Weirdly pretending—Brock, *Blinded by the Right.*

88  He disingenuously concluded—"The Foster Test," *Wall Street Journal,* January 14, 1994.

88  He'd been awarded a Pulitzer Prize—"The 1980 Pulitzer Prize Winner in Editorial Writing," The Pulitzer Prizes.

88  Robert Fiske, working industriously—"Foster's Death a Suicide," *Washington Post,* July 1, 1994.

88  in editorials with headlines—"From Scandal to Farce," *Newsweek,* August 14, 1994.

88  and he made his case—"Judge Met Sen. Faircloth Before Fiske Was Ousted," *Washington Post,* August 12, 1994.

88  Chief Justice Rehnquist had appointed—"Appointment in Whitewater Turns into a Partisan Battle," *New York Times,* August 6, 1994.

89  "The change came as a complete surprise"—Ibid.

### CHAPTER 8: August 1991: The Citizens United Filth Factory

90  Brown was the one to give us the infamous—"From Willie Horton to Western Journalism: Floyd Brown's Career in Media Manipulation," *Newsweek,* December 6, 2016.

91  Floyd Brown had founded a nonprofit—Ibid.

91  Brown told a *Washington Times* reporter—"The GOP's Own 'Dennis the Menace,'" *Washington Times,* July 10, 1992.

91  July 1988 *Reader's Digest* article—"Getting Away with Murder," *Reader's Digest,* July 1998.

92  working with TV ad maker Larry McCarthy—"Attack Dog," *The New Yorker,* February 5, 2012.

92  *Republic of Spin* author David Greenberg—"Bush Made Willie Horton an Issue in 1988, and the Racial Scars Are Still Fresh," *New York Times,* December 3, 2018.

92  "If I can make Willie Horton a household name"—Ibid.

92  Atwater even called Horton—Ibid.

92  Roger Ailes, then a Bush strategist—Ibid.

92   putting out a crude attack-ad smear-job—"Tables Turned in High Court Skirmish: Judiciary: Conservatives Are Running 'Attack Ads' Against Liberal Senators," *Los Angeles Times,* September 5, 1991.

93   with a narrator asking whether Kennedy and Biden—Ibid.

93   *The New York Times* reported—"Bush Criticizes Ad Backing Thomas," *New York Times,* September 5, 1991.

93   "We have what we need to turn ads around very quickly"—Ibid.

93   having just been denounced—Ibid.

93   said Arthur Kropp of People for the American Way—Ibid.

94   but the *Times* revealed that the White House—Ibid.

94   $15,000 to $20,000—Ibid.

94   "The latest advertisement shares another common feature"—Ibid.

94   even after a direct appeal—"Bush Acts to Quiet Storm over TV Ad on Thomas," *New York Times,* September 6, 1991.

94   "Unfortunately, the administration has no desire"—Ibid.

95   The week before the Clarence Thomas hearings—Ibid.

95   who was finance chair of Newt Gingrich's PAC—"Clinton Aides Step Up Attacks on Starr Inquiry," *New York Times,* April 8, 1998.

95   He had published a "book" that year—Floyd G. Brown, *Slick Willie: Why America Cannot Trust Bill Clinton* (Annapolis-Washington Book Publishing, 1993).

96   with chapters like—Ibid.

## CHAPTER 9: September 1994: Ken Starr's Sidekick

98   Author James B. Stewart was tart—"Innocence Betrayed," *New York Times,* October 13, 1996.

99   However, Stewart was pretty on target—Ibid.

100  basketball player Charles Ludington—Author interview.

101  even old pros like Pete Yost—Associated Press, "Hillary's Grand Jury Appearance Today," *Petoskey* (Michigan) *News-Review,* January 26, 1996. Accessed via newspapers.com.

101  You judge for yourself—Ibid.

102  Yost's account moved on—Ibid.

103  egged on by House Speaker Newt Gingrich—"Gingrich 'Not Convinced' Foster Death Was Suicide," *Washington Post,* July 26, 1995.

103  his voice no doubt cracking—"Foster Was 'Critical' to Travel Office Probe," *Tampa Bay Times,* January 18, 1998.

103  James Hamilton, had previously told—"Attorney Seeks Protection of Foster's Final Confidences," *Washington Post,* January 17, 1998.

104  "Mr. Kavanaugh, we'll hear from you"—*Swidler & Berlin v. United States,* Supreme Court.gov.

104  Seventy-six words into his debut—Ibid.

105   "They're not quite as well-known"—Ibid.

105   "Covering the Courts" columnist James J. Kilpatrick—"Does Death Put an End to 'Privileged' Talks?," *Binghamton Press and Sun-Bulletin,* June 15, 1998. Accessed via newspapers.com.

105   Stevens scolded Kavanaugh—*Swidler & Berlin v. United States,* Supreme Court.gov.

105   As David Savage wrote—"Justices Skeptical of Effort by Starr to Waive Privilege," *Los Angeles Times,* June 9, 1998.

105   Added Stephen Labaton—"Supreme Court Hears Case on Ex-White House Counsel's Notes," *New York Times,* June 9, 1998.

106   wrote Aaron Epstein—"Court Keeps Lawyer Notes from Starr," *Philadelphia Inquirer,* June 26, 1998. Accessed via newspapers.com.

106   A judge identified twenty-four news reports—"Secret Report on Starr Inquiry Leaks Is Released, but Doesn't Name Kavanaugh," *New York Times,* August 23, 2018.

106   *The Washington Post* reported on Kavanaugh—"Kavanaugh Is Not Mentioned in Once-Secret Report on Press Leaks," *Washington Post,* August 23, 2018.

106   The *Post* itself: Analysis by the author.

106   Sheldon Whitehouse laid out—"Confirmation Hearing on the Nomination of Hon. Brett M. Kavanaugh to Be an Associate Justice of the Supreme Court of the United States," United States Senate Judiciary Committee Transcript, Part 1, September 4, 5, 6, 7, 27, 2018.

107   but denied improper disclosures—Ibid.

107   Challenged by Whitehouse—Ibid.

107   admonished Starr's deputies—"Report of the Special Master on Rulthe(E) Inquiry," United States District Court of the District of Columbia, National Archives.

107   After breaching legal ethics—"Former Lawyer for Paula Jones Says He Consulted Starr About Case," *New York Times,* October 15, 1998.

107   Starr had been given secretly made tapes—"Starr Aides Trace Lewinsky's Steps," *Washington Post,* May 27, 1998.

107   who urged Starr to ask—"Brett Kavanaugh Urged Graphic Questions in Clinton Inquiry," *New York Times,* August 20, 2018.

107   Kavanaugh was also the principal author—"Brett Kavanaugh Memo Proposed Explicit Questions for President Bill Clinton," *Washington Post,* August 20, 2018.

108   reading like a bad pulp novel—"Narrative Pt. II: Initial Sexual Encounters," Starr Report.

108   when reports resurfaced—"Aspects of Gingrich Divorce Story Distorted," *Washington Post,* November 20, 2011.

108   the board of regents fired him—"Baylor Demotes President Kenneth Starr over Handling of Sex Assault Cases," *New York Times,* May 26, 2016.

108   Starr later joined Trump's legal team—"Texan Ken Starr Joins Donald Trump's Impeachment Defense Team," *Texas Tribune,* January 17, 2020.

108    also joined the team defending—"Ken Starr Waged 'Scorched-Earth' Campaign to Drop Federal Case Against Epstein: Book," *The Hill,* July 14, 2021.

108    involving a brutal smear—"Ken Starr Helped Jeffrey Epstein with 'Scorched-Earth' Campaign, Book Claims," *The Guardian,* July 13, 2021.

108    came forward to admit—"Ken Starr, Brett Kavanaugh, Jeffrey Epstein and Me," Judi Hershman via Medium, July 12, 2021.

108    also highlighting Brett Kavanaugh's—Ibid.

108    Hershman pinpointed the blatant hypocrisy—Ibid.

109    In his 2018 memoir—Ken Starr, *Contempt: A Memoir of the Clinton Investigation* (Sentinel, 2018).

### CHAPTER 10: June 1997: John Eastman and the Growing Thomas Network

110    led to his being indicted—"Attorney John Eastman Surrenders on Charges in Trump's Georgia 2020 Election Subversion Case," Associated Press, August 22, 2023.

110    another court ruling stating that Eastman—"Judge: Trump 'More Likely than Not' Committed Crimes Related to Jan. 6 Attack," *Roll Call,* March 28, 2022.

111    Thomas would tell his clerks—"Ginni Thomas's Close Ties with Husband's Law Clerks Highlighted in New Book," *The Hill,* June 21, 2022.

111    Thomas made a ritual—"7 Pols Who Praised Ayn Rand," *Politico,* April 26, 2012.

111    As film critic David Thomson put it—"Reach for the Skyscraper," *The Independent,* November 15, 1998.

111    Clarence Thomas said at a 2008 event—"The Second Annual William French Smith Memorial Lecture: A Conversation with Justice Clarence Thomas," *Pepperdine Law Review* 37, no. 5 (December 15, 2009).

111    In a 2022 book, *Created Equal*—Michael Pack and Mark Paoletta, *Created Equal: Clarence Thomas in His Own Words* (Regnery, 2022).

112    "Claremont is among the most influential"—"2 Wealthy Conservatives Use Think Tanks to Push Goals," *Los Angeles Times,* July 8, 1996.

112    studied economics and politics—"For John Eastman and Clarence Thomas, an Intellectual Kinship Stretching Back Decades," *Washington Post,* December 23, 2022.

112    His thesis advisor, Bill Allen—Ibid.

112    Allen, a member of President Reagan's—"Pomona Professor to Seek GOP Senate Nomination," *San Bernardino County Sun,* January 14, 1986. Accessed via newspapers.com.

112    Eastman, identified as Allen's—Ibid.

113    That June, he finished eleventh out of thirteen—"CA US Senate—R Primary," Our Campaigns.

113    the following April Reagan appointed him—"For John Eastman and Clarence Thomas, an Intellectual Kinship Stretching Back Decades," *Washington Post.*

113    Eastman moved to Washington—Ibid.

113    "In Washington, he was a gregarious go-getter"—Ibid.

113    Eastman would later talk of—Ibid.

113    he started hiring Claremont-affiliated scholars—Ibid.

113    was known at the time principally for—Ibid.

113    credited with supplying Goldwater—"The Goldwater Campaign," *New York,* October 12, 2012.

114    asked the Claremont scholars to tell him what he believed—"How the Claremont Institute Became a Nerve Center of the American Right," *New York Times Magazine,* June 15, 2023.

114    Thomas later praised an article—"Danforth: Thomas Speech Didn't Reflect Abortion View," *Washington Post,* July 18, 1991.

114    claiming it was a "throwaway line"—"Nomination of Judge Clarence Thomas to Be Associate Justice of the Supreme Court of the United States," United States Senate Judiciary Committee, Part 1, September 10, 11, 12, 13, 16, 1991.

114    Eastman completed his law degree—"Dr. John C. Eastman," The Federalist Society.

114    he was surprisingly generous—"Inside Professor Obama's Classroom," *New York Times,* July 30, 2008.

114    Law professor Garrett Epps—"The Dangerous Journey of John Eastman," *Washington Monthly,* April 4, 2023.

115    naming him one of his clerks—"For John Eastman and Clarence Thomas, an Intellectual Kinship Stretching Back Decades," *Washington Post.*

115    Eastman had also clerked for J. Michael Luttig—Ibid.

115    who would later speak out against—"A Conservative Judge Helped Stop Trump on Jan. 6. He Wants to Finish the Job," *Washington Post,* February 2, 2023.

115    Eastman for many years chaired—"Should the Federalist Society Reckon with Members Who Aided Trump's False Election Claims?," *ABA Journal,* January 19, 2021.

115    In 1990, two years after working on—"Challengers Find the Road to Congress Is Uphill Struggle," *Los Angeles Times,* October 25, 1990.

115    He finished well back—"Election Results for the U.S. Senate and the U.S. House of Representatives," Federal Election Commission, April 1991.

115    Eastman threw his name in the hat—"Court Orders Title Change for California Attorney General Candidate," *Los Angeles Times,* April 2, 2010.

116    Eastman ended up finishing second—"California Attorney General Election, 2010," Ballotpedia.

116    "I think I would've beaten"—"The Dangerous Journey of John Eastman," *Washington Monthly.*

116    recalls Republican consultant Wayne C. Johnson—Author interview.

116    Eastman struck Wayne Johnson—Author interview.

116    Among the contributors—Per California Secretary of State records.

116   *Los Angeles Times* editorial board—"Steve Cooley in Republican Race for State Attorney General," *Los Angeles Times,* April 29, 2010.

116   Eastman would finish with 737,025 votes—"California Attorney General Election, 2010," Ballotpedia.

117   In September 2011, Eastman was named chairman—"John Eastman Named National Organization for Marriage Chairman," *Huffington Post,* September 22, 2011.

117   when the chief justice resisted—"First Take: Justices Decide Gay Marriage by Not Deciding," *USA Today,* October 6, 2014.

117   even when he sounded pious—"Gay Marriage Fight May Hinge on Supreme Court's Anthony Kennedy," *Los Angeles Times,* February 8, 2012.

118   By December 2020, Eastman found himself—"What You Need to Know About John Eastman's 2020 Election Charges," PBS, September 21, 2023.

118   Trump lawyer Kenneth Chesebro—"Trump Lawyers Saw Justice Thomas as 'Only Chance' to Stop 2020 Election Certification," *Politico,* November 22, 2022.

118   To this fevered, arguably treasonous suggestion—Ibid.

118   was also in regular email contact—"Trump Lawyer Cited 'Heated Fight' Among Justices over Election Suits," *New York Times,* June 15, 2022.

## CHAPTER 11: December 2000: The Supreme Court Steals an Election

120   Sometimes referred to as "the Brooks Brothers riot"—"How the 'Brooks Brothers Riot' Set the Stage for Insurrection," *The Nation,* August 4, 2022.

120   who directed an aide to "shut it down"—"Pol Versus Pole," *New York,* March 19, 2001.

120   nickname "Congressman Kick-Ass"—"The 20th District in New York," Race Profile, *New York Times.*

120   the self-described "Republican hit man"—"Donald Trump Breaks with Longtime Aide Roger Stone," MSNBC, August 8, 2015.

120   key role in organizing the January 6 assault—"Revealed: Roger Stone's Secret Call with Proud Boys Leader in Lead-up to Jan. 6," *Rolling Stone,* January 4, 2024.

120   Bush was represented by—*Bush v. Gore,* 531 U.S. 98 (2000), *Justia.*

121   logic only applied to "the present circumstances"—Ibid.

121   "as we say in Brooklyn, a piece of shit"—"Scalia Thought *Bush v. Gore* Legal Rationale Was a 'Piece of Sh-t' but Backed It Anyway," *Washington Examiner,* March 7, 2019.

121   Republican senator Chuck Hagel—"The Rare Diplomat," *Salon,* November 20, 2000.

122   As one Supreme Court law clerk at the time—"The Path to Florida," *Vanity Fair,* October 2004.

122   summed up their sentiments—Ibid.

122   As one former clerk explained to Margolick—Ibid.

123   Evan Thomas wrote in his biography—Evan Thomas, *First: Sandra Day O'Connor* (Random House, 2019).

123    Kennedy's clerks were plugged into—"The Path to Florida," *Vanity Fair.*

123    Ginni was intimately involved—"Contesting the Vote: Challenging a Justice; Job of Thomas's Wife Raises Conflict-of-Interest Questions," *New York Times,* December 12, 2000.

123    Law clerks later leaked that O'Connor—"The Path to Florida," *Vanity Fair.*

123    Jeffrey Toobin reported that O'Connor—Jeffrey Toobin, *Too Close to Call: The Thirty-Six-Day Battle to Decide the 2000 Election* (Random House, 2001).

124    wrote Harvard Law professor Alan Dershowitz—Alan Dershowitz, *Supreme Injustice: How the High Court Hijacked Election 2000* (Oxford University Press, 2001).

124    the nonpartisan Florida Ballots Project concluded—"So, Who Really Won? What the *Bush v. Gore* Studies Showed," CNN, October 31, 2015.

## CHAPTER 12: October 2005: The Federalists Shoot Down Bush's Choice

125    She would be the first justice who would not have—"If Approved, a First-Time Judge, Yes, but Hardly the First in Court's History," *New York Times,* October 4, 2005.

125    served as Bush's personal lawyer—"Low-Profile Woman, High-Powered Job," *New York Times,* November 20, 2004.

125    first woman to serve as president—Ibid.

126    "Low-Profile Woman, High-Powered Job"—Ibid.

126    Bush referred to her as a—Ibid.

126    Robert Bork, now licking his wounds—"Robert Bork on Harriet Miers' High Court Bid," National Public Radio, October 11, 2005.

126    Eugene Delgaudio, president—"Senate Presses for Quick Miers Confirmation," NBC News, October 2, 2005.

126    from radio host Rush Limbaugh—"Rush Limbaugh Reacts to Miers Nomination," Fox News, October 5, 2005.

126    syndicated columnists Pat Buchanan—"Examining the Conservative Split over Miers," NBC News, October 11, 2005.

126    and Ann Coulter—"Private: Ann Coulter on Miers," American Constitution Society, October 6, 2005.

126    speculated that if confirmed—"GOP Senator Concerned About Miers' Abortion Views," ABC News, October 5, 2005.

127    Miers had indicated that she favored—"Questions for Harriet Miers," PBS, October 18, 2005.

127    leaked that in a meeting—"Specter, White House at Odds over Miers' Views," CNN, October 18, 2005.

127    Other nodes in the campaign—"Point Man for Miers Juggles Allegiances," *Wall Street Journal,* October 26, 2005.

127    the administration withdrew the nomination—"President's Statement on Harriet Miers' Supreme Court Nomination Withdrawal," White House Archives, October 27, 2005.

127    As Federalist Society expert Ann Southworth—"Justice Alito's Crusade Against a Secular America Isn't Over," *The New Yorker,* August 28, 2022.

128    As Federalist founder Steven Calabresi—"In Alito, G.O.P. Reaps Harvest Planted in '82," *New York Times,* January 30, 2006.

128    Democrat Harry Reid—"Lawmakers React to Miers' Withdrawal," CNN, October 27, 2005.

128    Charlie Savage of *The Boston Globe*—"Family Names, Fresh Faces Among Options," *Boston Globe,* October 28, 2005. Accessed via newspapers.com.

129    "Miranda Plan" of attack—"Getting Ready for the Supreme Court Battle," *The Hill,* November 30, 2004. Accessed via FreeRepublic.

129    When Miers was withdrawn—"Right Ponders Relations with White House," *Washington Post,* October 28, 2005.

129    The Associated Press posed the question—"Miers' Withdrawal May Spawn a New Verb," NBC News, October 27, 2005.

## CHAPTER 13: January 2006: Scalito

130    a conservative Catholic—"Opus Dei's Influence on the U.S. Judiciary," *Church and State,* December 21, 2018.

130    Nicknamed Scalito—"Opinion: Samuel Alito: One Angry Man," *Politico Magazine,* May 18, 2022.

130    Steinert High in Hamilton Township—"Supreme Court Justice Sam Alito Returns to Steinert High School for Library Dedication," *The Trentonian,* August 19, 2021.

130    later described by classmates—"A Tiger on the Court: Sam Alito '72 at Princeton," *Princeton Alumni Weekly,* March 8, 2006.

130    He supported Barry Goldwater's run—"Justice Alito's Crusade Against a Secular America Isn't Over," *The New Yorker,* August 28, 2022.

131    avid reader of William F. Buckley's *National Review*—Ibid.

131    joining a sexist campus organization—Ibid.

131    Interior Secretary Walter Hickel visited the campus—"A Tiger on the Court," *Princeton Alumni Weekly.*

131    one of only twelve members of his class—"Alito Is Seen as a Methodical Jurist with a Clear Record," *New York Times,* November 1, 2005.

131    when he joined the campus Whig-Cliosophic Society—"Justice Alito's Crusade Against a Secular America Isn't Over," *The New Yorker.*

131    settled for a meeting with Justice John Marshall Harlan II—Ibid.

131    George Pieler later recalled—"A Tiger on the Court," *Princeton Alumni Weekly.*

132    dense senior's thesis on Italian law—Ibid.

132    recalling that he researched his thesis—"1972 Nassau Herald."

132    Alito hoped to study with his intellectual hero—"A Tiger on the Court," *Princeton Alumni Weekly.*

132    Margaret Talbot wrote—"Justice Alito's Crusade Against a Secular America Isn't Over," *The New Yorker.*

132 Alito would draw puzzled stares—Ibid.

132 1985 application to be deputy attorney general—"Presidential Personnel Appointment form for Samuel A. Alito, Jr. for the Non-Career Position of Deputy Assistant Attorney General in the Office of Legal Counsel," United States Archives.

133 Bush nominated Alito to the U.S. Court of Appeals—"Justice Samuel A. Alito, Jr.," White House Archives.

133 he was approved unanimously—Ibid.

133 his ninety-year-old mother—"90-Year-Old Mother Mum, Except About Topic of Abortion," *The Sun Journal,* November 1, 2005.

133 "It was a done deal"—"In Alito, G.O.P. Reaps Harvest Planted in '82," *New York Times,* January 30, 2006.

133 "*Roe v. Wade* is an important precedent"—"Confirmation Hearing on the Nomination of Samuel A. Alito, Jr. to Be an Associate Justice of the Supreme Court of the United States," United States Senate Judiciary Committee, January 9–13, 2006.

134 he dismissed the Meese memos—Ibid.

134 An *Axios* analysis—"Supreme Court Ideology Continues to Lean Conservative, New Data Shows," *Axios,* July 3, 2023.

134 overturned longstanding court precedent—"Supreme Court Strikes Down Affirmative Action Programs in College Admissions," *SCOTUSblog,* June 29, 2023.

134 ruled that a private business owner—"Supreme Court Rules Website Designer Can Decline to Create Same-Sex Wedding Websites," *SCOTUSblog,* June 30, 2023.

134 weakened the Environmental Protection Agency—"Supreme Court Curtails EPA's Authority to Fight Climate Change," *SCOTUS blog,* June 30, 2022.

134 charge on requiring states to subsidize religious schools—"U.S. Supreme Court Backs Public Money for Religious Schools," Reuters, June 21, 2022.

134 weakening the Affordable Care Act—"Court Again Leaves Affordable Care Act in Place," *SCOTUSblog,* June 17, 2021.

134 expanding the right to carry firearms—"The Constitutional Right to Carry Firearms in Public Will Harm Public Health," Boston University School of Public Health, October 14, 2022.

135 he gave a blunt speech—"In Unusually Political Speech, Alito Says Liberals Pose Threat to Liberties," *New York Times,* November 13, 2020.

135 *ProPublica* broke the news—"Justice Samuel Alito Took Luxury Fishing Vacation with GOP Billionaire Who Later Had Cases Before the Court," *ProPublica,* June 20, 2023.

135 Alito ruled in a 7-1 case—"Justice Samuel Alito Took Luxury Fishing Vacation with GOP Billionaire Who Later Had Cases Before the Court," *ProPublica.*

135 Georgetown law professor Abbe Smith—Ibid.

135 Alito took the extraordinary step—"Justice Samuel Alito: ProPublica Misleads Its Readers," *Wall Street Journal,* June 20, 2023.

136    the Ethics in Government Act—"Code of Conduct for United States Judges," United States Courts.

136    Alito again appeared—"Samuel Alito, the Supreme Court's Plain-Spoken Defender," *Wall Street Journal,* July 28, 2023.

136    Congressional expert Norm Ornstein—"Samuel Alito Is Wrong and Arrogant—and Must Be Reined In," *The New Republic,* September 11, 2023.

137    Whitehouse lodged an ethics complaint—"Whitehouse Lodges Ethics Complaint Against Supreme Court Justice Samuel Alito," Sheldon Whitehouse Press Release, September 5, 2023.

### CHAPTER 14: The Three Amigas: Ginni, Cleta, and Connie

141    the man whose team identified—*60 Minutes,* CBS News, September 25, 2022.

141    Cleta Mitchell had the distinction—"Read the Report by the Special Grand Jury in Georgia That Investigated President Trump," *New York Times,* September 8, 2023.

141    As *The Intercept* wrote in September 2023—"Trump Lawyer Cleta Mitchell Escaped Georgia Indictment—And Still Leads Election Denial Movement," *The Intercept,* September 13, 2023.

141    Talking to the January 6th Committee—"Read: House January 6 Committee Releases More Transcripts, Including Jared Kushner and Ginni Thomas," CNN, December 30, 2022.

141    Added Riggleman—Author interview.

141    Riggleman and his data team—"Meadows' Texts Show 'Roadmap to an Attempted Coup,' ex-Jan. 6 Investigator Riggleman Says," *USA Today,* September 26, 2022.

141    calling that effort—"Read: House January 6 Committee Releases More Transcripts, Including Jared Kushner and Ginni Thomas," CNN.

141    she also referenced talking to her husband—Ibid.

141    Ginni Thomas forwarded to Meadows—Ibid.

142    came in a 1982 Pia Zadora vehicle—*Fake-Out,* IMDb.

142    including in *Death Wish 4*—*Death Wish 4: The Crackdown,* IMDb.

142    She started working with a rabidly anti-Clinton group—"The Nativists," Southern Poverty Law Center, November 2, 2006.

142    spoke at a so-called March for Justice rally—"Rally Supporting Clinton Investigation," C-SPAN, October 31, 1998.

143    Introducing Clinton-hating former FBI agent—Ibid.

143    Giddy and bouncy, she led cheers—Ibid.

143    Among the speakers that day was Alan Keyes—Ibid.

143    Connie Hair was his spokesperson—"Keyes Makes It Official: He's Out of Presidential Race," CNN, July 26, 2000.

143    even though Keyes had already lost Senate races—"Alan Keyes," *Encyclopaedia Britannica.*

143    when he did an interview with Michelangelo Signorile—"Senate Candidate Alan Keyes Calls Mary Cheney a 'Selfish Hedonist,'" *The Advocate,* September 2, 2004.

144 As reported in *The Southern Illinoisan*—"Keyes Comments on Homosexuality Stir Up Controversy," *Southern Illinoisan,* September 2, 2004. Accessed via newspapers.com.

144 there was Connie Hair—"U.S. Border Posse Sets Sights on 49th Parallel," *Globe and Mail* (Toronto), August 12, 2005.

144 Minutemen were riding a wave of interest—"Minutemen Go Back to Work," CBS News, April 2, 2006.

144 founder Chris Simcox told the Associated Press—Associated Press, "Minutemen Say Volunteer Calls Pouring In over Fencing Proposal," *Independent Record,* April 22, 2006.

144 "Minuteman spokeswoman Connie Hair"—Ibid.

145 Southern Poverty Law Center assessed the sequence of events—"The Nativists," Southern Poverty Law Center.

146 George F. Will, whose syndicated column—"Campaign Reform Seeks to Muzzle Free Speech," *Washington Post,* reprinted in *Northwest* (Illinois) *Herald,* March 31, 2001. Accessed via newspapers.com.

146 Will cited a *New York Times* formulation—Ibid.

146 Will resorted to the in-print version—Ibid.

146 Will's column turned for help—Ibid.

146 That "study," as Mitchell liked to term it—*Who's Buying Campaign Finance "Reform"?,* The American Conservative Union, 2001.

146 Chapter 3 of Mitchell's 2001 pamphlet—Ibid.

147 BCRA banned so-called soft money—"FEC Commissioner Blasts Campaign Finance Reform," Virginia School of Law, November 13, 2003.

147 starting in 1995 with an op-ed they wrote together—"Making Sense of McCain-Feingold and Campaign-Finance Reform," *The Atlantic,* July/August 2003.

147 *USA Today* wrote in 2002—"Passage Ends Long Struggle for McCain, Feingold," *USA Today,* March 20, 2002.

147 point of view of the argument—*Who's Buying Campaign Finance "Reform"?,* The American Conservative Union.

148 Or how about this astonishing acknowledgment?—Ibid.

148 photo of her at age fifteen—Northeast High School, Oklahoma City, Oklahoma, 1966 Yearbook, page 65. Accessed via ancestry.com.

148 missing out on a competition—"Senior at John Marshall City's First Junior Miss," *Daily Oklahoman,* December 3, 1967. Accessed via newspapers.com; "Teens Work Hard for News," *Oklahoma City Times,* January 11, 1968. Accessed via newspapers.com.

148 At the University of Oklahoma in 1971—"OU to Close for Teach-in," Sapulpa (Oklahoma) *Daily Herald,* February 17, 1971. Accessed via newspapers.com.

148 She ran that year for student body president—"1970s Activism Shaped State's Leaders," *The Oklahoman,* December 27, 1992.

148 She was known then as an outspoken feminist—Ibid.

149 she was ridiculed by opponents—Ibid.

149    Running as a Democrat, Cleta Deatheridge—"Mitchell, Cleta Deatherage (1950—)," Oklahoma Historical Society.

149    She was a Democrat for many years—Ibid.

149    she told the *Norman Transcript*—"Cleta Mitchell's Journey from Progressive Oklahoma Lawmaker to Trump Lawyer," *Norman Transcript,* January 9, 2021.

149    The sexual revolution, Magnet opined—Myron Magnet, *The Dream & the Nightmare: The Sixties Legacy to the Underclass* (Encounter Books, 2000).

150    Magnet, *PW* wrote—"The Dream and the Nightmare: The Sixties' Legacy to the Underclass," *Publishers Weekly,* March 1, 1993.

150    burbled syndicated columnist Mona Charen—Magnet, *The Dream and the Nightmare.*

150    Cleta Mitchell moved to Washington in 1991—"Meet Cleta Mitchell, the Conservative Movement's Anti-Gay Eminence Grise," *The Atlantic,* April 4, 2013.

150    As Denver Riggleman, an expert on Ginni Thomas—Author interview.

150    a story about Ginni asking him—Author interview, source anonymous.

150    Told the story, Denver Riggleman commented—Author interview; "Texts Show Ginni Thomas's Embrace of Conspiracy Theories," *New York Times,* March 26, 2022.

## CHAPTER 15: January 2010: Dark Money Unleashed

152    which Thomas shockingly failed—"Justice Clarence Thomas Failed to Disclose That Citizens United Foundation Supported His 1991 Nomination to the Supreme Court and Spent More Than $100,000 on Advertisements Attacking Opposing Senators, Says www.ProtectOurElections.org," *PR Newswire,* February 15, 2011.

152    now controls more than a billion dollars—"An Unusual $1.6 Billion Donation Bolsters Conservatives," *New York Times,* August 22, 2022.

153    outfit Floyd Brown founded—"From Willie Horton to Western Journalism: Floyd Brown's Career in Media Manipulation," *Newsweek,* December 6, 2016.

153    had moved on to a documentary-length attack—" 'Hillary: The Movie' Opens at the Supreme Court," National Public Radio, March 24, 2009.

153    McCain-Feingold, passed in 2002—"Bipartisan Campaign Reform Act of 2002," *Encyclopaedia Britannica.*

153    represented by none other than—*Citizens United v. FEC,* 558 U.S. 310 (2010), Justia U.S. Supreme Court Center.

153    The Supreme Court ruled that corporations—"*Citizens United* Explained," Brennan Center for Justice, December 12, 2019.

154    Jeffrey Toobin summed up—"Bad Judgment," *The New Yorker,* January 22, 2010.

155    Justice John Paul Stevens took note—*Citizens United v. FEC,* 558 U.S. 310 (2010), Justia U.S. Supreme Court Center.

155    President Barack Obama famously spoke out—"Obama Was Right About *Citizens United,*" Brennan Center for Justice, April 12, 2022.

155 Justice Samuel Alito, a man lacking—Ibid.

156 Justice Potter Stewart had famously observed of obscenity—"The Origins of Justice Stewart's 'I Know It When I See It,'" *Wall Street Journal,* September 27, 2005.

156 Stevens, born in 1920—"The Case That Changed John Paul Stevens's Life," *The Atlantic,* July 18, 2019.

156 he enlisted in the Navy—Ibid.

157 Gerald Ford appointed Stevens—"John Paul Stevens: Canny Strategist and the 'Finest Legal Mind' Ford Could Find," *New York Times,* July 16, 2019.

157 Ford later wrote—"The Case That Changed John Paul Stevens's Life," *The Atlantic.*

157 He actually wrote the first drafts—*Citizens United v. FEC,* 558 U.S. 310 (2010), Justia U.S. Supreme Court Center.

157 broke with his fellow ultraconservative judges—Ibid.

158 May 2023 analysis from Americans for Tax Fairness—"Travel Rewards: What the Crow Family May Have Bought by Hosting Those Luxury Trips for Justice Thomas," Americans for Tax Fairness, May 1, 2023.

158 As Stevens wrote in his opinion—*Citizens United v. FEC,* 558 U.S. 310 (2010), Justia U.S. Supreme Court Center.

159 Clarence Thomas, in contrast—Ibid.

159 accuser Christine Blasey Ford in the press—Author interview.

159 Citizens United spent more than $100,000 in support of him—"Justice Clarence Thomas Failed to Disclose That Citizens United Foundation Supported His 1991 Nomination to the Supreme Court and Spent More Than $100,000 on Advertisements Attacking Opposing Senators, Says www.ProtectOur Elections.org," *PR Newswire,* February 15, 2011.

159 a group called ProtectOurElections calling him out—Ibid.

160 Common Cause, cited Thomas's attendance—"Common Cause Seeks Details of Justice Thomas' Reported 'Drop-by' at Koch Industries Political Meeting," Common Cause, January 30, 2014

## CHAPTER 16: March 2016: The Art of the Deal

163 That was when President Barack Obama nominated—"President Obama Nominates Merrick Garland to the Supreme Court," *Washington Post,* March 16, 2016.

163 first elected to the U.S. Senate—"Mitch McConnell, Young and . . . Moderate?," *The New Republic,* March 21, 2019.

164 even though at that point Obama had—"Remarks by the President on the Passing of the U.S. Supreme Court Justice Antonin Scalia," White House Archives.

164 as Amy Howe wrote in an analysis—"Supreme Court Vacancies in Presidential Election Years," *SCOTUSblog,* February 13, 2016.

164 McConnell declared any appointment—"What Happened with Merrick Garland in 2016 and Why It Matters Now," National Public Radio, June 29, 2018.

164   blockade was unconstitutional—"McConnell's Unconstitutional Blockade of Garland Poisoned Subsequent Proceedings," *The Hill,* February 16, 2022.

165   McConnell argued, disingenuously—"Here's What Mitch McConnell Said About Not Filing a Supreme Court Vacancy in an Election Year," CBS News, September 19, 2020.

165   by invoking what he decided to call—"Senator Mitch McConnell Responds to Nomination," *SCOTUSblog,* March 16, 2016.

165   Joe Biden did give a speech on nominations—"Biden in '92: No Election-Season Supreme Court Nominees," *Politico,* February 22, 2016.

165   As Biden put it at the time—Ibid.

166   Biden observed, and went on to say—"Joe Biden Once Took GOP's Position on Supreme Court Vacancy," CBS News, February 22, 2016.

166   Vice President Biden commented in March 2016—"Joe Biden Says 'There Is No Biden Rule.' He's Right," *Slate,* March 24, 2016.

167   wondered New York senator Chuck Schumer—"Supreme Court Showdown Could Shape Fall Elections," *New York Times,* March 16, 2016.

167   Democratic senator Amy Klobuchar—"Obama Chooses Merrick Garland for Supreme Court," *New York Times,* March 16, 2016.

167   praised Garland about as lavishly as he praised—"Who Is Merrick Garland? Meet President Obama's Nominee to the Supreme Court," NBC News, March 16, 2016.

167   constitutional law scholar Laurence Tribe—"Harvard Law School's Laurence Tribe Talks Merrick Garland, Supreme Court Fight," NBC News, March 28, 2016.

168   had written at the time in a Kentucky journal—"Haynsworth and Carswell: A New Senate Standard of Excellence," *Kentucky Law Journal* 59 (1970–71).

169   The Religious Right was an important element—"In Alito, G.O.P. Reaps Harvest Planted in '82," *New York Times,* January 30, 2006.

170   included millions from close Leo associates—"Dark Money Group Received Massive Donation in Fight Against Obama's Supreme Court Nominee," Map-Light News Archive, October 24, 2017.

170   spearheaded a group called the Wellspring Committee—Ibid.

170   shut down in December 2018—"An Influential 'Dark Money' Group Turns Off the Lights for the Last Time," *OpenSecrets,* May 23, 2019.

170   According to Lisa Graves's Truth North Research—"Leonard Leo's Court Capture Web Raised Nearly $600 Million Before Biden Won; Now It's Spending Untold Millions from Secret Sources to Attack Judge Ketanji Brown Jackson," True North Research, March 22, 2022.

170   As *Politico* reported on March 24, 2016—"Group Blasts Garland in Colorado with Million-Dollar Ad Buy," *Politico,* March 24, 2016.

170   This was part of Judicial Crisis Network's first wave of ads—Ibid.

171   Carrie Severino a platform to froth about—Ibid.

171   The Judicial Crisis Network was founded—"The JCN Story: How to Build a Secretive, Right-Wing Judicial Machine," *The Daily Beast,* April 14, 2017.

171 Its key early supporters included—Ibid.

171 Media Matters reported in 2016—"Here Are the Big Players in the Inevitable Smear Campaign Against Judge Merrick Garland," Media Matters for America, March 16, 2016.

172 In 1990, Ann Corkery spoke—"Opus Dei: An Inner Resolve," *Palm Beach Post,* May 17, 1990. Accessed via newspapers.com.

172 As an Opus Dei flyer explained—Ibid.

173 Corkery spoke to a reporter—"Love of God Is Shrouded in Secrecy; Opus Dei Wants Others to Understand Devotion," *South Florida Sun Sentinel,* May 25, 1990.

173 Ann Corkery did share this glimpse—Ibid.

173 Leonard Leo—listed as the only trustee—"Leonard Leo's Court Capture Web Raised Nearly $600 Million Before Biden Won," True North Research.

173 more than $80 million in its first year—Ibid.

173 Exit polls showed the issue of the courts—"Polling Data Shows Republicans Turned Out for Trump in 2016 Because of the Supreme Court," *Vox,* June 29, 2018.

173 Democrats powerless to stop McConnell—"Fact Check: Republicans, Not Democrats, Eliminated the Senate Filibuster on Supreme Court Nominees," *USA Today,* October 1, 2020.

173 In a 2016 speech, he declared—"What Happened with Merrick Garland in 2016 and Why It Matters Now," National Public Radio.

173 McConnell said the decision not to act—"McConnell Points to 'the Most Consequential Decision' of His Career," MSNBC, April 5, 2018.

175 Then came a fateful meeting in March 2016—"Politico 50: Leonard Leo," *Politico Magazine,* 2018.

175 Trump released lists of potential high court nominees—"Trump Unveils His Potential Supreme Court Nominees," CNN, May 18, 2016.

175 All three future justices—"How Trump and Two Lawyers Narrowed the Field for His Supreme Court Choice," *Washington Post,* July 8, 2018.

176 They would, Trump promised—"Trump: I'll Appoint Supreme Court Justices to Overturn *Roe v. Wade* Abortion Case," CNBC, October 19, 2016.

176 Leo had hundreds of millions of dollars—"A Conservative Activist's Behind-the-Scenes Campaign to Remake the Nation's Courts," *Washington Post,* May 21, 2019.

176 By then, Leo had shepherded some 200 judges—"When Conservative Justices Revolt," *The Atlantic,* July 28, 2020.

176 Currently out of—Original research for this book.

176 Leo met with Trump in New York—"November 16, 2016: Clip of Trump Tower Web Stream," C-SPAN.

176 the list of guest speakers included—"Clarence Thomas, Samuel Alito, Ted Cruz head for Federalist Society Convention," *Washington Times,* November 16, 2016.

176    In other words: An enormous opportunity—"Justice Thomas: Honor Scalia by Reining in Government," *Seattle Times,* November 17, 2016.

## CHAPTER 17: April 2017: Gorsuch Gets Garland's Seat

177    appointed by Reagan as the first woman—"Neil Gorsuch's Mother Once Ran the EPA. It Didn't Go Well," *Washington Post,* February 1, 2017.

177    had a highly controversial tenure—"Remember When Neil Gorsuch's Mother Tried to Dismantle the EPA?," *Slate,* January 31, 2017.

177    and was forced out of her job—"Neil Gorsuch's Mother Once Ran the EPA," *Washington Post.*

177    "a member of a conservative group"—"Anne Gorsuch Burford, 62, Dies; Reagan EPA Director," *Washington Post,* July 22, 2004.

177    One fellow Colorado legislator found Gorsuch—Associated Press, "EPA Chief Anne Gorsuch—In Center of Swirling Torrent," *Miami Herald,* December 13, 1981. Accessed via newspapers.com.

177    a sobriquet that morphed into—"Neil Gorsuch's Late Mother Almost Annihilated the EPA. Is History Repeating Itself?," *Newsweek,* February 6, 2017.

178    surgeon father had instilled in her—"Anne Gorsuch Burford, 62, Reagan E.P.A. Chief, Dies," *New York Times,* July 22, 2004.

178    she completed her undergraduate studies—"Biography of Anne M. Gorsuch (Burford)," Environmental Protection Agency.

178    attorney for Mountain Bell Telephone—"Colorado News Briefs," *Greeley Daily Tribune,* October 26, 1976. Accessed via newspapers.com. "State representative David Gaon, D-Denver, Monday accused his Republican opponent with a conflict of interest in that she is seeking office while a corporate attorney and registered lobbyist with Mountain Bell. Gaon pointed to an interview in which Anne McGill Gorsuch said she would not abstain from voting on issues that could affect the financial interests of the phone company."

178    who could be counted on to horrify liberal proponents—"Remember When Neil Gorsuch's Mother Tried to Dismantle the EPA?," *Slate.*

178    Neil, attended Georgetown Prep—"Kavanaugh and Gorsuch Both Went to the Same Elite Prep School," *New York Times,* July 10, 2018.

178    A look through his 1984 high school yearbook tells a dramatic story—"Cupola 1984," Georgetown Prep. Accessed via Classmates.com.

178    As she wrote in her 1986 autobiography—Anne M. Burford, *Are You Tough Enough?* (McGraw Hill, 1986).

179    Gorsuch ran into trouble for her agency's handling—"Neil Gorsuch's Mother Once Ran the EPA," *The Washington Post.*

179    As *The New York Times* reported—"E.P.A. Chief Plans White House Legal Talks," *New York Times,* March 7, 1983.

180    Gorsuch had also been cited for contempt of Congress—"House Charges Head of E.P.A. with Contempt," *New York Times,* December 17, 1982.

180    she remarried and began going by the name—"Neil Gorsuch's Mother Once Ran the EPA," *Washington Post.*

180  As she wrote in her resignation letter—"Letter Accepting the Resignation of Anne M. Burford as Administrator of the Environmental Protection Agency," Ronald Reagan Presidential Library and Museum.

180  Summed up *The Washington Post*—"Burford Quits as EPA Administrator," *Washington Post,* March 9, 1983.

181  where soon after graduation he cowrote an essay—"Will the Gentlemen Please Yield?—A Defense of the Constitutionality of State Imposed Term Limitations," The Cato Institute, September 24, 1992.

181  earned the approving attention—"No More Careerists in Congress," *Washington Post,* September 30, 1992.

181  he also wrote opinion articles—"Liberals'N'Lawsuits," *National Review,* February 7, 2005.

181  In May 2006, Gorsuch was appointed—"Judge Neil Gorsuch—Colorado Native and Washington, D.C., Veteran," *SCOTUSblog,* January 30, 2017.

181  Linda Greenhouse would be describing Gorsuch—"Tragedy or Triumph," *New York Times,* September 3, 2014.

181  Gorsuch had received his right-wing legal establishment coronation—"Judge Neil Gorsuch—Colorado Native and Washington, D.C., Veteran," *SCOTUSblog.*

181  Joan Biskupic wrote in *Nine Black Robes*—Joan Biskupic, *Nine Black Robes: Inside the Supreme Court's Drive to the Right and Its Historic Consequences* (HarperCollins, 2023).

181  Earlier Olson lecture speakers included—"Barbara K. Olson Memorial Lecture Past Lecturers," The Federalist Society.

182  a surefire warm-up for that crowd—Ibid.

182  Gorsuch made the long list—"Donald Trump Expands List of Possible Supreme Court Picks," CBS News, September 23, 2016.

182  McGahn would later joke—"Trump's Fury at Don McGahn Is Misplaced," *The Atlantic,* May 22, 2019.

182  In late January 2017, Gorsuch was formally nominated—"President Donald J. Trump Nominates Judge Neil Gorsuch to the United States Supreme Court," White House Archives, January 31, 2017.

183  Gorsuch dressed the doctrine up this way—"Neil Gorsuch: An Eloquent Intellectual," The Hoover Institution, February 6, 2017.

183  eloquent, also backward—"Originalism: A Primer on Scalia's Constitutional Philosophy," National Public Radio, February 14, 2016.

183  The rise of originalism charted the rise—"Trump's Supreme Court Pick Is a Disciple of Scalia's 'Originalist' Crusade," National Public Radio, February 2, 2017.

183  Republican presidents had the good fortune—Ibid.

184  How had Gorsuch come to President Trump's attention—"In Gorsuch, Conservative Activist Sees Test Case for Reshaping the Judiciary," *New York Times,* March 18, 2017.

184 Leonard Leo, once again, said he was taking—"How Leonard Leo's Dark Money Network Orchestrated a New Attack on the Voting Rights Act," *Mother Jones,* December 18, 2023.

184 There would be no such doubts—"Neil Gorsuch Helped Defend Disputed Bush-Era Terror Policies," *New York Times,* March 15, 2017.

184 Gorsuch had been recommended—"Neil Gorsuch Has Web of Ties to Secretive Billionaire," *New York Times,* March 14, 2017.

184 who supported antigay causes and groups—"AEG Owner Phil Anschutz Is Still Donating to Causes Promoting Anti-LGBTQ Beliefs," *Billboard,* February 11, 2020.

184 Anschutz, a major donor—"The Anschutz Foundation 990, 2010."

184 also owns the right-wing *Washington Examiner*—"Phil Anschutz's Conservative Agenda," *Politico,* October 16, 2009.

184 Gorsuch misleadingly told—"Confirmation Hearing on the Nomination of Hon. Neil M. Gorsuch to Be an Associate Justice of the Supreme Court of the United States," United States Senate Judiciary Committee, March 20, 21, 22, 23, 2017.

185 Dick Durbin of Illinois then quizzed Gorsuch—Ibid.

185 asked by Sheldon Whitehouse—Ibid.

186 spoke in March 2022 about how Gorsuch—Senator Sheldon Whitehouse, "The Scheme 13: Auditioning," March 15, 2022.

187 Leo commented to *New Yorker* reporter Jeffrey Toobin—"The Conservative Pipeline to the Supreme Court," *The New Yorker,* April 10, 2017.

## CHAPTER 18: October 2018: Kavanaugh Channels Thomas

189 In July 2003, Bush nominated his close aide—"Nominations Sent to the Senate," White House Archives, July 25, 2003.

189 successfully stalled the confirmation—"Democrats' View of Kavanaugh Shaped by Bitter 2004 Hearing," *Washington Post,* September 2, 2018.

189 forward again for the post in January 2006—Ibid.

190 As *Newsday* explained the strategy—"GOP Using Court Nominee to Revitalize Conservatives," *Newsday,* May 10, 2006. Accessed via newspapers.com.

190 Democratic senator Dick Durbin of Illinois—"Is Brett Kavanaugh the 'Forrest Gump' of Washington?," *Washington Post,* July 12, 2018.

190 Durbin and other senators accused Kavanaugh—"Durbin Accuses Kavanaugh of Misleading Senators in 2006 Hearing," *The Hill,* September 11, 2018.

190 Memos later surfaced proving—"Document Shows Judge Kavanaugh Misled Durbin Under Oath About His Work on Controversial Judicial Nomination," Senator Dick Durbin Press Release, September 11, 2018.

190 singled out Brett Kavanaugh—Senator Sheldon Whitehouse, "The Scheme 13: Auditioning," March 15, 2022.

190 On March 30, 2015, for example, Kavanaugh delivered a speech—"The Judge as Umpire," *Catholic University Law Review,* June 22, 2016.

190 which has close ties to Leonard Leo—"Leonard Leo Has Reshaped the

Supreme Court. Is He Reshaping Catholic University Too?," *National Catholic Reporter,* December 15, 2022.

191   a former *Yale Daily News* sportswriter—"Decades Before Nomination Brett Kavanaugh Wrote About College Sports," *Yale Daily News,* July 10, 2018.

192   Ruth Marcus of *The Washington Post*—Ruth Marcus, *Supreme Ambition: Brett Kavanaugh and the Conservative Takeover* (Simon & Schuster, 2019).

192   Kavanaugh was not on the first list—"Trump Releases New List of Potential Supreme Court Nominees," *SCOTUSblog,* September 9, 2020.

192   "Like Barrett, Kavanaugh did his own publicity"—Senator Sheldon Whitehouse, "The Scheme 13: Auditioning."

192   the Trump family reportedly set their sights—"Inside the White House's Quiet Campaign to Create a Supreme Court Opening," *New York Times,* June 28, 2018.

193   First Daughter Ivanka Trump—"Book Reveals Trump Effort to Persuade Justice Kennedy to Step Aside for Kavanaugh," *The Guardian,* February 4, 2020.

193   In 2005, Justin Kennedy helped secure—"Inside the White House's Quiet Campaign to Create a Supreme Court Opening," *New York Times.*

193   *The New York Times* reported that Trump was able—"How Trump Maneuvered His Way Out of Trouble in Chicago," *New York Times,* October 8, 2021.

193   Justin Kennedy continued to help—"Donald Trump, Anthony Kennedy and the 'Boy' at Deutsche Bank: Not Just About the Money," *Salon,* July 2, 2018.

193   sitting Ivanka next to Justice Kennedy—"Inside the White House's Quiet Campaign to Create a Supreme Court Opening," *New York Times.*

193   Ivanka also visited Justice Kennedy—Ibid.

193   talking to Justice Kennedy—Ibid.

193   author David Enrich writes in his book—David Enrich, *Dark Towers: Deutsche Bank, Donald Trump, and an Epic Trail of Destruction* (Custom House, 2020).

194   Two law professors evaluated—"It's Hard to Find a Federal Judge More Conservative than Brett Kavanaugh," *Washington Post,* September 5, 2018.

194   The Trump vetting team also had access—"From the Bench: Judge Brett Kavanaugh on the Constitutional Statesmanship of Chief Justice William Rehnquist," American Enterprise Institute, September 18, 2017.

194   After their meeting, Collins issued an extraordinary statement—"Senator Collins Announces She Will Vote to Confirm Judge Kavanaugh," Senator Susan Collins Press Release, October 5, 2018.

194   Collins made another extraordinary statement—"Kavanaugh Gave Private Assurances. Collins Says He 'Misled' Her," *New York Times,* June 24, 2022.

195   Kavanaugh testified he respected *Planned Parenthood v. Casey*—"Kavanaugh, Who Told Senate *Roe v. Wade* Was 'Settled as Precedent,' Signals Openness to Overturning Abortion Decision," *Washington Post,* December 1, 2021.

195   Then news leaked in *The Intercept*—"Dianne Feinstein Withholding Brett Kavanaugh Document from Fellow Judiciary Committee Democrats," *The Intercept,* September 12, 2018.

195   hearings were to be held in only one day—"Dr. Blasey Ford, Judge Kava-
      naugh to Testify Thursday," United States Senate Judiciary Committee,
      September 23, 2018.

195   Taking the stand under oath—"Full Transcript: Christine Blasey Ford's
      Opening Statement to the Senate Judiciary Committee," *Politico,* Septem-
      ber 26, 2018.

196   A visibly emotional Kavanaugh—"Confirmation Hearing on the Nomina-
      tion of Hon. Brett M. Kavanaugh to Be an Associate Justice of the Supreme
      Court of the United States," United States Senate Judiciary Committee,
      September 4, 5, 6, 7, 27, 2018.

196   forced the Trump White House—"The FBI Investigation of Kavanaugh Was
      Doomed from the Start," *Vox,* October 5, 2018.

196   Deborah Ramirez, a Yale classmate—"Senate Democrats Investigate a New
      Allegation of Sexual Misconduct, from Brett Kavanaugh's College Years,"
      *The New Yorker,* September 23, 2018.

196   "I liked beer"—"Confirmation Hearing on the Nomination of Hon. Brett M.
      Kavanaugh to Be an Associate Justice of the Supreme Court of the United
      States," United States Senate Judiciary Committee, September 4, 5, 6,
      7, 27, 2018.

196   Ford's live testimony came across—"Full transcript: Christine Blasey Ford's
      Opening Statement to the Senate Judiciary Committee," *Politico.*

197   Timothy Don, a friend—"I Went to Georgetown Prep and Knew Mark
      Judge—and I Believe Christine Blasey Ford," *The Nation,* October 5, 2018.

197   following a similar playbook—Author interview.

197   who dismissed the Ford allegations—"Mark Judge Tells Senate He 'Has No
      Memory of Alleged' Incident with Kavanaugh," CNN, September 19, 2018.

197   New York's Chuck Schumer pointedly asked—"Brett Kavanaugh's Friend
      Mark Judge Breaks Silence About Alleged Sexual Assault Incident but Says
      He Will Not Testify," *Business Insider,* September 18, 2018.

198   Don observed recently—Author interview.

198   Judge, later a conservative writer—"Mark Judge," *The Daily Caller.*

198   wrote a memoir about his heavy drinking—Mark Judge, *A Tremor of Bliss:
      Sex, Catholicism, and Rock 'n' Roll* (Doubleday Religion, 2010).

198   Kavanaugh defender Ed Whelan—"Conservative Pundit Points Finger
      at Another Man to Deflect from Kavanaugh," *New York Times,* Septem-
      ber 21, 2018.

198   Whelan, president of the Ethics & Policy Center—Ibid.

198   where Leo sits on the board—"Leonard Leo, Architect of Conservative
      Supreme Court, Takes On Wider Culture," *National Catholic Reporter,* Janu-
      ary 4, 2024.

198   quickly shot down by Ford herself—"Conservative Activist Ed Whelan Apol-
      ogizes for Insinuating a Kavanaugh Doppelgänger Assaulted Ford," *Vox,*
      September 21, 2018.

198   Jake Tapper of ABC called them—"Kavanaugh Ally's Bizarre Mistaken

Identity Theory About Sexual Assault Accusation Blows Up in His Face," CNBC, September 21, 2018.

198  Whelan, clearly fearing Ford might sue—"Conservative Pundit Points Finger at Another Man to Deflect from Kavanaugh," *New York Times.*

198  Charles Ludington, the former basketball player—"Chad Ludington's Statement on Kavanaugh's Drinking and Senate Testimony," *New York Times,* September 30, 2018.

199  "I was just watching it"—Author interview.

199  Ludington called the FBI—Author interview.

199  In a statement shared with *The New York Times*—"Chad Ludington's Statement on Kavanaugh's Drinking and Senate Testimony," *New York Times.*

199  NBC News and other outlets picked up the story—"Yale Classmate to Tell FBI of Brett Kavanaugh's 'Violent Drunken' Behavior," NBC News, October 1, 2018.

199  Ludington said in a recent interview—Author interview.

200  They were simply forwarded to the Trump White House—"FBI Admits It Got 4,500 Tips on Brett Kavanaugh—Then Punted Them to Trump Team," *The Daily Beast,* July 23, 2021.

200  the White House announced that after reviewing—"White House Finds No Support in FBI Report for Claims Against Kavanaugh," *Wall Street Journal,* October 4, 2018.

200  the FBI belatedly responded to a letter—"After New Details on Kavanaugh Investigation Surface, Senators Call On FBI for Answers on Handling of 'Tip Line,'" Sheldon Whitehouse Press Release, July 22, 2021.

200  As Ruth Marcus wrote in *The Washington Post*—"The FBI's 'Investigation' of Kavanaugh Was Laughable," *Washington Post,* July 22, 2021.

201  remembers going to a September 25, 1985, UB40 concert—"Brett Kavanaugh Instigated Bar Fight After UB40 Concert, Police Report Reveals," *Rolling Stone,* October 1, 2018.

201  including one in November 1985—*Yale Daily News,* November 21, 1985.

201  Ludington explained, "Mostly I knew him"—Author interview.

202  especially in the case of an outrageous exchange—"Confirmation Hearing on the Nomination of Hon. Brett M. Kavanaugh to Be an Associate Justice of the Supreme Court of the United States," United States Senate Judiciary Committee, September 4, 5, 6, 7, 27, 2018.

203  Lisa Graves, a former Senate Judiciary Committee staffer—"Lisa Graves: Brett Kavanaugh Is Lying About Drinking, His Yearbook and Dr. Christine Blasey Ford," *Democracy Now!,* October 1, 2018.

203  has authored three books—Charles Ludington and Matthew Morse Booker, *Food Fights: How History Matters to Contemporary Food Debates* (University of North Carolina Press, 2019).

203  Looking back on his time knowing Brett Kavanaugh—Author interview.

204  Kavanaugh had cited Robert Bork—"Confirmation Hearing on the Nomination of Hon. Brett M. Kavanaugh to Be an Associate Justice of the Supreme

Court of the United States," United States Senate Judiciary Committee, September 4, 5, 6, 7, 27, 2018.

204  Gallup poll conducted in mid-September 2018—"Opposition to Kavanaugh Had Been Rising Before Accusation," Gallup, September 18, 2018.

204  whereas only 38 percent had supported confirmation for Bork—"Initial Views on Kavanaugh Confirmation Divided," Gallup, July 17, 2018.

204  As a point of comparison, Obama nominee Merrick Garland—"U.S. Support for Garland Average for Supreme Court Nominees," Gallup, March 21, 2016.

204  Retired justice John Paul Stevens—"Retired Justice John Paul Stevens Says Kavanaugh Is Not Fit for Supreme Court," *New York Times,* October 4, 2018.

205  with nearly $15 million—"Secretive Conservative Legal Group Funded by $17 Million Mystery Donor Before Kavanaugh Fight," OpenSecrets, May 17, 2019.

205  pushing saccharine blather—"Behind the Dark-Money Web That Put Barrett (and Kavanaugh and Gorsuch) on the Supreme Court," *Salon,* March 30, 2021.

205  Republicans sought to smear Ramirez—"Revealed: Senate Investigation into Brett Kavanaugh Assault Claims Contained Serious Omissions," *The Guardian,* April 28, 2023.

205  there was "no verifiable evidence" to support—Ibid.

205  *New York Times,* Stier—"Brett Kavanaugh Fit In with the Privileged Kids. She Did Not," *New York Times,* September 14, 2019.

205  Stier had agreed—"He Wanted Nonpartisan Federal Solutions. Now His Kavanaugh Tip Has Thrust Him into a Partisan Brawl," *Washington Post,* September 19, 2019.

206  he was confirmed 50–48—"Kavanaugh Confirmed: Here's How Senators Voted," *Politico,* October 6, 2018.

206  The following August a small item appeared—"Protesters Greet Collins Before Fundraiser at Mount Desert Island Home," *Portland Press-Herald,* December 27, 2019.

206  attended by C. Boyden Gray—"Collins Attends Fundraiser at $4m Mansion of Nation's Top Anti-Choice Judicial Activist," *Maine Beacon,* August 8, 2019.

206  JCN announced that it was launching—"JCN Launches 6-Figure Ad Buy in Maine Thanking Sen. Susan Collins," Judicial Crisis Network, October 9, 2018.

206  Kavanaugh had perjured himself—"Document Shows Judge Kavanaugh Misled Durbin Under Oath About His Work on Controversial Judicial Nomination," Senator Dick Durbin Press Release.

206  Kavanaugh again lied about his positions—"Confirmation Hearing on the Nomination of Hon. Brett M. Kavanaugh to Be an Associate Justice of the Supreme Court of the United States," United States Senate Judiciary Committee, September 4, 5, 6, 7, 27, 2018.

206  and he lied again, repeatedly—Ibid.

CHAPTER 19: **October 2020: The Handmaid**

207   Peter Baker and Maggie Haberman reported—"McConnell Vows Vote on Ginsburg Replacement as Her Death Upends the 2020 Race," *New York Times,* September 22, 2020.

208   "titanic partisan battle"—"McConnell Vows Vote on Ginsburg Replacement as Her Death Upends the 2020 Race," *New York Times.*

208   In an October 2018 interview with PBS—"Leonard Leo Flip-Flops on Trump Filling a Supreme Court Seat in 2020," *Huffington Post,* May 31, 2019.

208   Yet Leo soon began "amending his position"—Ibid.

208   lining up funds for ad buys—"Judge Amy Coney Barrett Confirmed," Judicial Crisis Network, 2020.

208   It was a "cynical attack—"Schumer: A Vote for Judge Amy Coney Barrett Is a Vote to Eliminate Health Care for Millions in the Middle of a Pandemic," Chuck Schumer Press Release, September 26, 2020.

208   since she had clashed with Democrats—"Amy Coney Barrett's Past Calls into Question Her Pledges of Impartiality," *The Guardian,* October 26, 2020.

208   protégée and former clerk—"Amy Coney Barrett, Supreme Court Nominee, is Scalia's Heir," Associated Press, September 26, 2020.

209   she sought to cast herself as an heir—"Supreme Court Nominee Amy Coney Barrett: 'Judges Are Not Policymakers,'" White House Archives, September 29, 2020.

209   in attendance stood a who's who—"A 'View' from the Rose Garden: The Nine," *SCOTUSblog,* September 26, 2020.

209   Barrett had signed political ads—"Barrett Signed Ad in 2006 Decrying 'Barbaric Legacy' of *Roe v. Wade,* Advocating Overturning the Law," *Washington Post,* October 1, 2020.

210   Trump reportedly told his inner circle—"Donald Trump Already Has Replacement Ready for Justice Ruth Bader Ginsburg's Post: Report," *Washington Times,* April 1, 2019.

210   Bridget Kelly of the Population Institute—"Replacing RBG with a Woman like Amy Coney Barrett Is Beyond Tokenism. It's an Affront: Opinion," *Newsweek,* October 1, 2020.

210   nominated by Trump in May 2017—"Some Worry About Judicial Nominee's Ties to a Religious Group," *New York Times,* September 28, 2017.

210   Sheldon Whitehouse said in his speech on auditioning—Senator Sheldon Whitehouse, "The Scheme 13: Auditioning," March 15, 2022.

210   UCLA law professor Adam Winkler—"Amy Coney Barrett's Long Game," *The New Yorker,* February 7, 2022.

211   reporter Margaret Talbot wrote—Ibid.

211   Barrett was a lifelong member of People of Praise—"Amy Coney Barrett Served as a 'Handmaid' in Christian Group People of Praise," *Washington Post,* October 6, 2020.

211   it embraced such intense practices—Ibid.

211 Mike Coney, offered this description—"February 2018: Mike Coney," St. Catherine of Siena Parish.

212 A 2010 directory of People of Praise listed Barrett—"Amy Coney Barrett Served as a 'Handmaid' in Christian Group People of Praise," *Washington Post.*

212 A 1986 community handbook—Ibid.

212 As recently as 2017, Barrett sat on the board—"Head of School Linked to Amy Coney Barrett's Faith Group Abruptly Resigns," *The Guardian,* July 3, 2023.

212 Tackling the taboo issue head-on—"'The Dogma Lives Loudly Within You': Revisiting Barrett's Confirmation Hearing," *New York Times,* September 26, 2020.

212 She wrote a letter to the Senate Judiciary Committee—"Former People of Praise Member Calls on Senators to Allow Her to Testify at Amy Coney Barrett's Confirmation Hearing," *Newsweek,* October 11, 2020.

213 plot took another turn—"New Role for Amy Coney Barrett's Father Inside Christian Sect Sparks Controversy," *The Guardian,* January 29, 2024.

213 said a spokesperson for PoP Survivors—Ibid.

213 She falsely told Feinstein she would—"Amy Coney Barrett Senate Confirmation Hearing Day 2 Transcript," *Rev,* October 13, 2020, https://www.rev.com/blog/transcripts/amy-coney-barrett-senate-confirmation-hearing-day-2-transcript.

213 While Barrett did concede she did not consider *Roe*—"Former People of Praise Member Calls on Senators to Allow Her to Testify at Amy Coney Barrett's Confirmation Hearing," *Newsweek.*

214 Meanwhile, right-wing dark-money groups—"Judge Amy Coney Barrett Confirmed," Judicial Crisis Network.

214 Senator Josh Hawley gave up the game—"Hawley Meets with Barrett, Won't Ask Whether She'd Overturn *Roe v. Wade,*" *Kansas City Star,* October 1, 2020.

214 Hawaii's Mazie Hirono retorted—"Amy Coney Barrett Senate Confirmation Hearing Day 2 Transcript," *Rev.*

214 Barrett was very narrowly confirmed, 52–48—"Amy Coney Barrett Confirmed to Supreme Court, Takes Constitutional Oath," National Public Radio, October 26, 2020.

214 79.9 years, as of 2020—"Hawaii Tops List of the 10 U.S. States Where Residents Can Expect to Live the Longest," CNBC, August 29, 2022.

## CHAPTER 20: June 2022: The *Dobbs* Earthquake and Beyond

217 they did so by a wide margin—"Ohio Election Results 2023," *New York Times.*

218 efforts to restrict abortion access—"Tracking Abortion Bans Across the Country," *New York Times.*

218 staked out a position on the stump—"Trump Calls DeSantis Abortion Ban 'a Terrible Mistake,' Sparking Anger from Some Key Republicans," Associated Press, September 18, 2023.

218 man who believes God speaks to him directly—"Mike Johnson Claims That God Prepared Him to Be a 'New Moses,'" *Slate,* December 7, 2023.

218 former Alito clerk J. Joel Alicea—"Dobbs and the Fate of the Conservative Legal Movement," *City Journal,* Winter 2022.

219 originally founded in 1993 in Phoenix, Arizona—Associated Press, "Coalition Raising Funds for 'Values,'" *Fort Worth Star-Telegram,* December 10, 1993. Accessed via newspapers.com.

219 Alan Sears, who would go on to coauthor—Alan Sears and Craig Osten, *The Homosexual Agenda: Exposing the Principal Threat to Religious Freedom Today* (B&H Books, 2003).

219 characterized by the Southern Poverty Law Center—"'Religious Liberty' and the Anti-LGBT Right," Southern Poverty Law Center, February 11, 2016.

219 As *The New Republic* put it—"How Leonard Leo Became the Power Broker of the American Right," *The New Republic,* July 11, 2022.

219 As *Politico* reported in December 2023—"'Plain Historical Falsehoods': How Amicus Briefs Bolstered Supreme Court Conservatives," *Politico,* December 3, 2023.

219 *Ms.* magazine, attempting to follow the money—"The Dark Money Fight Against Abortion Access," *Ms.* magazine, June 23, 2023.

220 the Gestational Age Act—"What to Know About the Mississippi Abortion Law Challenging *Roe v. Wade,*" *New York Times,* May 6, 2022.

220 a law that ADF staff attorneys helped draft—"Inside the Tactics That Won Christian Vendors the Right to Reject Gay Weddings," *Washington Post,* September 28, 2023.

220 ADF attorneys were also closely involved—Ibid.

220 Mississippi solicitor general Scott Stewart—*Dobbs v. Jackson Women's Health Organization,* 19-1392, Oyez.

220 As Justice Sonia Sotomayor—"Sotomayor Suggests Overturning *Roe* Would Cause SCOTUS Decisions to Appear Political," *Newsweek,* December 1, 2021.

221 When a draft of Samuel Alito's majority decision—"Read Justice Alito's Initial Draft Abortion Opinion Which Would Overturn *Roe v. Wade,*" *Politico,* May 2, 2022.

221 Alito asserted in the draft—Ibid.

222 University of Illinois law professor Leslie J. Reagan—"Opinion: What Alito Gets Wrong About the History of Abortion in America," *Politico Magazine,* June 2, 2022.

223 excoriated not only the *Dobbs* decision—"Behind the Scenes at the Dismantling of *Roe v. Wade,*" *New York Times,* December 15, 2023.

223 Expanding on the point—Richard Re, *Should Gradualism Have Prevailed in Dobbs?* (Oxford University Press, 2024).

223 The *Journal* urged the two possibly wavering justices—"Abortion and the Supreme Court," *Wall Street Journal,* April 26, 2022.

224 Aaron Tang, a law professor—"Did the Supreme Court's Leak Investigation Let the Justices off the Hook?," *New York Times,* January 20, 2023.

224    *New York Times* report—"Former Anti-Abortion Leader Alleges Another Supreme Court Breach," *New York Times,* November 19, 2022.

224    According to the *Times*—Ibid.

225    Alito or his wife had told conservative donors—Ibid.

225    testifying in December 2022—"Hearing on Politics and the Supreme Court," C-SPAN, December 8, 2022.

225    quixotic efforts to work with Justice Stephen Breyer—"5 Takeaways from Inside the Overturning of *Roe v. Wade*," *New York Times,* December 15, 2023.

225    Breyer, in an interview for his book—"Former Justice Stephen Breyer Reflects on 'Unfortunate' Supreme Court Leak Before Dobbs Abortion Ruling," NBC News, March 22, 2024.

225    Roberts had directed the marshal—"Roberts Orders Leak Investigation as Court Confirms Authenticity of Draft Opinion," *SCOTUSblog,* May 3, 2022.

226    Supreme Court justices themselves were apparently not subjected—"Inside the Supreme Court Inquiry: Seized Phones, Affidavits and Distrust," *New York Times,* January 21, 2023.

226    Curley, responding to a media furor—"Statement from Marshal Gail A. Curley," United States Supreme Court, January 20, 2023.

226    former Supreme court clerk Daniel Epps—"Supreme Court Says It Can't Determine Who Leaked Draft Dobbs Opinion," *Washington Post,* January 19, 2023.

226    *The Hill* was particularly excoriating—"What Happened to the Investigation into the Dobbs Draft Leak?," *The Hill,* December 3, 2022.

227    Roberts had the court issue a statement—"Supreme Court Press Release," United States Supreme Court, May 3, 2022.

227    right is not "deeply rooted"—*Dobbs v. Jackson Women's Health Organization,* 19-1932, Oyez.

227    made a highly unusual move at one point—"Five Takeaways from the *Dobbs v. Jackson* Oral Arguments," Alliance for Justice, December 6, 2021.

228    Stewart argued in Mississippi's main brief—"Behind the Scenes at the Dismantling of *Roe v. Wade*," *New York Times.*

228    The month that Stewart brief was filed—Ibid.

228    As *The New York Times* reported—Ibid.

228    polls showed women didn't believe—"Broader Support for Abortion Rights Continues Post-Dobbs," Gallup, June 14, 2023.

229    Representative Ted Lieu said in a tweet—"Post from @tedlieu," X, May 7, 2022.

229    At least twenty-one states with Republican leadership—"Tracking Abortion Bans Across the Country," *New York Times.*

229    Thirteen states had so-called trigger laws—"What Is a Trigger Law? And Which States Have Them?," *New York Times,* May 4, 2022.

229    Another nine states had never repealed—"With *Roe v. Wade* Overturned, Here's Where Things Stand with 'Trigger' Laws and Pre-*Roe* Bans," NBC News, June 24, 2022.

229 Several states adopted, or began to enforce—"Where Abortion Law Stands in Every State a Year After the Supreme Court Overturned *Roe*," Associated Press, June 22, 2023.

229 As of December 2023, fully twenty-one states—"Tracking Abortion Bans Across the Country," *New York Times.*

229 an Idaho woman who took to TikTok—"Idaho Woman Shares 19-Day Miscarriage on TikTok."

229 Heartbreaking stories from Texas—"Denied Abortion for a Doomed Pregnancy, She Tells Texas Court: 'There Was No Mercy.'" National Public Radio, July 20, 2023.

229 Amanda Zurawski of Austin, Texas, testified—"Texas Woman Denied an Abortion Tells Senators She 'Nearly Died on Their Watch,'" CNN, April 26, 2023.

230 polling firm PerryUndem found that voters—"Why Democracy Hasn't Settled the Abortion Question," *New York Times,* December 17, 2023.

230 Kate Zernike wrote in *The New York Times*—Ibid.

231 *Dobbs* made abortion a major issue—"'The Central Issue': How the Fall of *Roe v. Wade* Shook the 2022 Election," *Politico,* December 19, 2022.

231 Exit polls attributed the Democratic surge—"Inflation and Abortion Lead the List of Voter Concerns, Edging Out Crime, NBC News Exit Poll Finds," NBC News, November 8, 2022.

231 They showed voters highly motivated by *Dobbs*—"Abortion Access Proved to Be a Powerful Force in 2022 Midterm Elections," CBS News, November 11, 2022.

231 A clear majority of all Americans disapproved—"Majority of Public Disapproves of Supreme Court's Decision to Overturn *Roe v. Wade*," Gallup, July 6, 2022.

231 approval ratings of the court hit a record low—"Views of Supreme Court Remain Near Record Lows," Gallup, September 29, 2023.

232 Dan Balz wrote in *The Washington Post*—"Dobbs Changed Abortion Politics. One Year Later, It's Still Potent," *Washington Post,* June 24, 2023.

232 disapprove of the Supreme Court by 73 percent—"Is Democracy in the U.S. Working? It's a Toss-Up, but Voters Don't See It Ending in Their Lifetimes, Quinnipiac University National Poll Finds; 51% Support House Bill That Could Lead to TikTok Ban, 2024 Race: Biden vs. Trump Too-Close-to-Call," Quinnipiac University Poll, March 27, 2024.

232 Senator Chris Murphy of Connecticut—"Democratic Senator: GOP Will '100 Percent' Pass National Abortion Ban with Control of Congress," *The Hill,* July 17, 2023.

233 Securities and Exchange Commission could lead—*Securities and Exchange Commission v. Jarkesy,* 20-61007, *SCOTUSblog.*

233 Consumer Financial Protection Bureau in its crosshairs—*Consumer Financial Protection Bureau v. Community Financial Services Association of America, Limited,* 21-50826, *SCOTUSblog.*

234   right-wing-dominated Fifth Circuit Court of Appeals—"The Supreme Court Will Decide If a Whole Federal Agency Is Unconstitutional," *Vox,* February 27, 2023.

234   articulated his new standard writing—*New York State Rifle & Pistol Association, Inc. v. Bruen,* 597 U.S. ___ (2022)," Justia U.S. Supreme Court Center.

234   As *Politico* noted, highlighting the obtuseness—"Clarence Thomas Created a Confusing New Rule That's Gutting Gun Laws," *Politico Magazine,* July 28, 2023.

234   from the right-wing Fifth Circuit—*United States v. Rahimi,* American Civil Liberties Union, September 13, 2023.

234   As the Brennan Center succinctly pointed out—"Second Amendment Meets Domestic Violence in the Supreme Court," Brennan Center for Justice, November 3, 2023.

235   involving the federal government's approval of mifepristone—"Justices Will Review Lower-Court Ruling on Access to Abortion Pill," *SCOTUSblog,* December 13, 2023.

235   A new right-wing organization formed as an umbrella group—"New SCOTUS Anti-Abortion Case Forced to High Court by Leo, Far-Right Orgs," Accountable.us, December 13, 2023.

235   The group was secretly funded by Leonard Leo—"Dark Money Is Flowing to Groups Trying to Limit Medication Abortion. Leonard Leo Is Again at the Center," *The 19th,* January 4, 2024.

235   The money trail began with the Catholic Association Foundation—Ibid.

235   Matthew Kacsmaryk, a Trump appointee—Ibid.

235   founded a lawyers chapter in Fort Worth—"Federal Judge at Center of FDA Abortion Drug Case Has History with Conservative Causes," *Texas Tribune,* March 15, 2023.

235   He ruled that the FDA—"Dark Money Is Flowing to Groups Trying to Limit Medication Abortion," *The 19th.*

236   antiobscenity law from 1873—"Takeaways from the Supreme Court Arguments over the Abortion Drug Mifepristone," CNN, March 27, 2024.

236   the Chicago financier and antiabortion activist Barre Seid—"How a Secretive Billionaire Handed His Fortune to the Architect of the Right-Wing Takeover of the Courts," *ProPublica,* August 22, 2022.

236   Leo told *The New York Times*—"Leonard Leo Pushed the Courts Right. Now He's Aiming at American Society," *New York Times,* October 12, 2022.

237   As Cardozo Law School professor Kate Shaw—"Supreme Court Gavels in 2023 with Major Decisions Ahead," ABC News, January 10, 2023.

## CHAPTER 21: Real Reform Starts with Expanding the Supreme Court

238   issued Executive Order 14023—"Presidential Commission on the Supreme Court of the United States," The White House.

238   *Wall Street Journal* editorial page immediately branded—"Biden Commissions the Supreme Court," *Wall Street Journal,* April 9, 2021.

239   As Epps himself observed in a *Washington Post* column—"Major Supreme Court Reform Is Unlikely. But These Changes Would Be a Good Start," *Washington Post,* July 15, 2021.

239   March 1937 Fireside Chat radio address—"March 9, 1937: Fireside Chat 9: On 'Court-Packing,'" University of Virginia, Miller Center.

240   which struck them as a power grab—"1937 Democrats Had the Best Response to Court-Packing," *National Review,* April 13, 2021.

240   As Biden's Supreme Court Commission wrote—*Presidential Commission on the Supreme Court of the United States, Final Report,* December 2021.

241   Congressman Hank Johnson introduced—"H.R.2584—Judiciary Act of 2021," United States Congress, 117th Session.

241   Ro Khanna of California, a creative thinker, introduced—"H.R.5140—Supreme Court Term Limits and Regular Appointments Act of 2021," United States Congress, 117th Session.

241   Sheldon Whitehouse introduced a Senate bill—"S.359—Supreme Court Ethics, Recusal, and Transparency Act of 2023," United States Congress, 118th Session.

241   Senator Chris Murphy of Connecticut also introduced—"S.325—Supreme Court Ethics Act," United States Congress, 118th Session.

241   In May 2023, Senator Ed Markey reintroduced—"S.1616—Judiciary Act of 2023," United States Congress, 118th Session.

241   the sponsors noted—"Bush, Johnson, Markey, Smith, Schiff Announce Legislation to Expand Supreme Court," Congresswoman Cori Bush Press Release, May 16, 2023.

242   As *The Washington Post* wrote—"Biden's Supreme Court Commission Endorses Final Report Noting Bipartisan Public Support for Term Limits," *Washington Post,* December 7, 2021.

242   offered devastating support—*Presidential Commission on the Supreme Court of the United States, Final Report,* December 2021.

243   the two wrote in a December 2021—"Opinion: The Supreme Court Isn't Well. The Only Hope for a Cure Is More Justices," *Washington Post,* December 9, 2021.

244   The court issued a statement explaining—"Statement of the Court Regarding the Code of Conduct," United States Supreme Court, November 13, 2023.

244   Supreme Court did, theoretically at least—"Code of Conduct for United States Judges," United States Courts.

244   for example in this provision—"Statement of the Court Regarding the Code of Conduct," United States Supreme Court.

245   his own wife was an acknowledged co-conspirator—See Appendix.

245   Here was the language the Supreme Court unveiled—"Statement of the Court Regarding the Code of Conduct," United States Supreme Court.

245   *Politico* made a point on many minds—"Embattled Supreme Court Adopts Code of Conduct," *Politico,* November 13, 2023.

245　Simon Lazarus argued that seen in the broader context—"Liberals Are Wrong to Trash the Supreme Court's New Code of Ethics," *The New Republic,* November 30, 2023.

246　"They don't give a damn": Author interview.

246　He stated at the time—"When John Roberts Wants Things Done, He Acts. What That Means for Ethics Rules," CNN, September 1, 2023.

247　Roberts in 2007 pulled in only a paltry $212,100—"Judicial Compensation," United States Courts.

247　agreeing that it would be "awkward"—"At the Supreme Court, Ethics Questions over a Spouse's Business Ties," *New York Times,* January 31, 2023.

247　according to information revealed—"Jane Roberts, Who Is Married to Chief Justice John Roberts, Made $10.3 Million in Commissions from Elite Law Firms, Whistleblower Documents Show," *Business Insider,* April 28, 2023.

247　Kendal Price, the whistleblower—Ibid.

248　he spurned a request—"Chief Justice Roberts Declines to Testify About Ethics Before Senate Judiciary Committee," CBS News, April 25, 2023.

248　included with his letter to Durbin—Ibid.

250　was already framing the issue—"I Spent 7 Months Studying Supreme Court Reform. We Need to Pack the Court Now," *Time,* December 10, 2021.

251　says Senator Ed Markey, cosponsor—"Democrats Reintroduce Supreme Court Expansion Legislation," *The Hill,* May 16, 2023.

252　a 2023 poll by the University of Massachusetts Amherst—"Majority of Americans Support Supreme Court Reforms, Including Term Limits and Ethics Requirements, According to New UMass Amherst Poll," University of Massachusetts Amherst, June 16, 2023.

252　A 2022 Associated Press–NORC Center for Public Affairs Research poll— "AP-NORC Poll: 2 in 3 in US Favor Term Limits for Justices," AP-NORC, July 25, 2022.

252　The average American life expectancy—Data from United Nations—World Population Prospects.

253　Larry Sabato noted—Author interview.

## CHAPTER 22: The Continuing Danger of Ginni Thomas

254　Ginni Thomas, wife—"Virginia Thomas Urged White House Chief to Pursue Unrelenting Efforts to Overturn the 2020 Election, Texts Show," *Washington Post,* March 24, 2022.

255　Thomas had texted Meadows—See Appendix.

255　she forwarded a YouTube link—See Appendix.

255　best known up to then for pushing the conspiracy theory—"Ginni Thomas' Election Fraud Guru Claims He Arrested Pope," *The Daily Beast,* March 25, 2022.

255　burbling to Meadows in the same text—See Appendix.

256　she wrote Meadows a straightforward directive—See Appendix.

256　On November 10, having apparently exercised—See Appendix.

256 Nancy Schulze, cochair—"Videos Show Closed-Door Sessions of Leading Conservative Activists: 'Be Not Afraid of the Accusations That You're a Voter Suppressor,'" *Washington Post,* October 14, 2020.

256 Trump lost the popular vote—According to the Federal Election Commission, Biden finished with a record 81,268,924 votes, 51.31 percent of the total, to 74,216,154 for Trump.

256 Here was Meadows's reply—See Appendix.

257 verbatim, was Thomas's response—See Appendix.

257 the night of November 10—See Appendix.

257 In particular, a text from Connie Hair—See Appendix.

257 Fox News had called Arizona for Biden—"Fox News and AP Scrutinized for Projecting Arizona While Other Outlets Hold Off," CNN, November 5, 2020.

258 chief of staff to House Freedom Caucus—See Appendix.

258 Thomas forwarded it to Meadows—See Appendix.

258 As Hair's Louisiana Freedom Caucus State Chair bio reads—State Freedom Caucus Network.

258 nursing imagined grievance—See Appendix.

258 Hair wrote and Ginni Thomas forwarded—See Appendix.

259 Hair's boss Gohmert would echo—"Capitol Police Intelligence Analysts Worried a Member of Congress Was Actually Encouraging Violence in the Days Leading Up to the January 6 Attack: Louie Gohmert," *Politico,* January 5, 2022.

259 Sheila Jackson Lee later said during—United States House Judiciary Committee meeting, December 8, 2022.

259 who as a University of Virginia law student—Ibid.

259 Ginni Thomas's role in January 6—Ibid.

259 Denver Riggleman, the head of the data team—Author interview.

259 the linking of all three branches of government—Author interview.

260 Riggleman says it was—Author interview.

260 Former Clarence Thomas aide Armstrong Williams—"Party On, Judge," *Kansas City Star,* October 1, 2007. Accessed via newspapers.com.

261 As Williams wrote at the time in *The Hill*—"Vice President Cheney," *The Hill,* October 10, 2007.

262 even Trump called her schemes "crazy"—"January 6 Report Reveals Trump Laughed About Sidney Powell's 'Crazy' Election Fraud Claims," *The Independent,* December 23, 2022.

262 Lee wrote Meadows at 10:23 p.m.—"Read: Mark Meadows' Texts with Mike Lee and Chip Roy," CNN, April 15, 2022.

262 Ginni Thomas herself would push Sidney Powell—See Appendix.

262 Meadows received a text—Original reporting for this book.

262 Not only would Farris draft the legal brief Texas—"Christian Conservative Lawyer Had Secretive Role in Bid to Block Election Result," *New York Times,* October 7, 2021.

263  Farris would also recruit—Original reporting for this book.

263  Farris grew up a Baptist—"Liquor Ban Plea Fails," *Spokesman-Review*, October 3, 1976. Accessed via newspapers.com.

263  A political science major at Western Washington University—"Leadership," Patrick Henry College.

263  he harangued the Spokane City Council—"Liquor Ban Plea Fails," *Spokesman-Review*.

263  In 1983 he moved from a Washington State leadership post—Associated Press, "Ex-Moral Majority Leader in New Area," *Spokane Chronicle*, January 2, 1985. Accessed via newspapers.com.

263  Farris left the Moral Majority—Ibid.

263  Republicans and Democrats were all the same—Ibid.

263  Farris founded the Home School Legal Defense Association—"Leadership," Patrick Henry College.

263  he cofounded a group called the Convention of States Project—"Michael Farris, Convention of States Co-Founder and Senior Advisor," Convention of States Project, January 12, 2023.

263  a campaign summed up in a *Richmond Times-Dispatch*—"Effort Seeks to Reset Course for America," *Richmond Times-Dispatch*, January 19, 2014.

264  Farris served as CEO of Alliance Defending Freedom—"Michael Farris," Alliance Defending Freedom.

264  submitted on December 9—"Motion of Donald J. Trump, President of the United States, to Intervene in His Personal Capacity as Candidate for Re-Election, Proposed Bill of Complaint in Intervention, and Brief in Support of Motion to Intervene," December 9, 2020.

264  "Prayer for Relief"—Ibid.

264  As Reuters reported, the Supreme Court—Reuters, "U.S. Supreme Court Rejects Texas Lawsuit Seeking to Undo Trump Election Loss," Yahoo News, December 11, 2020.

265  often called "The Coup Memos"—"Who Is 'Coup Memo' Author John Eastman and What Role Did He Play in Pushing Trump's Plan to Derail Democracy?," *The Independent*, June 17, 2022.

265  In a tell of how weak an argument—"Read: Trump Lawyer's Memo on Six-Step Plan for Pence to Overturn the Election," CNN, September 21, 2021.

265  the data investigative team found its moves—Original for the book.

266  she referenced a conversation—See Appendix.

266  Shortly before 10 p.m.—See Appendix.

267  Clarence Thomas himself emphasized—"Defiant Clarence Thomas Fires Back," *Politico*, February 27, 2011.

268  she repeatedly claims to have no memory—Select Committee to Investigate the January 6th Attack on the U.S. Capitol, U.S. House of Representatives, Washington, DC, Interview of Virginia L. Thomas, September 29, 2022.

268  in a momentary flash of honesty—Ibid.

268  The "best friend" remark?—Ibid.

268  she continued in the "best friend" text—See Appendix.

269  Ankush Khardori argued—"Ginni Thomas Is a Victim of Donald Trump's Alleged Crimes," *Politico Magazine,* December 21, 2023.

269  Former Clinton administration official Robert Reich—Robert Reich, Twitter, January 3, 2024, 3:22 p.m.

269  New York congressman Dan Goldman—"Congressman Dan Goldman Demands Justice Clarence Thomas Recuse Himself from Upcoming Colorado Ballot Case," Press Release, January 5, 2024.

## CHAPTER 23: Time to Impeach Clarence Thomas

271  advocating for the impeachment of Thomas—"David Brock Penned Memo on Impeaching Clarence Thomas," *Politico,* September 1, 2015.

272  was pegged to a new interview in *The New York Times*—"Ex-Companion Details 'Real' Thomas," *New York Times,* October 22, 2010.

272  Thomas categorically denied—"Nomination of Judge Clarence Thomas to Be Associate Justice of the Supreme Court of the United States," United States Senate Judiciary Committee, Part 4, October 11, 12, 13, 1991.

272  In August 2022, I published an op-ed—"Opinion: David Brock Believed in Clarence Thomas. Now He Wants Him Impeached," *Huffington Post,* September 16, 2022.

273  At the time, Ginni Thomas was serving—"A Rare Peek Inside the Vast Right-Wing Conspiracy," *The New Republic,* August 26, 2022.

273  Clarence Thomas was the sole dissenter—"Fact Check: Was Clarence Thomas Lone Dissenter on Trump Jan. 6 Documents?," *Newsweek,* June 17, 2022.

273  Federal law says judges and justices must recuse—"Code of Conduct for United States Judges," United States Courts.

273  Harvard Law professor Laurence Tribe concluded—"What Clarence Thomas Did Was Illegal Says Laurence Tribe," MSNBC via YouTube, March 29, 2022.

273  In 2011, seventy-four House Democrats—"Dems: Thomas Should Recuse Himself," *Politico,* February 9, 2011.

274  Ginni Thomas was a highly paid lobbyist—Ibid.

274  Thomas also failed to recuse himself—"Is Ginni Thomas a Threat to the Supreme Court?," *The New Yorker,* January 21, 2022.

274  according to *The New Yorker*—Ibid.

274  Thomas also ran afoul of the law—"Clarence Thomas Has for Years Claimed Income from a Defunct Real Estate Firm," *Washington Post,* April 16, 2023.

274  The Ethics in Government Act requires—"S.555—Ethics in Government Act," United States Congress, 95th Congress.

274  University of Colorado law professor Paul Campos—"Clarence Thomas' Criminal Behavior on Financial Disclosure," *The Daily Beast,* July 13, 2017.

274  Thomas's self-justification—"Clarence Thomas Defends Undisclosed 'Family Trips' with GOP Megadonor. Here Are the Facts," *ProPublica,* April 7, 2023.

# INDEX

A NOTE ON THE TYPE

Benton Modern, first published through Font Bureau in 1997, was designed by Tobias Frere-Jones as a text face for *The Boston Globe* and the *Detroit Free Press*. Its design was inspired by Century Expanded, a news text typeface created by Morris Fuller Benton in 1900 for the American Type Founders Company. The italic draws on the design of Century Schoolbook. Display cuttings were later designed by Dyanna Weissman and Richard Lipton.

Composed by North Market Street Graphics,
Lancaster, Pennsylvania

Printed and bound by Berryville Graphics,
Berryville, Virginia

Designed by Marisa Nakasone